HATTERS
HEROES

An A – Z of Luton Town players since 1946

Roger Wash

First published in 2008 by Roger Wash
5 Downing Close
Newmarket
CB8 8AU

Copyright 2008 Roger Wash

ISBN 978-0-9560832-0-3

Luton Town Post-War A to Z

■ Nathanael (Nathan) ABBEY.

Islington born Nathan joined the Hatters as a trainee before signing professional forms in May 1996. After making his league debut in goal at Burnley, and playing a blinder, in February 1999 he became the regular goalkeeper the following season after the departure of Kelvin Davis.

Nathan was dropped after a 1-4 home defeat at the hands of Bristol Rovers in February 2000 but bounced back during the relegation season of 2000/01.

Joining the mass departure from Kenilworth Road in the summer of 2001, Nathan has subsequently turned out for Chesterfield, Northampton, Boston, Leyton Orient and Bristol City and is currently with M K Dons.

■ James (Jimmy) ADAM.

Scot Jimmy Adam was spotted by the Town whilst playing for Spennymoor and despite fierce opposition from several top flight clubs they got their man when he signed on the dotted line in July 1953.

Enjoying skill in abundance and able to play on either wing, his only fault was a lack of finishing power which meant that he had long spells out of the side. Miffed at not being part of the 1959 Cup final team he left Luton that summer for Aston Villa and from then on to Stoke and Falkirk before emigrating to Australia where he played for his adopted country as well as becoming a successful coach.

Now retired in Australia, Jimmy was recently a welcome guest of the club alongside his Luton born wife Enid.

■ Terence (Terry) ADAMSON

After appearing for Sunderland in the 1966 Youth Cup final, Terry was not retained by the Roker Park outfit and was snapped up, along with Brian Johnson, by Luton manager George Martin in July 1966 as cover for full-backs Bobby Thomson and Fred Jardine.

Terry made his Luton debut nine months later in a 1-1 home draw with Port Vale and made one further appearance that season, in a 0-2 defeat at Southend, before moving on to Hartlepools United that summer.

Linking up with his older brother Keith at Scarborough soon afterwards, he then played for South Shields and spent 12 seasons with Murton. He is now an upholstery supplier based in Sunderland.

■ Anthony (Tony) Charles ADCOCK

Bethnal Green born Tony was an experienced goalscorer with two good feet and a respectable strike rate who was signed by Luton manager David Pleat in the summer of 1994 for £20,000 as forward cover.

Unfortunately, a series of injuries meant that he was restricted to only two substitute appearances, at Notts County and at home to Charlton in 1994/95, and he was allowed to leave that summer, returning to Colchester with whom he had started his career in 1981.

After being released by Colchester in 1999, Tony wound down his football career at Heybridge Swifts and still lives in that area working for an air conditioning installation firm.

■ Thomas (Bud) AHERNE

Although born in Limerick, Bud moved to the North in 1946, after leaving the army, to turn out for Belfast Celtic.

Following the infamous riot in 1949, which ended with Belfast Celtic being thrown out of the Irish League, the Hatters were first to offer the established international full-back terms.

Bud gave the Town ten years service with many cultured and reliable displays and was proud of the fact that he was always able to keep wing maestro Stanley Matthews quiet each time they met.

After retiring from the professional game he looked after the Town's youth side for a while but still continued to play for Luton Celtic until well into his forties. Bud passed away in 1999.

■ Mark AIZLEWOOD

Born only a stone's throw from Somerton Park, Newport, Mark joined his local club from school before making his league debut as a 16 year old in March 1976.

Luton manager David Pleat paid £50,000 for his services two years later and he made 98 league appearances for the Hatters in a variety of defensive and midfield roles before losing his place to Richard Money in 1982.

He moved to Charlton that summer and then enjoyed relatively big money moves to Leeds and Bradford City before winding down at Bristol City and Cardiff having racked up over 500 league appearances in a magnificent career.

After a variety of coaching roles Mark is now an agent.

■ Milija Antony ALEKSIC

Born of a Yugoslav father, Milija made his goalkeeping name with Stafford Rangers leading to a move to Plymouth in February 1973.

His bravery and sharp reflexes came to the attention of Hatters manager Harry Haslam who needed a replacement for the injured Keith Barber and after signing for Luton in December 1976 he remained virtually ever present for two years, earning the nickname 'Elastic' along the way, before a big money offer from Tottenham became too good to turn down.

Unfortunately, he was beset with injuries at White Hart Lane and although appearing in the 1981 F.A.Cup final, the signing of Ray Clemence meant his relegation and after a short loan spell back at Luton he drifted off to South Africa where he sells golf equipment.

■ Graham ALEXANDER

Coventry born Graham signed on for Scunthorpe in March 1990 from youth trainee making his League debut the following season.

After over 150 League appearances for the Iron he became one of ill-fated Luton manager Terry Westley's signings over the summer of 1995. The £100,000 was well spent, however, as Alexander soon displayed sound defensive qualities as well as showing he was the best dead ball kicker at the club.

Sadly, finances dictated that the Hatters had to accept a cut-price £50,000 offer from Preston in March 1999 and the full-back went on to become a crowd favourite at Deepdale as well as picking up caps for Scotland.

Graham made a surprise move to Burnley in the summer of 2006.

■ Derrick (Sos) Sydney ALLEN

Although born in Luton, Sos was playing for Alton Town when he was spotted by Hatters scouts and invited to Kenilworth Road where he signed on as an amateur whilst still keeping up a day job as a driver.

After signing full time he made only one appearance, on the wing, in a mid-week game at Derby during the Town's promotion season of 1954/55.

Realising his chances at Luton were limited he played six games for Watford before moving back into non-league. He was still playing Sunday football right up until his death in 1978.

■ Christopher (Chris) Anthony ALLEN

Chris signed professional forms for his local club, Oxford United, in May 1991 and soon made a name for himself as a speedy winger leading to England under-21 caps and a big money move to Nottingham Forest.

Unfortunately he lost his way at the City Ground leading to a loan spell at Lennie Lawrence's Luton where he failed to pull up any trees, scoring once in 14 appearances.

After failing to win back a first team slot at Forest, Chris moved to Port Vale and then Stockport before dropping down to Slough, Dover and Aldershot Town.

■ Keith ALLEN

The fourth of seven sons who all played football at varying levels, Keith was not given a first team chance at local club Portsmouth but made his name at Stockport where he was a mainstay in the side that walked away with Division Four in 1967.

Surprisingly transferred to Luton in exchange for forward Derek Kevan he never regretted the move as he became an instant terrace hero at Kenilworth Road with his 100% all-action style of play.

'Spider' became the perfect foil to both Bruce Rioch and Malcolm Macdonald as the Hatters won two promotions in three seasons before leaving on a free transfer to Plymouth.

Keith is now back on his native Isle of Wight.

■ Paul Kevin ALLEN

Busy midfielder Paul was part of the Allen clan that has produced so many footballers since the War.

Famous for becoming the youngest player to appear in the F.A.Cup final, when turning out for his first club West Ham, he subsequently enjoyed a long stay at Tottenham followed by a less successful time at Southampton.

It was while at the Dell that he was encouraged to come to David Pleat's Luton on loan in December 1994 when he made four appearances. He then wound down his career at Swindon, Bristol City and Millwall before working for the PFA and subsequently coaching at Tottenham's academy.

■ Rory William ALLEN

The Hatters were struggling at the wrong end of the Division Two table as the 1997/98 season drew to a close when ex-manager David Pleat offered one of his Tottenham youngsters on loan.

Rory Allen was recovering from a serious ankle injury and Luton were a little reluctant to take on a crock but it was a good job they did as he was a revelation and his six goals in eight appearances ensured survival.

Unable to stake a regular first team place at White Hart Lane, Rory was transferred to Portsmouth for £1 million but a succession of injuries cut short his career.

■ Ian James Robert ALLINSON

Hitchin born Ian had racked up over 300 appearances for Colchester, who he had joined from school, when he was amazingly snapped up by Arsenal on a free transfer in 1983.

Although never a regular at Highbury he made over a century of appearances for the Gunners before moving to Stoke and then on to Luton in October 1987.

A clever footballer, Ian weighed in with some vital goals for the Hatters but was sadly cup-tied for the successful Littlewoods cup run.

After returning to Colchester, where he finished his League career, Ian managed Baldock and Stotfold and is now in charge at Borehamwood.

■ Timothy (Tim) John ALLPRESS

Hitchin born Tim came through the youth ranks at Kenilworth Road before making his League debut for the Hatters alongside Ceri Hughes and Neil Poutch in an injury ravaged side at Aston Villa in March 1990.

Unable to dislodge Richard Harvey from the Luton defence, Tim enjoyed a loan spell at Preston and a period in Germany before moving to Colchester United in 1993. After two years at Layer Road the tall full-back had three separate spells at Hitchin Town wrapped around interludes in Hong Kong and St Albans.

Tim is now a police officer stationed in Hitchin.

■ Benjamin (Ben) Robert ALNWICK

After joining his local club Sunderland from school, Ben picked up England Youth international caps and started the 2006/07 campaign as the Black Cats regular goalkeeper despite still being a teenager.

After being replaced by the more experienced Darren Ward, Ben was suddenly transferred to Tottenham in January 2007 for £900,000 where he is regarded as one for the future.

In order to gain more first team experience Ben was loaned to Luton in September 2007 and went on to make four appearances before being re-called to White Hart Lane due to an injury to England goalkeeper Paul Robinson.

Ben was on loan at Leicester City for the remainder of the 2007/08 campaign.

■ Adrian ALSTON

Going nowhere at Preston and working in an egg packing factory it did not take much persuading for Adrian to try his luck in Australia where he became a great success, culminating in playing for his adopted country in the 1974 World Cup finals.

Adrian was about to sign for Hertha Berlin that summer when Luton stepped in and the tricky forward starred as the Hatters made a brave but unsuccessful attempt to avoid relegation from Division One.

Surprisingly transferred to Cardiff for £20,000 in October 1975, Adrian helped the Bluebirds to promotion before joining the exodus to the USA where a knee injury ended his career.

Adrian then returned to Australia where he has a job caring for people with intellectual difficulties as well as a coaching post with Bulli F.C.

■ Peter Thomas ANDERSON

Trained chartered accountant Peter was happily playing for Hendon when he was given the opportunity to go full-time at Kenilworth Road. He did not regret the decision though, making 181 League appearances for the Hatters as a tenacious and competitive midfielder and helping his side to promotion to Division One in 1974.

As Christmas 1975 approached, the Town were in dire financial straights and the transfer of Peter to Antwerp saved the club from liquidation. After coming back, Peter turned out for Sheffield United interspersed with spells in the USA.

A surprise choice as player-manager at Millwall, Peter lasted two years at the Den. He is now CEO of the Bayshore Technologies Group in Tampa Bay, Florida..

Luton Town Post-War A to Z

■ Calvin ANDREW

Local youngster Calvin came through the ranks at Kenilworth Road before making his League debut at Brentford in December 2004.

Loaned out to Grimsby at the start of the 2005/06 season he scored his first League goal, against Barnet, and played against mighty Newcastle in the Carling Cup for the Mariners. Another loan spell followed, this time at Bristol City, before he returned to Luton coming on as substitute at Plymouth in April 2006 and netting the winner.

After being in and out of the side at Kenilworth Road in 2007/08, Calvin jumped at the chance of a move to Championship side Crystal Palace in July 2008.

■ Radomir (Raddy) ANTIC

Raddy will always go down in Kenilworth Road folklore for his magical goal at Maine Road on the final day of the 1982/1983 season which kept the Hatters in Division One.

David Pleat's first foray into the foreign transfer market brought the Yugoslav international sweeper to Bedfordshire but as the Hatter's manager rarely played with a sweeper Raddy's cultured play, superb technical skills and powerful shot graced the Luton midfield instead.

After retiring from playing in 1984, Raddy arguably built up an even greater career as manager/coach of amongst others, Real Zaragoza, Celta Vigo, Atletico Madrid, Barcelona and Real Madrid.

■ Joseph William (Billy) ARNISON

South African born Billy first came to prominence with Glasgow Rangers from whom the Hatters paid £8,000 for his services in 1948. Scoring a hat-trick in the 3-0 home win over Cardiff in only his fourth game Billy soon became a crowd favourite finishing as top scorer in 1948/49 despite missing a large part of the season with a right knee injury.

Because of this injury Billy was never able to repeat his scoring feats and after three major operations decided to call it a day at the age of 27.

After a well deserved testimonial, Billy returned to South Africa where he practised as a physiotherapist.

■ Edward (Ed) ASAFU-ADJAYE

Quick and aggressive defender Ed worked his way up through the youth ranks at Kenilworth Road before being loaned out to Walton & Hersham. After building on his football experience at Stompond Lane he returned to Luton to earn a place on the first-team bench when the Hatters were struggling through injury and suspension under previous manager Mike Newell.

After being awarded a professional contract at Luton, Ed was loaned out to Conference side Salisbury during the 2007/08 campaign before being recalled to make his League debut at full-back in the 2-1 home win over Crewe in March 2008.

■ Alec ASHWORTH

Everton reserve Alec jumped at the chance to come to Kenilworth Road as part of the deal that took Billy Bingham to Goodison Park in 1960.

Immediately setting up a fine understanding with ace Luton marksman Gordon Turner the duo scored goals for fun and it was disappointing when Alec asked for a transfer over the summer of 1962.

Joining Northampton of Division Three it came as no surprise when he banged in the goals that earned the Cobblers immediate promotion. He than accepted a move to Preston in 1963, picking up an F.A.Cup runners-up medal in his first season.

A knee injury brought an early end to his League career before his untimely death at only 55.

■ John ASTON

It was a major coup by Luton manager Harry Haslam when he managed to entice the holder of both a League Champions and European Cup medal to Kenilworth Road.

Still only 25 when he came to Luton from Manchester United in 1972, John soon became a crowd favourite with his clever wing play encompassing a deceptive turn of pace, a tremendous left foot and an ice-cool temperament.

After helping the Hatters to the top flight in 1974, his knack of scoring vital goals almost saved the Town from their ultimately unsuccessful bid to avoid immediate relegation.

After leaving Luton, John had brief spells at Mansfield and Blackburn before concentrating on his Stalybridge business 'Pet World'.

■ Geoffrey (Geoff) Edward Ramer AUNGER

Canadian international Geoff came to the U.K on the recommendation of Craig Forrest, a fellow countryman who was goalkeeper for Ipswich.

Geoff failed to make the grade at Portman Road but managed to persuade Hatters manager David Pleat to offer him a contract after a series of goalscoring performances for Luton reserves.

Handed a first team debut at Crystal Palace in November 1993, Geoff scored with his first kick of the game. The Town eventually went down 2-3 as did the career of Geoff who made only four more appearances for Luton before brief stays at Sudbury, Chester and Stockport.

Since leaving these shores he has turned out for several sides in the USA with Kansas City Wizards the last known.

■ Trevor Keith Charles AYLOTT

The phrase 'much-travelled striker' was invented for Bermondsey born Trevor who turned out for nine League clubs in a long and fruitful career.

Starting out at Chelsea, it was from Millwall that Luton manager David Pleat signed the big target man for £55,000 in March 1983 when it was realised that a 'presence' was needed in the Hatters forward line to help the nippy but small Paul Walsh.

A superb hold-up player, Trevor aided the Hatters in their bid to avoid relegation in 1982/83 then weighed in with eight top-flight goals in 1983/84 before surprisingly moving to Crystal Palace in exchange for Vince Hilaire.

Trevor is now a London black cab driver.

■ Herve BACQUE

Bordeaux born Herve came to Luton on trial from AS Monaco in the summer of 1998 and won the supporters over with a couple of brilliant displays in pre-season games at Kenilworth Road against Arsenal and Coventry.

It may have been fan power that forced Luton manager Lennie Lawrence's hand to sign the slight forward but it soon became obvious that Herve did not like the 'muck and bullets' of lower-League football and after only a handful of games he moved on to Motherwell.

Herve is now back in France with FC Bassin D'Arcathon.

■ Jack BANNISTER

Part of a successful Chesterfield Boys team, Jack was invited to West Bromwich for trials and signed on for the Baggies in 1959.

After only nine appearances for West Brom, Jack accepted a move to Scunthorpe in 1964 and then Crystal Palace a year later where he finally enjoyed a settled and sustained period of first team football.

Jack was surprised to see Palace accept Luton's bid of £10,000 for his services in November 1968 but he did not regret the move as the Town enjoyed almost unbroken success in his three seasons at Kenilworth Road.

The cool and cultured left-back moved to Cambridge United in 1971 and was still playing Sunday football at the age of 48.

■ Jairzinho (Rocky) Alon BAPTISTE

On the books of both Chelsea and Brentford as a junior, Rocky failed to make the grade at either club and instead played for a succession of non-League outfits where his goalscoring abilities increasingly caught the eye.

He probably thought his chances of League football were over though, before Luton manager Ricky Hill gave him a chance at the age of 28 in October 2000.

Sadly, the tall and skilful striker came to Kenilworth Road at a time of great turmoil on and off the pitch and he made only three substitute appearances before moving to Hayes on loan in March 2001 and then on to Farnborough Town.

Rocky was at Havant & Waterlooville in 2007/08.

■ Keith BARBER

Although born in Luton, Keith was spotted by the Hatters while playing local football in London and signed professional forms in April 1971.

A brave goalkeeper, Keith shared duties in the early part of his Luton career but soon made the position his own and was virtually always first choice until sustaining a bad chest injury at Notts County in November 1976.

When he returned to fitness he could not unseat his replacement Milija Aleksic and so joined Swansea. It was while on loan at Cardiff that he made his final League appearance, deciding to hang up his gloves after a 1-7 defeat at Kenilworth Road!

A Newmarket resident for over 20 years, Keith works for a racecourse starting stalls firm.

■ Leon Peter BARNETT

A product of the Luton Town youth system, local boy Leon became the first person to represent the club at Under-17, Under-19, Reserve and Senior level within one season when coming on as a substitute in a LDV Vans Trophy game at Woking in October 2002.

Although favouring the centre-half position, where due to his amazing spring and pace he is able to dominate forwards, he can play anywhere along the back line.

It came as no real surprise when Leon was transferred to West Brom in July 2007 for a big fee and he is now looking forward to his Premiership debut having helped the Baggies to promotion in 2007/08.

■ Kenneth (Ken) Rees BARTON

Following a glittering schoolboy career in his native Wales, Ken joined Tottenham after a successful trial in 1954 but had to wait seven years before making his League debut which came at Old Trafford during Spurs' double winning season of 1960/61.

After only three more appearances, the strong full-back decided to try his luck at Millwall in September 1964 before joining Luton three months later.

The Hatters were in the final leg of their drop from Division One to the football basement in five years and Ken's 11 starts could not stop the rot. He joined Dunstable in the summer of 1965 before working as a representative for a pharmaceutical company. Ken was only 44 when he died in 1982.

■ William (Billy) Henry BATES

Billy was spotted by the Town while playing local football for Eaton Bray. A strong and fast winger he played regularly for the Hatters during the war years as well as turning out once for Watford after they had arrived at Kenilworth Road a man short!

His only League appearance for Luton came in a 0-2 defeat at Millwall in October 1946 and, with his chances of first team football dwindling, he moved to Vicarage Road to pick up from where he left off during the war and made 13 League appearances in 1948/49.

He finished his football career at Dunstable and lived in the town until his death in 1997.

■ David Anthony BAYLISS

Liverpool born Dave joined Rochdale from school and made over 200 first team appearances for the Spotlands side as a tough tackling, no-nonsense central defender.

His refusal to sign a new contract at Rochdale worked to his advantage as Luton manager Joe Kinnear, suffering from an injury crisis and desperately looking for defensive cover, snapped him up in December 2001 and he helped the Hatters to immediate promotion from Division Three.

Sadly, Dave was then hit by a succession of injuries and after returning to full fitness was unable to command a regular first team place. He was firstly loaned to Chester in 2004 and then transferred to Wrexham the following year.

Dave is now joint manager at Barrow.

■ Ronald (Ron) Leslie BAYNHAM

Ron did not take up goalkeeping seriously until a stint in the army on National Service and declined a trial at Wolves because he did not think himself good enough.

After starring at Worcester City he now felt confident in accepting a move to Luton in 1951 and then spent the next four years sharing the goalkeeping duties with Bernard Streten before making the position his own.

Extremely brave and an expert cross taker, Ron won three caps for England and appeared for the Hatters in the 1959 F.A.Cup final before presiding over the club's drop to Division Four.

Ron was a welcome visitor to Kenilworth Road in September 2005 as part of the ground's centenary celebrations.

■ Douglas (Doug) Frederick BEACH

Spotted by Luton manager George Martin, while partnering another future Hatter Billy Cooke in an army representative match, Doug was a regular full-back at Kenilworth Road during the last war-time season as well as the first peacetime campaign.

A tough full-back who could play on either flank, Doug was transferred to Southend in July 1947 after the Hatters signed the expensive Billy Hughes and from there he moved to non-League sides Colchester, Chelmsford and Biggleswade.

After leaving the game, Watford born Doug became a private gardener at Bricket Wood and on retiring in 1985 settled in Callington, Cornwall.

■ David Alan BEAUMONT

After understudying Scottish International pair David Narey and Paul Hegarty at Dundee United, Edinburgh born David accepted a £150,000 move to Luton in January 1989 and stepped straight into the Hatters side that beat West Ham 3-0 in a Littlewoods Cup semi-final first leg.

Such was his assured performance that day at the heart of the Luton defence alongside Steve Foster he became a regular in the side for over two top-flight seasons at Kenilworth Road.

After losing his place during the relegation season of 1991/92 he moved on to Hibernian for £110,000 where he graced the Scottish Premier League for three more years.

David is now a police officer in Fife.

■ George David BEAVAN

Central defender George was spotted by Luton Town's former youth team coach Marvin Johnson and impressed after being given a trial at Kenilworth Road.

The Bexley born teenager soon became a consistent member of the Hatters youth side during the 2006/07 campaign and his aerial power and strength in the tackle earned him promotion to the reserve team. A combination of injuries and player sales saw him awarded an unexpected League debut, coming on as substitute for Keith Keane in a home game against Bournemouth in February 2008.

After impressing on his debut, George was given a start the following week and is predicted to have a bright future in the game.

■ Kenneth (Ken) BEAVEN

Early in the 1967/68 Fourth Division promotion season the Hatters suffered a mini injury crisis with wingers Ray Whittaker and Graham French both sidelined. For the important mid-week trip to Southend, manager Allan Brown decided to blood 17 year old apprentice Ken Beaven based on several outstanding wing performances for the reserve side.

The Town went down 0-3 to a strong Shrimpers outfit and Ken 'without much support, showed up better on the left'. This was to be his sole first team appearance and he was eventually released and joined Chesham United.

Ken now lives in Hemel Hempstead close to his Bovingdon birthplace.

■ Robert (Rob) BECKWITH

With Luton goalkeeper Mark Ovendale injured in the warm-up before a clash with Bristol City at Kenilworth Road in April 2003, 18 year old Rob Beckwith was thrust in at the deep end.

Acquitting himself well, he held on to the goalkeeping slot for the remainder of that season and suddenly, in view of the Hatters' receivership, found himself the senior goalkeeper at the club that summer!

The London born shot-stopper, who had been at Luton since leaving school, was eventually replaced by Marlon Beresford and, following a serious knee injury, fell way down the pecking order leading to his release in the summer of 2006.

Rob is now between the sticks at Barnet.

■ Ian Tracey BENJAMIN

Ian Benjamin scored goals for twelve League clubs over a long career and would probably class his ten months at Luton Town as one of the least successful of his time in the game.

He will, however, hold a place in the hearts of Hatters' fans due to scoring against Watford, in a 2-0 victory, in only his second game for the club!

Ian enjoyed his greatest successes at Northampton and Southend, with Luton, needing a replacement for Steve Claridge, paying £50,000 for his services from the latter in November 1992.

Unfortunately, he was unable to build upon his goalscoring start and moved on to Brentford before finishing his career at Wigan.

Ian is now manager of Soham Town Rangers.

■ Edgar William BENNETT

Outside-right Edgar contested a first team slot with Mick Cullen and Roy Davies whilst at Luton Town. Initially with local junior side West Park, he then played for Vauxhall Motors in the Spartan League and gained representative honours.

He joined the Hatters in September 1952 whilst on National Service based in Gainsborough and made his solitary Second Division appearance in the Town's 2-1 victory at Notts County in October 1953. After spending the 1954/55 promotion campaign in the reserves he joined Dunstable in July 1955 and worked as a jig and tool fitter for Vauxhall Motors until retirement. Edgar still lives in Luton.

■ Marlon BERESFORD

Marlon holds the distinction of being the oldest goalkeeper to turn out for the Hatters in League football.

In a career that has seen him appear between the sticks for ten clubs, including 240 League starts for Burnley, Lincoln born Marlon started off as a youth trainee at Sheffield Wednesday before making his first appearance in the League whilst on loan at Bury in August 1989. A transfer to Burnley saw him become a cult hero at Turf Moor before he tasted Premiership action at Middlesbrough after a fee of £400,000 enticed him away.

Marlon enjoyed two spells at Kenilworth Road, after initially joining the club in October 2003, and was released in the summer of 2008.

■ Cedric BERTHELIN

Luton Town used six goalkeepers over the course of the 2002/03 season with probably the best being big Frenchman Cedric Berthelin.

Signed initially on a two month contract, the ex-Lens shot stopper made a shaky Hatters debut in a 3-2 win at Stockport but eight games later had done enough for manager Joe Kinnear to offer him an 18 month deal.

Unfortunately, finances dictated that the offer had to be withdrawn with Cedric then moving on to Crystal Palace where he starred in an epic win at Liverpool in the F.A.Cup.

Cedric moved to Belgian side Mons in October 2004 and is now their manager.

■ Wayne BIGGINS

A strong and powerful striker, Sheffield born Wayne scored goals for nine League clubs, as well as making a surprise move to Glasgow Celtic, over a long playing career.

It was while at Stoke that Wayne enjoyed his most prolific scoring run and it was from that club, while in his second spell there, that he came to Luton Town in January 1995 on loan.

Signed to strengthen the Luton forward line following the sale of John Hartson to Arsenal, Wayne scored once in seven appearances before returning to Stoke after the Hatters signed John Taylor on a permanent deal.

Wayne then turned out for a variety of non-League clubs and finally hung up his boots only five years ago. He now runs a pallet business.

■ Hugh John Richard BILLINGTON

Although born in Ampthill, Hugh was raised in Luton and was picked up by the Hatters from Waterlows (Dunstable) for whom he had scored over 80 goals in the 1937/38 season.

He then banged in 14 goals in 15 reserve team games for the Town at the start of the following campaign before scoring twice on his League debut at Tranmere and finishing up with 28 strikes from 27 Division Two matches. A truly remarkable record!

Sadly, the war then took away the best of his playing days although he did net regularly for the Hatters over the first two post-war seasons before transferring to Chelsea for £8,000.

Hugh remained in Luton until his death in 1988.

■ William (Billy) Laurence BINGHAM

The Hatters tried to sign Belfast boy Billy in 1950 but he opted to go to Division One Sunderland instead. When the Rokermen were relegated eight years later the Town got their man for £15,000 and he proved a revelation on the right wing in the 1958/59 season as the Town fought through to the F.A.Cup final.

Fast, clever and elusive, Northern Ireland international Billy could not save Luton from relegation from Division One on his own the following season and he moved to Everton in 1960 where he won a League Championship medal.

Billy's second career came in management when he oversaw, amongst others, Plymouth and Everton as well as his country. Billy now lives in Southport in retirement.

■ Alan John BIRCHENALL

Much travelled midfielder Alan came to Luton in the twilight of his career, brought in by rookie manager David Pleat for his experience, as the Hatters fought against the drop to Division Three in 1979.

Alan calmed things down during his ten games at Kenilworth Road and, with his job done, moved on to Hereford, his last League club.

Starting with Sheffield United and then on to Chelsea and Crystal Palace, Alan probably enjoyed his greatest success at Leicester where his cultured left foot helped make the Foxes one of the most attractive sides of the mid-1970's.

Alan is still involved at the Walkers Stadium in his role as on-pitch announcer.

Kingsley Terence BLACK

Local boy Kingsley signed on for Luton Town after leaving college and following a series of brilliant displays on the left wing for the reserves was awarded a League debut at QPR in September 1987 while still only 19.

Seven months later he starred as the Hatters lifted the Littlewoods Cup leading to a fight between Billy Bingham of Northern Ireland and Bobby Robson of England for his international services. He chose the former and eventually earned 30 caps for the country of his father.

An inevitable big money move to Nottingham Forest in 1991 was never entirely successful, leading to a drifting down through the divisions. Kingsley now owns tanning studios in Luton.

Matthew (Matt) David BLINKHORN

Signing professional for his home town side, Blackpool, in June 2003 striker Matt featured in the Tangerine's 2004 LDV Vans Trophy final triumph.

Remembered by Luton manager Mike Newell from his spell at Bloomfield Road, Matt went on loan to the Hatters at the start of 2004/05 but could not displace Steve Howard and Rowan Vine and made only two substitute appearances, at Hull and at home to Bradford City, before returning to Blackpool where a shoulder injury virtually ended his season.

Matt moved to Morecambe on loan before accepting a permanent transfer to Christie Park in June 2007.

Philip (Phil) BOERSMA

After signing professional for Liverpool in 1966, midfielder Phil helped the Reds to lift the League Championship and UEFA Cup in 1972/73 before moving to Middlesbrough for £72,000 in December 1975.

Luton Town manager Harry Haslam lost out to Boro that time but eventually got his man in August 1977 in exchange for £35,000. A quick and skilful player, Phil netted some memorable goals for the Hatters, non more so that the diving header which saw off Brighton in front of the 'Match of the Day' cameras in December 1977.

After one season with Luton, new manager David Pleat transferred Phil to Swansea where a broken ankle ended his career.

In recent times Phil has assisted Graeme Souness at various clubs.

Emmerson Orlando BOYCE

Aylesbury born Emmerson was one of the many players to come through Luton Town's schools and youth development programme prior to signing YTS forms in the summer of 1995.

He made the breakthrough into the Hatters' League side at home to Lincoln in April 1999 before becoming a regular and crowd favourite during the following season. A fast and reliable overlapping right back, 'Boycie' saw an offer from Premiership Crystal Palace in the summer of 2004 as too good to turn down but even he was surprised when he found himself catapulted into the first team following a series of injuries to established regulars, a place he held on to.

Emmerson made a big money move to Wigan in the summer of 2006 and is now a Barbados international.

Adam Mark BOYD

Adam signed his first professional contract for his home town club, Hartlepool United, in 1999 and was gradually introduced to the first team after making his debut at home to Barnet in November of that year.

A change of manager saw Adam loaned out to Boston in 2003 but fortunately a proposed transfer fell through and on his return to Victoria Park he could not stop scoring and his goals helped Pool to the play-offs.

He finished top scorer the following season as Hartlepool reached the play-offs once more before a bad knee injury severely limited his appearances in 2005/06.

Once over his injury problems he was subject to a big money move to the Hatters over the summer of 2006. The transfer did not work out and Adam was on his way again in 2007, this time to Leyton Orient.

John BRAMWELL

Tough tackling full-back John came to Luton as part of the deal that took Billy Bingham to Everton in October 1960.

Starting off with Wigan, John then moved to Goodison Park where he enjoyed a good run in the Toffees Division One side. On coming to Kenilworth Road he was virtually ever present for five seasons and was even watched by the England selectors on one occasion such was his form in a struggling Hatters side.

John left Luton as the club slid into Division Four in 1965 and joined Rugby Town for a brief stint before emigrating to Australia.

■ Terence (Terry) George BRANSTON

Northampton Town finally got their man in October 1958 with the reluctant centre-half joining at a time when the Cobblers were about to sweep from Division Four to Division One in five years.

When Northampton started to fall back just as rapidly, Luton manager Allan Brown stepped in and brought Terry to Kenilworth Road in the summer of 1967. A born leader and hard as nails, terrace favourite Terry skippered the Hatters to the Division Four title in 1968 and further promotion two years later.

After a short spell at Lincoln, Terry retired to his established driving school in Rugby and is still an occasional visitor to Kenilworth Road.

■ Timothy (Tim) Sean BREACKER

Tim joined Luton from school in St Neots and made his Hatters debut in a 0-3 defeat at Ipswich in March 1984 while still only 18.

A fast and strong full-back who loved to overlap, Tim soon made the right back position his own, as well as picking up England u-21 caps, and was the only player to turn out in all 58 League and cup games in the momentous 1987/88 season which ended with the Hatters lifting the Littlewoods Cup.

Finances dictated that a reluctant Tim was sold to West Ham for £600,000 in September 1991, but he enjoyed eight years at Upton Park before finishing his career at QPR. In recent times Tim has worked as number two to Ian Holloway at various clubs with the last being Leicester in 2007/08.

■ Friedrich Johann BREITENFELDER

A summer 2000 signing by Luton manager Ricky Hill, this tall, right sided midfielder bizarrely let it be know that he liked to be called 'Ratz Fetz'!

Previously with NCN St Polten, the Vienna born 'Ratz' was beset with injury and made only two starts (against Wrexham and Wycombe Wanderers at Kenilworth Road) and three substitute appearances in a struggling Hatters side before returning to Austria in 2001. A year later he came back to England to sign on for Enfield before moving to German side Eintracht Bad Kreuznach. Subsequently, he has been with Rapid Vienna since August 2003.

■ Dean James Gary BRENNAN

Dublin born Dean joined Sheffield Wednesday from the exotically named Stella Maris Youth Club but found it impossible to fight his way into the side at Hillsborough.

When Ricky Hill became manager at Luton in the summer of 2000 he went back to Wednesday, where he had been coaching, and brought back Dean along with Peter Holmes.

A hard running left sided midfield player and occasional striker, Dean did not make much impact in an, admittedly, poor Hatters team and left to join Hitchin in 2002.

Since then Dean has been with Stevenage, Hendon, Grays, Lewes and AFC Wimbledon before linking up with Hemel Hempstead. Dean is now with Halesowen Town.

■ Matthew (Matt) Hyland BRENNAN

Spotted by Luton Town scouts while playing for St Roch, a junior club in his native Glasgow, Matt signed on at Kenilworth Road in the summer of 1962.

Getting his chance at the back end of the following campaign, as the Town were slipping out of Division Two, Matt put in some impressive performances and scored one of the goals of the season in the 3-0 home win over Plymouth before injury struck.

Sadly, Matt had to drop down to non-League level firstly with Chelmsford and later with Cambridge City and Bury Town.

Matt worked for Whitbread in Luton and now lives in Kempston.

■ Robert (Bobby) Anderson BRENNAN

It was a smart piece of business for Luton Town when they brought the clever inside forward over from Belfast Distillery in October 1947 for £2,000.

Once he had established himself in the Hatters side, his quality and opportunist goalscoring was plain to see and it was with regret that a record offer from Birmingham two years later was too good to refuse although it caused much anger amongst the supporters at the time.

He did not settle well at St Andrews or at his next club Fulham but then went on to enjoy seven years with Norwich, for whom he turned out against the Town, and scored, in the 1959 F.A.Cup semi-final.

He settled in Norfolk where he remained until his death in 2002.

■ Gordon Harry Joseph BRICE

Bedford born Gordon signed on for the Hatters during the war but was called up to the Marines almost immediately.

In the first post-war season Gordon had made only 13 appearances for the Town, mostly as understudy to centre-half Horace Gager, when mighty Wolves paid out a staggering £11,000 for his services seeing him as the successor to Stan Cullis.

It did not work out at Molineux and in March 1948 he signed for Reading where he became a terrace favourite. Moving up a grade to Fulham in 1952, Gordon had four years at Craven Cottage before being transferred to Ayr where he also ran an hotel.

Gordon was also a county cricketer for Northants and was living in Bedford at the time of his death in 2003.

■ Dean Michael BRILL

Local lad Dean signed on for the Hatters from school and made his Luton debut in a Division Two game at Oldham in September 2003, whilst still only 17, coming on in goal for Robert Beckwith who had been dismissed for handling outside the area.

Dean played four more times that season, none in the next, and five in 2005/06, including the first three games of the campaign when the Town took the Championship by storm. Then regarded as understudy to the experienced Marlon Beresford, the young shotstopper has subsequently made the Luton goalkeeping position his own.

■ Ahmet BRKOVIC

The 'Croatian Sensation' came to England after meeting a Romford girl who was on holiday in Croatia. The former Dubrovnik midfielder had trials at both Millwall and Luton before accepting a contract with Leyton Orient in November 1999.

In East London he starred as the 'O's won through to the 2001 play-off finals, where they lost 2-4 to Blackpool, before signing for Luton that summer on a 'Bosman' free transfer.

He then became a regular in a Hatters side that climbed from the basement to the Championship and won the fans over with his clever footwork, intelligent use of the ball and occasional spectacular goals from overhead kicks!

Brko sadly moved to Millwall during the 2007/08 campaign.

■ David BROGAN

Only a month after signing from Scottish junior club St Anthony, David was thrust into the Luton first team and scored on his debut, a last minute effort in a League Cup tie at Liverpool in October 1960, the club's first ever goal in the competition.

A clever inside-forward, David kept his place in the League side for four consecutive games before the heavy pitches began to tell and he returned to the reserves.

It was while playing for the Town's reserves that he badly fractured a leg which failed to heal properly and he reluctantly had to give up the game.

After receiving a testimonial in 1962, David returned to his native Glasgow.

■ Allan Duncan BROWN

Allan Brown became a record Scottish export, when leaving East Fife for Blackpool in exchange for £25,000 in 1950, due to his pace, power and subtlety in the forward line.

A Scottish international, he was regarded as a major coup by the Hatters in 1957 and became part of the Luton side that won through to Wembley for the 1959 F.A.Cup final making up for the two finals he missed with Blackpool due to injury.

After spells at Portsmouth and Wigan, Allan returned to Kenilworth Road as manager in 1966 and steered the club to the Division Four championship. Following several more managerial posts Allan now lives in Lytham St Annes in retirement.

■ Michael (Micky) John BROWN

Slough born Micky joined Fulham from school but played only a handful of games in the Cottagers Division One side in four years so moved on to Millwall in 1965 where he was a regular in the team which won promotion from Division Three a year later.

Following promotion, Micky found his chances at the Den limited so stepped down a level and came to Kenilworth Road in 1967.

A short, solid forward Micky played in four different positions in his first five games for the club but was unable to stake a permanent place in the side that won the Division Four championship.

After a year at Colchester, Micky played for several non-League clubs before settling in Harrow where he became a newsagent. Now retired, Micky lives in Spain.

■ Steven (Steve) BUCKLEY

One of the best left-backs in the Town's history, Steve was signed by Luton manager Harry Haslam from Burton Albion in 1974 and it was not long before his cultured left foot and surging runs down the wing became a feature of the Hatter's play.

Steve was a virtual ever-present in the Luton side until an offer of £165,000 from Tommy Docherty's Derby in January 1978 was too tempting to turn away.

Becoming just as popular at Derby, Steve enjoyed eight remarkably consistent years at the Baseball Ground before taking up a succession of managerial roles at non-League level.

In recent years Steve has scouted for older brother Alan as well as working as a lorry driver.

■ Frank (Frankie) Stephen BUNN

Joining Luton straight from school after being spotted playing for his district team in Birmingham, Frankie made his Hatters debut against Derby in August 1980 while still 17 and scored a point saver against Oldham two games later.

Big and strong, Frankie was not a prolific goalscorer and was never able to command a permanent place in Luton's eventual top flight side so moved down the leagues to join up with his old team-mate Brian Horton, by now manager at Hull, in 1985.

After some success at Boothferry Park he moved to Oldham for £90,000 two years later where his claim to fame was scoring six goals in a League Cup tie against Scarborough, still a record in the competition.

Frankie's football career was cut short by injury and he is now first team coach at Coventry.

■ Mark Stephen BURKE

Great things were predicted for Solihull born Mark after he starred for England schoolboys and then, after signing professional terms with Aston Villa, earned Youth caps.

Sadly, he failed to establish himself at Villa Park and moved to Middlesbrough before coming back nearer home to sign on for Wolves in 1991.

Luton Town manager David Pleat, desperately looking to bolster his squad at a time when the Hatters were fighting through to the F.A.Cup semi-final in 1994, took Mark in on a months loan.

Obviously blessed with wing skills, he did not make a good enough impression at Kenilworth Road and finished his League days with Port Vale.

Mark then went on a nomadic career abroad and was last seen playing in Sweden.

■ Charles (Charlie) Edward BURTENSHAW

After breaking scoring records with his local side, Southwick, Charlie was snapped up by Luton Town in January 1948 but had to wait over a year before making his first team debut at home to Barnsley.

Charlie then enjoyed a good run in the side, mainly on the wing as he was deemed too small to play up front, but was then surprisingly transferred to non-League Gillingham in October 1949 along with his brother Bill and Billy Collins for a joint fee of £10,000.

The three players then moved en bloc to Snowdown Colliery Welfare in 1953 where Charlie became player-manager.

After hanging up his boots Charlie returned to his native Portslade and was working for Metal Box on his retirement.

■ William (Bill) Frederick BURTENSHAW

Younger by three years than Charlie, and five inches taller, Bill came to Luton on the recommendations of his brother over the summer of 1948 and was immediately thrust into the first team on the opening day of the 1948/49 campaign.

Sadly, the powerful inside-forward did not make any further first team appearances for the Hatters but finished up as leading scorer for the reserves in his first season. The triple transfer of the two Burtenshaws and Billy Collins to Gillingham was big news at the time but the deal ensured that the Gills were treated seriously enough to be re-elected to the Football League in 1950.

Bill stayed in Gillingham after retiring from the game and spent over 30 years fixing meters for Seeboard.

■ Vivian (Viv) Dennis BUSBY

As a youngster Viv signed on for his home town club Wycombe Wanderers where his goalscoring exploits came to the attention of Luton Town manager Alec Stock who signed him in January 1970.

He did not wait long for his first team chance and by the end of that season had written himself into Hatters folklore by scoring the all-important goal against Southport which virtually assured promotion to the old Division Two.

A linking up on loan with his ex-strike partner Malcolm Macdonald at Newcastle did not work and he eventually moved to Fulham for whom he appeared in the 1975 F.A.Cup final.

After finishing playing, Viv moved into scouting, coaching and managing various clubs and is now assistant manager at Workington.

■ Barry Desmond BUTLIN

Unable to stake a claim to a regular spot in Derby County's Division One side, Barry was tempted to Luton in November 1972. Amazingly the £50,000 fee was a record for the Rams at the time!

Although his first season was cut short by knee injury he top scored in 1973/74 as the Hatters won promotion to the top flight. Brilliant in the air and no slouch on the ground it came as a major shock when 'Bullet' was sold to Nottingham Forest for £122,000 in October 1974 with the Town desperate for goals at the time.

Barry played for a variety of clubs after leaving Forest but was never quite so productive as in his days at Luton. He is now the secretary for the ex-Derby County Players Association.

■ Ian Raymond BUXTON

Ian was one of the last sportsmen to combine professional football with top level cricket which he managed throughout his long career.

Starting with his local side Derby in 1959, Ian was not a prolific scorer but brought others into the game. It was for this reason that Luton manager Allan Brown paid out £11,000 to bring the 29 year old to Kenilworth Road in September 1967 where his experience proved the final piece in the jigsaw as the Hatters walked away with the Division Four championship at the seasons end.

After hanging his football boots up, Ian continued with County Cricket for Derbyshire, who he had also joined in 1959, and eventually became chairman of the committee as well as running a sports shop in Chesterfield.

■ Noel Leslie (Les) BYWATER

Lichfield born Les guested for Luton Town during the war and when a new goalkeeper was needed to replace George Duke early in 1946/47 the Hatters picked up the agile shotstopper for a nominal fee from Huddersfield.

Les would probably have remained first choice goalkeeper for some time but the Hatters were given the chance to sign England amateur international Bernard Streten and his days at Kenilworth Road were numbered.

After playing briefly for Rochdale, Les became a police officer and remained in the Manchester area until his death in 1998.

The goalkeeping gene continues to run in the family as grandson Steve is current Derby goalkeeper.

■ Graham Stuart CALEB

Signed from Oxford City as a youngster, Graham was a prominent member of the strong Hatter's youth side of the early 1960's.

The Town had not won away for 16 months when Graham made his first team debut at Brentford in February 1964 but his display at centre-half helped steady the ship leading to an amazing 6-2 victory!

He kept his place for eight games before being replaced by the experienced Gordon Fincham as the Town fought to avoid relegation. He made a further 12 appearances in a struggling Luton side the following season before moving to Kettering and then Banbury.

Graham now lives in Witney.

■ Jamie CAMPBELL

Snapped up by Luton Town as a youth trainee, Birmingham born Jamie was regarded as a utility man at Kenilworth Road with his versatility meaning that he was used mainly as a substitute, which sadly ensured that he could never claim a permanent position in the Hatters side.

After making his Town debut as the team were slipping out of the old Division One in 1991/92 Jamie found his chances increasingly limited and moved on to Barnet, followed by Cambridge, Brighton and Exeter where he enjoyed a fair amount of success.

Jamie has recently retired from the game after a long, and ultimately fruitful, career and is now back in the Luton area.

■ Clarke James CARLISLE

Vastly experienced and commanding central defender Clarke started his career at Blackpool where his performances earned him a £250,000 move to QPR in May 2000.

After helping the Loftus Road outfit into the Championship, Clarke transferred to Leeds and then on to Watford in 2005 where he assisted his new side into the top flight.

Clarke suffered a thigh strain at the start of 2006/07 and in order to build up his match fitness he was loaned to Luton in March 2007 where his whole-hearted performances quickly earned the respect of the Hatters supporters.

After returning to Vicarage Road, Clarke was pitch-forked into the Watford side that took on Manchester United in the FA Cup semi-final but then decided to move back to the north-west when Burnley tabled a £200,000 bid last summer.

■ David CARR

David was another player whose career at Luton was somewhat compromised by his ability to play in several positions. Aylesham (Kent) born, David came to Luton as a trainee and signed professional forms in January 1975 all the time learning from reserve team coach David Pleat.

After making his League debut on the final day of 1976/77, David went on to make 43 appearances in seven different positions spread over the next two seasons.

A £20,000 transfer to Lincoln saw him miss only one match in his first three years at Sincil Bank as the Imps won promotion from Division Four. A season at Torquay then followed before he returned to his native Kent.

David sadly died in June 2005, age 48, following a brave fight against cancer.

■ William (Willie) Francis CARRICK

Willie was one of the many boys hooked out of schools football in Dublin and whisked straight over to Old Trafford to join Manchester United.

After five years there, the young goalkeeper found himself way down the pecking order and so took up the offer by Luton manager Harry Haslam to move to Kenilworth Road.

Unfortunately, he found his opportunities at Luton limited to four League outings in the 1972/73 season, including the brilliant televised 2-2 home draw with Burnley, and with Graham Horn coming on the scene to vie with number one Keith Barber he moved on to Chelmsford and also had a spell as manager of Witham Town before finishing with the game.

Willie still lives in Essex and has worked for Proctor and Gamble in Thurrock for 28 years.

■ Alec Francis Roy CHAMBERLAIN

Fen boy Alec first made a name for himself as a teenage goalkeeper at Colchester but a dream move to Everton did not work out, leading to him signing as number two to Les Sealey at Luton in July 1988.

Alec waited patiently for his chance and when it came he did not miss a game for almost three seasons. A brave goalkeeper with superb reflexes, Alec seemed set to stay at Kenilworth Road for life and it was a major disappointment when he decided to join Sunderland under freedom of contract in 1993.

Since then Alec has now been at Watford for eleven years and was still ready to keep goal at the age of 42. He is now on the coaching staff at Vicarage Road.

■ Brian Mark CHAMBERS

Midfielder Brian, an England schoolboy international, signed professional for Sunderland in August 1967 before making a surprise £30,000 move to Arsenal six years later.

It did not happen for Brian at Highbury and so he accepted a transfer to Luton who had just been promoted to the top flight. The clever ballplayer really came into his own though, after the Hatters were relegated in 1975 and for the next two seasons he was a regular in the side and also weighed in with some spectacular goals.

Brian then went on to give good service to Millwall, Bournemouth and Halifax over the next four years before turning out for several non-League clubs finishing up as player-manager of Poole in 1991.

Now living in Ferndown, Brian is a financial adviser for Zurich.

■ Robin Anthony Sydney CHANDLER

An old boy of Dunstable Road school, Robin was destined for greatness after appearing for England schoolboys but it was not until December 1961 that the Hatters managed to get his signature, albeit as a part-time professional.

By this time Robin had appeared in the Luton first team and after starring in an F.A.Cup trilogy against Ipswich in 1962 it seemed that the Town had secured a goalscoring centre-forward for years to come.

Inexplicably it all went wrong at Kenilworth Road and Robin left Luton for Stevenage in 1965 having made only 13 League appearances in five years.

Robin made up for lost time by becoming a prolific scorer in non-League circles, particularly for Romford in the 1970's, before coaching Baldock Town. He still lives in Luton.

■ Ryan Andrew CHARLES

Enfield born Ryan has been at Kenilworth Road since the age of nine after turning down the chance to join local rivals Watford.

A pacy, energetic striker, Ryan scored 17 goals in his debut season for the Luton youth side and followed it up with 12 strikes during the 2007/08 leading to a first team debut, coming on as a second half substitute at Southend in March 2008.

Ryan was then given his full debut at Carlisle on the following Tuesday before scoring on his introduction to the home fans four days later.

His clever strike, the opening goal in a 3-0 victory over Oldham, brought the house down.

■ Benjamin (Ben) Roger CHENERY

Taken on as a youth trainee by Luton from under the noses of home town club Ipswich, Ben made his Hatters debut playing at right-back in an F.A.Cup replay at Bristol Rovers in 1995.

He had to wait for his League debut until the end of the following season, with the Town already relegated, but finding places at Kenilworth Road still limited he joined Cambridge United in 1997 where he enjoyed a regular full-back position over the next three years.

It was after leaving League football that Ben enjoyed his greatest successes though. With Canvey Island he scored the winner in the 2001 F A Trophy final and starred as the Essex club rose up the leagues.

With Canvey folding, Ben joined the exodus of players and staff to Chelmsford in the summer of 2006 and is now at Braintree Town.

■ Daniel (Danny) Robert CLAPTON

Stepney born Danny combined a job as a Billingsgate market porter with amateur football for Leytonstone before being snapped up by Arsenal in 1953.

A quick and tricky right-winger, Danny graced Highbury for eight years, winning an England cap along the way, before finally losing his place at the age of 28 and moving on to Luton for £5,000 in September 1962 at a time when the Hatters were about to be relegated to Division Three.

He did not have much chance to shine in a poor side and made only ten League appearances in an injury hit season before emigrating to Australia. Upon his return to the U.K he ran a pub but died in tragic circumstances in 1986.

■ Stephen (Steve) Edward CLARIDGE

Steve has played for 15 League clubs – a record for an outfield player – in a long career which started out at Bournemouth in 1984.

During his career, Steve had two spells at Cambridge and sandwiched in between was a period at Luton with David Pleat paying £160,000 for his services in July 1992. By his own admission the goalscoring inside-forward hardly pulled up any trees at Kenilworth Road and moved back to the Abbey in November 1992 for £195,000!

Although now a pundit for Sky TV a return to League action at the age of 41 is not out of the question.

■ Alan CLARKE

Local boy Alan shone as a youth and joined the Hatters as an amateur straight from school before finally signing professional forms in October 1961.

Although regarded as a tough tackling wing-half it was on the wing that he made five first team appearances towards the back end of the 1961/62 season. Sadly, he failed to win a regular place the following campaign and moved to Dunstable.

Whilst with Dunstable, Alan gained the distinction of becoming the first ever scorer in a Sunday professional match when netting at Wisbech in March 1967. Alan also played cricket for Dunstable.

■ Gary Edward COBB

Right sided midfielder Gary joined his local side, Luton Town, from school and after a series of sound displays in the reserves made his League debut at Charlton in May 1987 where he set up Mick Harford for the only goal of the match.

After this bright start, Gary drifted down the pecking order and, following loan spells at Northampton and Swansea, moved permanently to Fulham in 1990.

Gary then combined working for the Chelsea community scheme with playing for, amongst others, Chesham, Berkhamsted and Bedford whilst still living in Luton.

■ Alan Stanley COLLIER

Markyate born Alan won England schoolboy and youth caps before signing for Luton Town as a 17 year old in 1955 but found his way blocked by international goalkeepers Bernard Streten and Ron Baynham at Kenilworth Road.

When Baynham fractured his skull early in the 1960/61 campaign, Alan was unable to take advantage as he was suffering from a broken arm at the time. Realising that it was not going to happen for him at Luton he moved on to Chelmsford and then to Bedford in time to star in their epic run in the F.A.Cup in 1965/66.

After retiring from the game, Alan worked in the printing trade in Luton and has recently moved to Reading to be near to his grandchildren.

■ John William COLLINS

On leaving school, clever forward John signed on for QPR where he made a name for himself as a scorer of important goals. Spells at Oldham and Reading then followed and it came as a surprise when he was allowed to move to Luton in August 1969 especially as he had finished top scorer at Elm Park the previous season.

Hatters manager and ex-QPR boss Alec Stock knew who he was signing, and the £11,000 fee was money well spent as John netted 10 goals, mainly from the right wing, as the Town won promotion to Division Two.

After finishing playing, John was assistant to old colleague Mike Keen at Watford and coach to Alec Stock at Fulham before running a building firm in West London.

■ Michael (Mick) Joseph Anthony COLLINS

Although born in London, Mick was brought up in Wellingborough and came to the attention of Luton after playing for the Northants youth side.

Signing on at Kenilworth Road in 1955, Mick had to bide his time as his favoured centre-half position was always taken by skipper Syd Owen or understudy Terry Kelly. When he eventually got his chance it was in an ageing team which was about to tumble through the divisions.

He reluctantly went to Chelmsford, joining up with Alan Collier and then moved to Bedford to be followed by Collier before both played in the Eagles 1965/66 F.A.Cup run.

In later years Mick became manager of Dunstable Town and is now back in Wellingborough.

■ William (Bill) Hanna COLLINS

Bill was invited over from Belfast by Luton Town for a months trial in early 1948 and the 27 year old ended up signing almost immediately and then making his Hatters debut at the end of the 1947/48 season.

Able to play as a right-half as well as in the forward line Bill could not keep up his early promise and was sold to Gillingham in October 1949 in a triple transfer with the Burtenshaw brothers.

After five years at Snowdown Colliery Workers, Bill returned to Priestfield where, over the next 40 years, he ran the reserves and youth team followed by first team trainer and kit manager. Bill, who enjoyed the benefit of two testimonial matches, still lives in Gillingham.

■ Francis (Frank) Joseph Anthony CONBOY

After signing professional for Tommy Docherty's Chelsea in 1965 Frank unfortunately failed to secure a First Division slot at Stamford Bridge and moved to Luton on a free transfer in October 1966.

Becoming Hatters manager George Martin's last signing, Frank made his debut in a 2-5 home defeat at the hands of Notts County and made a total of 19 League appearances, mostly as right-half, during the club's worst ever season.

After being released in 1967, Frank spent a year out of the game working as a painter and decorator with his father before joining Southern League Cheltenham for three successful years.

Frank now lives in Tadworth and is still a self-employed painter and decorator.

■ Edward (Eddie) John CONNELLY

A feisty ball-playing Scottish inside-forward, Eddie was snapped up by Newcastle in 1935 from Rosslyn Park for £90 and although he could be a match winner on his day he failed to fulfil his potential and was allowed to move to Luton for £2,100 in March 1938.

At Kenilworth Road he soon became a crowd favourite for his trickery and it was a surprise when he was sold to West Brom just before war broke out. At the Hawthorns his temper got the better of him and he was banned sine die in 1940 after two dismissals.

The ban was later lifted and he guested for the Town during the war and rejoined the club in 1946 but a cartilage injury led to him moving down the divisions.

Eddie continued to live in Luton until his death in 1990.

■ Richard Edward COOKE

Islington born Richard signed on for Tottenham after leaving school and made his Spurs debut at Luton in November 1983, scoring in a 4-2 win.

He failed to make his mark at White Hart Lane, though, and moved to Harry Redknapp's Bournemouth where his clever wing play attracted Luton manager Ray Harford who signed him for £75,000 in March 1989.

He featured regularly as substitute for the Hatters in the top flight but rejoined Bournemouth where his League career was ended by a knee injury in 1993.

Richard still lives in Bournemouth but commutes to London where he is a taxi driver.

William (Billy) Henry COOKE

After guesting for the Hatters during the war, it took some persuading and a substantial fee to prise Billy away from Bournemouth.

The effort was worthwhile, though, as crowd favourite Billy made over 200 League appearances for the Town as a rugged, no-nonsense full-back who took no prisoners. Remarkably consistent, Billy invariably came out on top against the finest wingers of the day with Preston's Tom Finney, a prime example, being kept quiet on more than one occasion.

After finally leaving Kenilworth Road in 1953, age 34, Billy had spells at Shrewsbury, Watford and Bedford before working at Electrolux until retirement. Billy sadly died in Luton in 1992.

Ronald (Ron) COPE

England schoolboy international Ron enjoyed eleven years at Manchester United and was centre-half for the Old Trafford side in the 1958 F.A.Cup final and was a regular in the team the following season when the Reds finished runners-up to Wolves in Division One.

After losing his place to Bill Foulkes, it did not take Ron long to accept a £10,000 transfer to Luton in August 1961 but he did not have the happiest of times at Kenilworth Road making only 28 appearances in two seasons.

A talented, footballing centre-half, Ron became national news as a prize example of the wrongs of the retain and transfer system but eventually was able to secure a move to Northwich Victoria where he stayed 14 years in all capacities.

Ron is now retired and living back in his native Crewe.

David John COURT

Joining Arsenal from school, David earned an occasional first team place at Highbury as a forward but after manager Billy Wright moved him to the half-back line in 1964 he became a regular member of the side for the remainder of the decade.

It was regarded a major coup by Luton manager Alec Stock when the Mitcham born midfielder was enticed to Kenilworth Road in 1970 for £35,000 but he did little to enhance his reputation and moved on to Brentford two years later.

After a spell at Barnet, David retired to look after his Brookmans Park delicatessen and is now back at Arsenal coaching in their academy as assistant to Liam Brady.

James (Jimmy) Darryl COX

Joining Luton as a youth trainee and signing professional forms in May 1998, Jimmy looked to have a long career in front of him when he burst on the scene as an 18 year old in a Worthington Cup tie at Ipswich early in the following season.

Showing pace and dribbling skills, Jimmy made eight League appearances over the 1998/99 campaign in midfield and attack but was surprisingly released the next summer and opted to go back to his native Gloucester where he joined the local City side.

Jimmy then went on to play for Bishops Cleeve and was at Yate Town in 2007.

Christopher (Chris) John COYNE

Brisbane born Chris came to these shores in 1996 following a £150,000 transfer from Perth SC to West Ham. Frustratingly, the tough tackling defender could only manage one substitute appearance for the Hammers and after loan spells at Brentford and Southend he joined Dundee on a free transfer in 2000.

Seeking a commanding centre-half to help secure the Luton Town back line as they attempted to win promotion from Division Three in 2001, manager Joe Kinnear paid £50,000 to bring Chris to Kenilworth Road and rarely has that sum of money been better spent.

After racking up over 200 first team games for the Hatters, and having been part of two promotion sides, all at Kenilworth Road were sad to see him leave for Colchester in January 2008.

Dean Anthony CROWE

Mobile and speedy forward Dean signed on for Stoke from school and was regarded as one to watch, with the teenager starring in his early days in the Potters side.

He was, though, unable to maintain this momentum and after moving out on loan to three clubs signed for Luton Town on a free-transfer in September 2001.

Signed as a replacement for the injured Carl Griffiths, Dean was virtually ever present as the Hatters won promotion from Division Three and finished second top scorer behind his strike partner Steve Howard.

In his second season at Kenilworth Road, the signing of Tony Thorpe and injury problems saw Dean move down the pecking order followed by an eventual transfer to Oldham in 2004.

Dean was with Stockport in 2006 before moving to Witton Albion a year later.

■ Peter Leonard CRUSE

England amateur international Peter failed to make the grade at Arsenal and was glad to move to Luton in 1973 for the chance of first team football.

Hatters manager Harry Haslam put the graceful inside forward into the side on the opening day of the 1973/74 campaign at Nottingham Forest but the Town were thrashed 0-4 and Peter was one of the casualties, being dropped from the team that beat Carlisle 6-1 the following week!

Peter found it difficult to win back a place in the side and so was loaned to Shrewsbury where he badly injured an ankle which effectively ended his League career.

After spells at Enfield and Staines and a year in Malta, Peter retired from the game and for the last 30 years has been a London cabbie.

■ Michael (Mike) Joseph CULLEN

Scout and ex- Town player Doug Gardiner recommended 17 year old Glaswegian Mike to the Hatters as a centre-forward but manager Dally Duncan soon moved him out to the wing.

A handful for any defender with a unique shuffle, Mike starred for the Town as they won promotion to Division One in 1955 and picked up a Scottish cap, the only Luton player to ever do so, the following season even though he was in the reserves at the time!

Surprisingly transferred to Grimsby in 1958, Mike went on to become virtually ever present over four years at Blundell Park before finishing his League career at Derby.

Mike remains in Luton after working at Vauxhall and the railway station car park.

■ George Patrick CUMMINS

George was a schoolboy sensation in Dublin and was wanted by most of the big English clubs but decided to choose Everton because of their strong Irish contingent.

Although an inside forward of skill and vision and blessed with the ability to carve open a defence with a single touch, George found it difficult to retain a regular first team place amongst the 52 professionals at Goodison Park and was happy to come to Luton in 1953.

George enjoyed eight years at Kenilworth Road as the Hatters won promotion to the top flight and reached the F.A.Cup final during his stay and he also earned 19 Eire caps along the way.

Leaving Luton in 1960 to join Cambridge City, George came back into the League with Hull before working as an electrician on Merseyside where he still lives.

■ Darren Paul CURRIE

London born Darren has been on the books of eleven League clubs in a career which started at West Ham in 1993. Unable to win a first team place at Upton Park, Darren took in some loan moves before signing for Shrewsbury and then on to Plymouth and Barnet where his silky skills brought the scouts flocking.

A £200,000 move to Wycombe followed and after a short spell at Brighton, Ipswich put in a big bid to take him to Portman Road where he initially won several 'Man of the Match' awards leading to loan spells at Coventry and Derby last season.

With the talent to win a match on his own, Darren joined Luton on a free transfer in 2007 before moving to Chesterfield in July 2008.

■ Alan Winstone DANIEL

Ashford born Alan moved to Luton at an early age when father Mel signed on for the Hatters. When Mel left Kenilworth Road the family settled back in Ashford leaving son Alan to be picked up by Bexleyheath and Welling where he played in an F.A.Youth Cup match against Manchester United losing 1-11!

Alan was, however, a good defender and was snapped up by the Hatters from under the noses of several clubs and after working his way up through the youth and reserve sides made his first team debut at West Brom in 1959 as a 19 year old.

A long and successful livelihood seemed assured but sadly, Alan's football career ended four years later with a mis-diagnosed snapped Achilles tendon.

Now in retirement, Alan lives in Dunstable.

■ Melville (Mel) Verdun Reginald John DANIEL

Welshman Mel unfortunately saw the best years of his footballing career lost to the war and after spells at Llanelli and Swansea was picked up by the Hatters from Ashford Town as the war drew to a close.

Prized for his versatility, Mel scored a hat-trick against Sheffield Wednesday on the opening day of the 1946/47 season but was equally adept in the half-back line and even as a full-back!

Leaving Kenilworth Road in 1949, Mel turned out for Aldershot, Newport and Betteshanger CW before hanging up his boots. A qualified carpenter, Mel later moved back to this area to be near his son, by now at Kenilworth Road, and scouted for the Town in his spare time.

■ Raymond (Ray) Christopher DANIEL

Local boy Ray made his way up through the ranks at Kenilworth Road before making his Luton debut at home to Sunderland in March 1983 as substitute.

At home in any position down the left hand side Ray could never carve out a regular place in Luton's top flight side and moved to Hull in 1986 where his career took off and he then enjoyed extended spells at Cardiff, Portsmouth and Walsall over the next ten years with only a succession of injuries keeping his appearances down.

After being connected with various clubs in the Hull area, Ray now coaches the Hall Road Rangers side.

■ Alexander (Sandy) Grimmond DAVIE

Scottish u-23 international goalkeeper Sandy had enjoyed seven years at Dundee United before being enticed to Luton in October 1968 for £8,000 and his form for the Hatters over the remainder of that season was a revelation.

Keeping 11 clean sheets in 27 starts, his campaign ended at the feet of a Southport forward over Easter 1969 and although he returned to the side the following campaign he was never quite the same player and it therefore came as a surprise when he was transferred to Southampton.

Sandy only managed one start for the Saints before returning to Dundee United and then emigrating to New Zealand in 1974 where he still lives.

■ William (Willie) Clark DAVIE

St Mirren forward Willie was attracting scouts from many big clubs but Luton manager Dally Duncan won the day and a cheque for £7,500 plus Tom Kiernan brought the clever player to Kenilworth Road where his goals and 'assists' kept the club in Division Two in the miserable 1950/51 season.

When panicking Huddersfield put in a £23,000 bid for the player in December 1951, a record for both clubs, it was too good to turn down and although Willie could not prevent the Terriers from suffering relegation from Division One they bounced back at the first attempt.

After five years at Huddersfield, Willie played for Walsall and Bath City before returning to Yorkshire where he worked in local hospitals before his death in 1996.

■ Curtis Eugene DAVIES

Luton Town trainee Curtis Davies showed maturity beyond his years when making his Hatters League debut as an 18 year old in a 2-2 draw with Stockport in January 2004 and it was only a matter of time before he won a regular spot in the first team.

Almost ever present during the Town's tremendous 2004/05 championship winning season his displays in central defence alongside Chris Coyne quickly caught the eye of Premiership clubs but it took a massive £3 million to prise him from Kenilworth Road.

A credit to his profession, Curtis moved to West Bromwich in September 2005 where he took to the top flight like a duck to water and it came as no surprise to Luton supporters when he subsequently made another big money move to Aston Villa.

■ Ronald (Roy) Alfred DAVIES

Cape Town born Roy decided to try his luck in the U.K and after unsuccessful trials at Manchester City joined Clyde where he soon built up a solid reputation as a quick two-footed winger.

Snapped up by the Hatters in May 1951, Roy went on to give sterling service over the next six years with only a succession of injuries preventing him from being one of the first names on the first team list.

A fast bowler for Bedfordshire and a good golfer, Roy finished his football career with Bedford Town but died tragically young at the age of only 49.

■ Ronald (Ron) Tudor DAVIES

Ron joined Chester as a £3 a week groundstaff boy and reputedly trained in army boots to improve his already prodigious leaping skills. The Hatters took a £10,000 gamble on the 20 year old in October 1962 and he rewarded them with 21 goals in 29 League appearances as a poor Luton side sunk to Division Three.

In September 1963 a £35,000 bid from Norwich, against whom Ron had scored six goals the previous season, had to be accepted and his career then went from strength to strength taking in Southampton, Portsmouth and Manchester United along the way.

One of the best headers of a ball the game has ever seen, Ron now lives in Florida.

■ Simon Ithel DAVIES

Winsford born Simon was taken on by Manchester United as a Youth Trainee, signing professional forms in July 1992, but in five years at Old Trafford was only able to make 11 League appearances.

Even so it was regarded as a coup by Luton Town when they paid £150,000 for the strong midfielder in 1997 but he sadly failed to live up to his reputation and moved on to Macclesfield a year later, inevitably scoring against the Hatters when the two sides met!

After a period at Rochdale, Simon went on to play for Bangor and Total Network Solutions (TNS) before going into management. Simon is currently in the hot seat at Chester City

■ Kelvin Geoffrey DAVIS

Kelvin made his Luton Town debut whilst still a Youth Trainee, appearing between the sticks in a 2-2 draw at Stoke in May 1994, two months before signing a professional contract at Kenilworth Road.

It took some time for Kelvin to claim a regular goalkeeping slot, needing to understudy both Juergen Sommer and Ian Feuer first, but once he became number once choice his shot stopping skills, allied to incredible reflexes, had the big clubs beating a path to Luton's door.

A £600,000 bid from Wimbledon took Kelvin into the Premiership in 1999 and since then his career has taken him to Ipswich, Sunderland and currently Southampton.

■ Solomon (Sol) Sebastian DAVIS

Cheltenham born Sol signed professional forms for Swindon in May 1998, after coming up through the ranks at the County Ground, making his League debut at home to QPR in November 1997, soon after his 18th birthday.

Forging a reputation for himself as a committed and tough tackling left sided player he was brought to Luton by Joe Kinnear in August 2002 soon after the Hatters were promoted from Division Three.

Something of a cult hero at Kenilworth Road, a stroke suffered on the way to Ipswich in 2006 shocked all Luton supporters but true to form he made a complete recovery and was soon back in the Luton defence.

■ Stephen (Steve) Mark DAVIS

Although coming from the North-East, Steve was a junior at Southampton but found first team opportunities hard to come by at the Dell so accepted a £60,000 move to Burnley in 1991 where he became a crowd favourite, helping the Clarets to successive promotions.

A £750,000 cheque took him to Kenilworth Road in 1995 where his astute reading of the game and power in the air in both penalty areas made him indispensable in over three seasons at Luton. An £800,000 bid from Burnley, and the players desire to return, saw Steve move back to Turf Moor in December 1998.

After a spell at Blackpool, Steve is now back at Turf Moor as first team coach.

■ Mervyn Richard DAY

Goalkeeper Mervyn played almost 650 League games for a variety of clubs over a distinguished 20 year career after coming up through the ranks at West Ham and making his debut in the 1973/74 season.

Long spells at Orient and Leeds then followed and it was from the latter club that he came on loan to Luton in 1992 just as he was coming to the end of his career and the Hatters were about to be relegated from the top flight.

The Luton supporters were aggrieved that previous loanee Steve Sutton had not been allowed to sign, leaving Mervyn to be seen as a poor replacement but he did little wrong in a four game spell.

Mervyn has gone back to his roots and is now assistant to Alan Curbishley at West Ham.

■ John (Dixie) Kelty DEANS

Dixie was a scoring revelation in Scotland for both Motherwell and Celtic and bagged a hat-trick for the latter in a Scottish Cup final and six in a league game against Partick Thistle in 1973.

It was regarded as a big coup by Luton manager Harry Haslam when he brought the 30 year old to Kenilworth Road in 1976 and he did not disappoint scoring 6 goals in 14 appearances including two on his debut against Sheffield United.

Short and squat and the complete opposite of a lithe athlete, Dixie was a bull of a striker and brilliant in the air but indiscretions both on and off the pitch saw Haslam lose patience and he was packed off to Carlisle.

After a time playing in Australia, Dixie settled back in Scotland where he is still a publican.

Peter Robert DENTON

Peter had difficulty in earning a regular right wing slot at Coventry, such was the form of Ronnie Rees, and managed only ten starts in four years at Highfield Road as the Sky Blues moved up through the divisions.

Thoughts that a move to Fourth Division Luton in January 1968 would re-boot his career proved incorrect as he could never hope to displace the mercurial Graham French and he remained, as he had at Coventry, a good squad player who would never let the side down.

After spells with Margate and Canterbury as well as coaching at Kenilworth Road, Peter worked at Vauxhall, is now retired, and still lives in the Luton area.

Andrew (Andy) Gerald DIBBLE

Andy will always hold a special place in the hearts of Luton supporters due to his heroic display in goal during the 1988 Littlewoods Cup final when the Hatters beat Arsenal 3-2.

Welshman Andy started out with Cardiff, before moving to Luton for £125,000 in 1984 but early on in his Hatters career he suffered a bad injury at Manchester United and was from then on trying to get his place back from the remarkably consistent Les Sealey.

An injury to Sealey gave him his Littlewoods Cup chance but knowing he was likely to be back on the bench, Andy opted for a £240,000 move to Manchester City and from there a dozen League clubs in a long career. Andy is now goalkeeping coach at Peterborough.

Paul DICKOV

Although born in Scotland, Paul started with Arsenal and it was while with the Gunners he came to Luton on loan in October 1993 to gain experience and scored once (a 1-0 home win over Notts County) in 15 whole hearted appearances.

A £1 million move to Manchester City followed in 1996 along with ten Scottish caps and, later on, further transfers to Leicester and Blackburn leading up to a return to the blue half of Manchester in 2006.

Feisty forward Paul was still giving defenders nightmares with his 'in your face' displays and total commitment last season at the age of 35 after signing for Championship side Blackpool.

Kerry Michael DIXON

Kerry became the 'one that got away' with Luton Town rejecting the local lad, and Hatters fan, as a youngster leaving him to make a name for himself at Dunstable Town before moving to Reading for £20,000.

A goal every other game for the Royals earned the big striker a dream move to Chelsea in 1983 where he became a terrace hero netting 147 league goals and winning eight England caps in nine years at Stamford Bridge before entering in to another big money move, this time to Southampton.

The move did not work out and Kerry's career then turned full circle with a free transfer to Luton where he weighed in with 19 goals and an appearance for the Town in an F.A.Cup semi-final against Chelsea in the twilight of his career.

Kerry is now actively involved with Dunstable Town.

Michael (Mike) DIXON

Although born in Willesden, Mike was brought up in Luton signing on professional terms at Kenilworth Road in 1957. Although a regular goalscorer for the reserves, Mike managed only three League games up front for the Hatters but his career was hampered by a fractured kneecap sustained at a Combination game at Southampton.

Moving to Coventry in 1961, Mike had scored 12 goals in 18 starts for the Bantams when a change of manager, with Jimmy Hill taking over the hot seat, and a further injury meant his days at Highfield Road were numbered.

A succession of non-League clubs than followed, including Cambridge United and Dunstable, but Mike drew consolation from son Kerry's later career in the game.

Gary Michael Thomas DOHERTY

Coming up through the ranks at Kenilworth Road the Eire born but locally raised Gary formed part of a formidable Luton Town Youth side that reached the F.A. Youth Cup semi-finals in 1997.

Luton supporters could never be sure which was Gary's best position as he was equally adept in central defence and as a striker and the same could be said after a big money move to Tottenham in April 2000 saw him appear all over the pitch at White Hart Lane.

A broken ankle saw the big Eire international out for a long spell and after returning to fitness he reluctantly accepted a move to Norwich where he has decided to concentrate on defending, becoming a mainstay in the Canaries back line.

Malachy (Mal) Martin DONAGHY

Luton Town boss David Pleat stole Mal from Northern Irish side Larne for £20,000 in 1978 while their manager was on holiday and he proved to be one of the bargains of all time, playing well over 400 league games for the Hatters and winning 58 caps for his country while at Kenilworth Road.

Best remembered for his central defensive partnership with Steve Foster, the consistent and remarkably injury free defender actually started his Luton career at left-back.

It was a sad day when Mal eventually got his dream move to boyhood favourites Manchester United and after a spell at Chelsea he hung up his boots and returned to Northern Ireland where he coaches with his country's F A.

Maxwell (Max) Spalding DOUGAN

Scottish amateur international centre-half Max moved from Queens Park to Leicester City in 1963 but the consistency of Ian King and John Sjoberg at Filbert Street limited his first team appearances.

In December 1966, Fourth Division Luton lost 1-8 at bottom club Lincoln and the signing the following week was just what the Hatters defence needed. Max converted to right back the following season, as the Town walked away with the Division Four title, before he bowed out in 1970 to join Dunstable.

Max eventually returned to Scotland and was a welcome guest of the Hatters for the Kenilworth Road Centenary celebration in 2005.

Stuart Anthony DOUGLAS

Wholehearted and brave forward Stuart came up through the ranks at Kenilworth Road before making a dream League debut as a 17 year old, scoring in a 1-1 home draw with Oldham in November 1995.

Never a prolific goalscorer, Stuart was often introduced from the bench by successive Luton managers when his enthusiasm and speed troubled opposition defences late in a game.

After being loaned to both Oxford and Rushden, he was made surplus to requirements by Hatters manager Joe Kinnear in 2002. Stuart then enjoyed a couple of seasons at Boston before a spell in Finland and then back to this country with Dagenham & Redbridge.

Stuart is currently at Bath City combining playing with a role as physiotherapist.

Iain DOWIE

Hatfield born Iain was a Development Engineer with British Aerospace and banging in the goals for Hendon when a £30,000 bid from Luton gave him the chance to ply his trade in the top flight.

After signing on in December 1988 Iain played only a bit part in his first season but in the following campaign he made the strikers position his own and it was a great shame when this scorer of vital goals was reluctantly sold to West Ham for £480,000 in March 1991.

Since that time the Northern Ireland international enjoyed another ten years at the top before taking up another career as a coach and manager. Iain is now manager at QPR.

John Dennis DOWNIE

John was snapped up by Bradford Park Avenue during the war becoming a goalscorer of renown and after a particularly good performance against Manchester United in the F.A.Cup the Reds paid £18,000, a record, for his services.

At Old Trafford he won a League championship medal in 1952 and it came as a surprise when he was allowed to move to Luton for £10,000 a year later.

Scoring a hat-trick on his Hatters debut, his future at Kenilworth Road seemed secure but a major row involving the provision of a club house meant that he stayed only twelve months before transferring to Hull at a loss.

John was still playing football until his forties and now lives in retirement in Bradford.

John Brian DREYER

A versatile defender and midfield player, John or 'Tumble' as he was affectionately known, almost perfected the one step penalty kick while at Kenilworth Road until warned off by manager David Pleat. It was also reckoned that the nets above the boxes were put up for his benefit!

Starting his professional career with Oxford, John came to Luton in June 1988 in exchange for £140,000 and became a regular in the side for six seasons before moving to Stoke under freedom of contract.

Further moves to Bradford City and Cambridge followed before he dropped down into non-League and then became manager of Maidenhead United.

John is now assistant to Graham Westley at Stevenage Borough.

■ Allenby (Allen) DRIVER

Allen was one of the many footballers who lost their best playing years to the war. After starting to make a name for himself at Sheffield Wednesday in the late 1930's, Allen had to make do with a diet of games for the Royal Artillery during hostilities and guest appearances for a wide variety of clubs.

Luton Town paid £4,000 for his services early in the 1946/47 season and he showed the ability to play either centre or inside forward netting 13 goals in 41 league appearances before he moved to Norwich after the Hatters signed Bobby Brennan.

Allen subsequently turned out for Ipswich and Walsall before playing non-League and then spending over 20 years working for a confectionary company. Allen sadly died in Sheffield in 1997.

■ Michael (Micky) Robert DROY

Giant centre-half Micky had enjoyed almost 15 years as a terrace favourite at Chelsea when he was asked to come to Luton on loan in 1984 to cover for broken leg victim Paul Elliott and shore up a woeful Hatters defence.

Micky made his Luton debut at Old Trafford in a 0-2 defeat but the following week, with the Hatters at home to West Ham, he limped off early with a hamstring injury. The Town then signed Steve Foster and Micky's days at Kenilworth Road were over.

After recovering from his injury Micky went on to Crystal Palace and Brentford before serving Kingstonian in various capacities. Micky is now living in retirement in Florida.

■ Richard Andrew DRYDEN

Starting off as a winger with his first club Bristol Rovers, Stroud born Richard gradually moved back and by the time he had signed on with his eleventh club, Luton Town, he was known as a tough, but skilful centre-half.

Along the way, big money transactions had taken him to, amongst others, Notts County, Birmingham and Southampton but he could do little to keep the Hatters in Division Two after signing in February 2001 despite remaining ever present until the end of that campaign.

Richard could not stake a regular place the following season and eventually joined Scarborough and subsequently Worksop Town before becoming manager of Worcester City in December 2007.

■ Edward (Ted) John DUGGAN

Ted became Luton Town's first ever groundstaff boy when signing on for the Hatters as a 15 year old in 1938 after being spotted starring for a successful West Ham Schools X1.

Another player who lost seven years to the War, Ted was, however, tipped for England honours once hostilities had ceased but the clever inside-forward suffered a series of injuries, including two cartilage operations on the same knee, and sadly failed to fulfil his great potential.

Transferred to QPR in 1949, Ted played for three years at Loftus Road before subsequent moves to Worcester City and Bedford.

After hanging up his boots Ted was for many years trainer-coach to the Hatters youth side and was instrumental in bringing through the likes of Bruce Rioch and Alan Slough. Ted was only 60 when he died in 1982.

■ George Edward DUKE

Southwick born George signed professional forms for the Hatters just before the outbreak of the war whilst still a teenager and built up his experience guesting for several London teams during the hostilities as well as turning out for the Town.

A sound goalkeeper, George was the Town's acknowledged number one at the start of the first post-war season but was then called up for overseas service in the Army. By the time of his return George found that Bernard Streten had made the goalkeeping position his own so he had to be content with reserve team football.

A move to Bournemouth was accepted in 1949 and from there on he went to Guildford, Snowdown CW and Ramsgate. George passed away in 1988.

■ Douglas (Dally) DUNCAN

Scotsman Dally had already crammed in a full career by the time he came to Luton as player/coach in October 1946. A pre-War Scottish international, he had starred for Derby as a mercurial winger picking up an F.A.Cup winners medal along the way.

When Luton manager George Martin went to Newcastle in 1947, Dally was asked to take over at Kenilworth Road but soon hung his boots up to concentrate on the job full-time.

He oversaw the Town's rise to Division One in 1955 with a young, keen and talented side and then left in controversial circumstances three years later to join Blackburn who he guided to the 1960 F.A.Cup final.

Following his dismissal from Ewood Park, Dally ran a guest house in Brighton for many years. He died in a Brighton hospital in 1990 aged 80.

■ Seamus DUNNE

After a glittering youth career in his native Ireland, Seamus was playing for Shelbourne when the Hatters managed to snap up his services from under the noses of a host of bigger clubs.

After one season in the reserves he earned his first team debut on Boxing Day 1951 and from then went on to break the 300 appearance barrier for his only league club. A fast and strong right back he became a fixture in the Town side for ten years and picked up 15 caps for his country.

After finally leaving Kenilworth Road, Seamus played for three years at Yiewsley and was then player/manager at Dunstable whilst working at Vauxhall.

In 1970 a chance to move back to Ireland to work in a chemical plant was too good to turn down and Seamus now lives in retirement in Bray.

■ Sean Mark DYCHE

Unable to make the grade at Nottingham Forest, the Kettering born central defender went on a free transfer to Chesterfield in 1990 and soon became a mainstay in the Spireites rearguard and had made over 200 appearances for the Derbyshire club before a £350,000 move to Bristol City in 1997.

Sadly, injury problems at Ashton Gate meant the Robins faithful never saw the best of the powerful stopper and he was loaned to Luton in January 1999 where he was able to regain his fitness, confidence and form as well as help the Hatters to escape relegation.

With the Town in receivership the funds to purchase Sean could not be found and so he went to Millwall and from there to Watford and then Northampton. Sean is now on the academy coaching staff at Vicarage Road.

■ Akenhaton Carlos EDWARDS

Already an established international for Trinidad and Tobago, Carlos was signed by Wrexham, along with Hector Sam, for £125,000 from Defence Force (Trinidad) in 2000.

Due to skill, pace and trickery, Carlos is able to unsettle the strongest of defences and it was for this reason that Luton manager Mike Newell enticed him to Kenilworth Road in the summer of 2005 just as the Hatters were promoted to the Championship.

Carlos instantly became a crowd pleaser at Kenilworth Road, proving virtually unplayable on occasions, and continued to play regularly for his country with whom he enjoyed a memorable World Cup finals in 2006.

Luton supporters were disappointed to see the mercurial Carlos move to Sunderland in January 2007 where he has predictably proved to be a big hit.

■ David Alexander EDWARDS

David joined Shrewsbury Town from school before making his League debut as substitute on the last day of the 2002/03 season whilst still 17 and not even a full-time professional.

A tireless midfielder with boundless energy, David signed professional forms in January 2004 and it was not long before he attracted widespread attention with Luton the eventual winners of the unofficial auction, signing him for £200,000 last summer.

Sadly, Luton supporters did not get to see much of David as finances dictated that he should be sold in the January 2008 transfer window. By now a Welsh international, David moved to Wolves for a large fee and Championship football.

■ Richard (Dick) Leonard EDWARDS

Dick was playing for Addmult (Hemel Hempstead) in the South Midland League when the Hatters spotted him and signed him on amateur forms in October 1963.

The tough tackling full-back then signed part-time professional forms in June 1964 before making his full debut for the Town on the final day of the 1964/65 season just as the club was relegated to Division Four for the first time in its history.

During the following season Dick signed a full-time contract and was able to make 16 appearances, plus score a goal in the 2-2 draw at Colchester, as the Town tried for promotion at the first attempt.

Released at the end of that campaign, along with many others, Dick then signed on for Kettering Town. Dick now lives back in Hemel Hempstead.

■ Paul Marcellus ELLIOTT

Paul failed a trial at Luton Town as a striker and signed forms for his local club Charlton instead and converted to a central defender.

With the Hatters needing a strong and commanding centre-half to bolster their defence as they attempted to avoid relegation from the top flight in 1983 they paid a cut price £95,000 to cash strapped Charlton to achieve their aims.

Unfortunately Paul broke his leg in a League Cup tie with Leicester in 1984 and by the time of his return the Town had signed Steve Foster. Unable to keep both players happy the Hatters sold Paul to Aston Villa for £400,000 and from there he sampled life in Italy with Pisa and then turned out for Celtic and Chelsea where another bad injury ended his career.

Paul is now a football pundit regularly seen on television.

■ Stephen (Steve) Blair ELLIOTT

A true journeyman striker, Steve started off as an apprentice at Nottingham Forest but to get regular football accepted a move to Preston where his career took off.

Managing 70 goals in over 200 League appearances for Preston, Steve hankered after a move up the football ladder but was surprised when a bid from top flight Luton took him to Kenilworth Road in 1984.

Steve knocked in six goals in 15 starts for the Hatters but became surplus to requirements when Luton wanted David Preece from Walsall and the Saddlers insisted on Steve as part of the deal.

This move then became one of many for Steve as he continued to bang in the goals for Bolton, Bury, Rochdale and Guiseley. Steve is now a Leisure Centre manager for South Ribble Borough Council.

■ Lars ELSTRUP

Although Luton Town had dipped into the foreign player market before, the signing of an established Danish international for a club record fee in 1989 took transfers up to a completely different level.

Lars had played for Feyenoord, but established himself with Odense from where he was signed by the Town. His first season at Kenilworth Road was beset by injury but in the 1990/91 campaign supporters could finally see that he was a class act with his speed, intelligence and finishing ability.

Sadly, a row over money saw him return to Odense in controversial fashion and within two years he had dropped out of football altogether, changing his name to Darando and joining the anarcho-Buddhist Wild Goose sect. Lars apparently now offers seminars on new age topics!

■ Carl Wayne EMBERSON

Epsom born Carl was unable to make an impression at first club Millwall and signed on for Colchester in July 1994 where he became a crowd favourite. At Layer Road he was first choice for most of his five years there as well as being voted 'Man of the Match' in the 'U's play-off final win over Torquay in 1998.

A move to Walsall a year later did not work out and he accepted a transfer to Luton in 2001, initially as understudy to Mark Ovendale, but he soon took over the number one spot as the Town won promotion from Division Three at the first attempt.

A good shot stopper, Carl was allowed to move to Southend in 2003 and from there he has appeared for Grays and latterly Sutton United.

■ Lewis James EMANUEL

Bradford born Lewis joined Bradford City as a Youth Trainee before making his debut for the Bantams in a Worthington Cup tie at Macclesfield in August 2001.

A tough tackling, speedy left sided player, Lewis soon became a mainstay in the City side but decided to try his luck in the Championship with Luton Town in the summer of 2006, signing a two year contract after a successful trial period.

Since joining the Hatters, Lewis became an instant crowd favourite when scoring the only goal of the game at Sheffield Wednesday in only his second outing. He has also now added a Republic of Ireland 'B' cap to the Youth caps already won.

■ Sean Anthony EVERS

A tremendous 'box-to-box' player with superb stamina, Sean signed professional forms for the Hatters in May 1996 shortly after making his League debut in a Luton side that was just about to be relegated from Division One.

It was, though, two years later that Sean saw scouts flock to Kenilworth Road, due to his displays in a long Worthington Cup run and a sparkling performance for the Nationwide League representative team in Italy.

Cash-strapped Hatters reluctantly accepted a £500,000 offer from Reading in March 1999 but Sean was beset with injuries at the Madejski and after a loan spell at St Johnstone joined Plymouth on a free-transfer where further injury put paid to his League career.

Since leaving Plymouth, Sean turned out for Stevenage and Woking and is now an Estate Agent.

■ Michael (Mick) Peter FAIRCHILD

Born in Northampton, went to school in Gt Yarmouth and spotted while playing for Lowestoft, Mick came to Kenilworth Road in November 1960 and made a scoring debut for the Hatters at a wet Southampton the following April.

As the Town dropped through the divisions, pacey winger Mick had difficulty in winning a regular place and moved to Reading in 1964 where his chances were still limited. After a short spell at Cambridge United, Mick joined Hillingdon where he found his niche.

Mick's main claim to fame at Hillingdon was in being part of the side that knocked the Hatters out of the F.A.Cup in 1969. An embarrassing afternoon for Luton supporters!

Mick returned to Lowestoft in 1972 and still resides in the area.

■ Sean Paul FARRELL

Big, strong striker Sean was probably too brave for his own good as he missed a large chunk of his footballing career due to injury.

Watford born, but signing on for Luton Town from school, Sean made his debut for the Hatters in the top flight and during the 1990/91 campaign made 20 appearances and seemed to have carved out a regular slot in the side. A change of manager saw David Pleat transfer Sean to Fulham for £100,000 and from there he moved to Peterborough and Notts County scoring plenty of goals along the way.

After leaving Meadow Lane, Sean moved on to Burton Albion but had to retire through inevitable injury.

■ John Gilbert FAULKNER

'Maxie', to all at Kenilworth Road, decided to qualify as a Quantity Surveyor and play non-League for Sutton United rather than join Charlton.

A commanding performance at centre-half against Leeds in the F.A.Cup saw him succumb to temptation and join the professional ranks at Elland Road but in only his second start he broke a kneecap.

With Luton Town selling Chris Nicholl a vacancy arose at Kenilworth Road in March 1972 and John accepted the offer with both hands and with it over 200 League appearances, a promotion to Division One and cult status amongst the Hatters fans.

A spell in the USA followed before he returned to Luton as youth team coach and then first team coach under Jim Ryan. After Ryan's departure, John went to Norwich under Mike Walker before scouting for, amongst others, ex-Town star Danny Wilson.

John is now a sports psychologist.

■ Warren James FEENEY

After being watched by many clubs while playing in his native Belfast, Warren decided to opt for Leeds, then one of the powers in the land. Working his way up through the youth system at Elland Road, Warren was frustrated by big money imports being introduced and so decided to try his luck elsewhere and joined Bournemouth in March 2001.

Warren enjoyed a successful time with the Cherries where his speed and persistence brought him a clutch of goals. Finances dictated that Warren be transferred to Stockport where he finished as top scorer in a relegated side but he was then rescued by Luton manager Mike Newell who remembered him as a thorn in the side of various Hatters' teams.

Unfortunately, Northern Ireland international Warren could never command a regular spot at Kenilworth Road and moved on to Cardiff, Swansea and latterly Dundee United.

■ Rodney Alan FERN

Capable of the sublime or the ridiculous, quite often in the same game, Rodney was a playmaking inside forward who joined Leicester in 1966 eventually winning a regular place and finishing top scorer for the Foxes in 1969/70. A superb display at Luton in a 3-1 Leicester win over Easter 1971 was remembered by all at Kenilworth Road leading to a £45,000 transfer a little over a year later.

Rodney did not enjoy the best of times at Luton and was glad to accept a cut price move to Chesterfield in 1975 where he netted regularly and then four years later to Rotherham who he helped to the brink of the top flight.

Rodney now runs pubs and a fuel business in Leicestershire.

■ Ian Anthony FEUER

Giant American goalkeeper Ian was playing for West Ham's third team when Luton Town manager Terry Westley invited him to Kenilworth Road on loan to take the place of another American, Juergen Sommer.

Quickly becoming a favourite, Ian was eventually signed for £580,000 and was virtually ever present as the Hatters were relegated from Division One in 1996 and then almost bounce back at the first time of asking the following year.

At the start of the 1997/98 campaign Ian badly injured a shoulder, was out for a long time and then struggled to regain his form leading to him leaving the club and returning to the States.

Subsequently Ian made brief attempts at comebacks in the U.K and, according to his website, is now available for personal coaching in the USA.

■ Gordon Richard FINCHAM

Tough, uncompromising centre-half Gordon joined Leicester as a 17 year old in 1952 and after working his way up through the ranks at Filbert Street seemed to have claimed a regular first team spot three years later only for serious injury to strike.

By the time he gained full fitness others had overtaken him in the pecking order so he accepted a move to Plymouth where he enjoyed five good seasons before joining Luton Town in 1963.

Gordon battled manfully as the Hatters escaped relegation in 1964 but following the inevitable drop a year later he emigrated to South Africa where he turned out for Port Elizabeth and ran a sports shop.

Gordon is now retired and back in his native Peterborough.

■ John (Jake) Williamson FINDLAY

Aston Villa manager Tommy Docherty fought off a shoal of clubs to sign goalkeeper Jake as a 15 year old but although he starred in the Villans 1972 Youth Cup triumph he found it difficult to displace Jim Cumbes and Jimmy Rimmer.

It took a lot of pestering by Luton manager David Pleat though, to get Villa to release Jake to replace Milija Aleksic in 1979 but once he came to Kenilworth Road he became a terrace favourite and starred as the Hatters won promotion to Division One in 1982. A badly broken thumb then effectively ended his Luton career as by the time he was fit the Town had signed Les Sealey and after a brief spell at Swindon he hung up his gloves.

Jake is now assistant manager at Stourport Swifts.

■ Thomas (Tom) FINNEY

A pipefitter by trade and playing part-time for Crusaders in his native Belfast, Tom was quietly signed by Luton manager Harry Haslam over the summer of 1973 and became an instant sensation for the Hatters.

Scoring twice on his full debut against Carlisle in September 1973 he then netted in his next three games but no sooner had his star risen than it started to wane and the following summer he was transferred to Sunderland.

He fared little better at Roker Park but won the first of his Northern Ireland caps while he was there. It was his next move, though, where he found his niche, making over 300 appearances for Cambridge United in ten years at the Abbey.

Tom now works for Securicor in Cambridge.

■ James (Jim) Paterson FLEMING

Tricky winger Jim was signed by Luton Town in 1960 from Partick Thistle in a straight swap deal involving Joe McBride. Still a teenager when he came to Kenilworth Road Jim was one of the stars of a poor Luton side and if his finishing had matched his approach play he undoubtedly would have picked up caps for Scotland.

As the Hatters were about to drop to Division Three, Jim returned to Partick and then moved on to Dunfermline, with whom he played in Europe, before transferring to Hearts.

Jim finished his career at Ross County and now lives in Inverness.

■ Jaroslaw FOJUT

Giant central defender Jaroslaw earned Polish Youth international caps and had turned out for several clubs in his homeland before being spotted by Bolton during one of their many sweeps through Europe looking for bargains.

After signing on at the Reebok in 2006, the 18 year old was introduced gently into the first team and by the end of 2006/07 had made four appearances spread across three different competitions for the Trotters.

In order to gain further experience Bolton decided to loan Jaroslaw out, with Luton the fortunate recipients. A towering, skilful presence in defence who seemed genuinely pleased to be at Kenilworth Road, Jaroslaw soon became a crowd favourite and it was desperately disappointing for both club and player when he was forced to return to Bolton in January 2008.

■ Kevin Patrick FOLEY

Luton boy Kevin first came to the attention of the local newspapers when skippering Cardinal Newman RC school who won the Heinz Ketchup Cup, the schools equivalent of the F.A. Cup, at Highbury.

Snapped up by the Hatters, Kevin made his League debut coming on as substitute in a 2-2 home draw with Bristol City in April 2003 and scored his first goal early in the following season during a Carling Cup clash with Yeovil at Kenilworth Road.

Since that time, Kevin became virtually ever present in the Luton side as a right sided defensive player and, following a big money move to Wolves in 2007, all Town supporters would be unsurprised should the modest defender add full Eire caps to his Under-21 appearances.

■ Adrian Emmanuel FORBES

West London born Adrian joined Norwich from school and made over 100 League appearances for the Canaries, albeit many as substitute, before a shock £60,000 move took him to Luton in 2001 just as the Hatters were about to embark on their first season in the basement since 1968.

A fast, strong player who is equally at home on the wing or in a central striking role, Adrian was a regular as the Town won immediate promotion but then a bad knee injury in a pre-season friendly killed the following campaign and when he came back he was not an automatic choice.

A move to Swansea followed in 2004 from where he was surprisingly in 2006 but he soon found further employment at Blackpool before joining up with Millwall in January 2008.

■ David FORDE

Goalkeeper David started with his home town team Galway United before joining up with Welsh club Barry Town where his performances between the sticks led to West Ham paying £75,000 for his signature in 2002.

After failing to win a first team spot at Upton Park, David was loaned out to Conference side Barnet before helping Derry City to an FAI Cup final success.

Deciding to try his luck in the English League once more, David was picked up by Cardiff in January 2007 and by the end of that campaign was regarded as first choice goalkeeper at Ninian Park.

After falling out of favour, David came to Luton on loan at the start of this 2007/08, making six appearances, and is now on the books of Millwall.

■ Stephen (Steve) Brian FOSTER

An inspirational skipper and leader, Steve was the Luton Town captain during arguably their finest hour, lifting the Littlewoods Cup in 1988.

Portsmouth born, Steve started with his home town club as a forward but reverted to centre-half and was then sold on to top flight Brighton for £150,000 in 1979.

Steve won England caps whilst at the Goldstone and was virtually ever present during the Seagulls four year stay at the top but a change of manager saw him move to Aston Villa in March 1984, where he was unhappy, and then to Luton in November of that year.

At Luton, Steve formed a tremendous central defensive pairing with Mal Donaghy and with it came the most successful period in the Hatter's history.

A move to Oxford followed in 1989, and then back to Brighton three years later. Steve now runs his own insurance business and is heavily involved with Luton 2020.

■ Panos Andrew FOTIADIS

Despite winning England Schools caps at both under-15 and under-21 level, Andrew decided to stay on at school to gain his GCSE A-levels before taking up full-time football with Luton Town.

Hitchin born, Andrew came to Kenilworth Road at the same time as his close school friend Sean Evers and made his League debut on the opening day of the 1996/97 campaign. Much was then expected of Andrew as he possessed the good technique, pace and power needed by an old fashioned centre forward but he was beset by a string of injuries which meant that he made less that 150 appearances in seven seasons.

A move to Peterborough in 2003 saw him fare little better and after a spell with Heybridge Swifts in 2004 he dropped out of the game to concentrate on his property portfolio.

■ Stuart Thomas FRASER

Edinburgh born Stuart joined Luton Town from school and skippered the Hatter's youth team before making his League bow on the closing day of the 1997/98 campaign in a 3-2 home win over Carlisle.

Within a year the stylish full-back had become a regular member of the Luton squad and had won Scotland U-21 caps but then suffered a broken leg in an F.A.Cup replay at Q.P.R. in January 2001.

Unfortunately, by the time he had recovered, new manager Joe Kinnear had decided that Emmerson Boyce and Matthew Taylor were his preferred full-back partnership leading to Stuart moving to Stevenage.

Stuart left Stevenage in 2004 to join the Royal Marines.

■ Graham Edward FRENCH

A member of the squad that won the Little World Cup at Wembley in 1963 Graham's suspect temperament put off a host of clubs leading to him turning out for Wellington Town where he was spotted by Luton Town and soon became a favourite at Kenilworth Road.

For a big man, Graham had pace and two footed ability on the wing and set up many goals for a succession of Luton strikers. After helping the Town to two promotions he was sentenced to three years in prison following a shooting incident.

The Town were happy to let him try again on his release but the deprivations of prison life left him a shadow of his former self and he drifted out of the game before re-surfacing under the assumed name of 'Lafite' at Southport in 1976.

The poor man's George Best now lives in Wolverhampton.

■ Barry Francis FRY

England schoolboy international Barry signed on as an apprentice at Manchester United in 1960 before turning professional two years later. Sadly, the abundance of riches at Old Trafford meant that he failed to make a first team appearance there and after a short spell at Bolton the Bedford born inside forward moved back home and joined Luton in 1965.

His stay at Kenilworth Road was short, one season six League games, and after a similar spell at Leyton Orient he next surfaced as the successful manager of Dunstable Town.

Barry had now found his niche and managerial appointments at Hillingdon and Maidstone followed before he guided Barnet into the Football League. Saving Southend from relegation and seeing Birmingham promoted were feathers in his cap before he ended up at Peterborough where this larger than life character is to this day.

■ Pasquale (Lil) FUCCILLO

Another Bedford boy who made his way up through the ranks at Kenilworth Road before making his debut as substitute during the Town's Division One season of 1974/75.

A powerful midfielder with a strong shot, Lil became a permanent feature in the Luton side a year later and there was talk of him being picked for Italy before a badly broken leg at Brighton in 1978 effectively took two years out of his career as he broke his leg again on his comeback.

Bravely, he eventually re-established himself in the Luton side and helped the Town to promotion from Division Two in 1982. After a spell in the States, Lil turned out for Southend, Peterborough and Cambridge before taking up various management positions including a short spell at Kenilworth Road.

Lil is now scouting for Newcastle.

■ Paul Anthony FURLONG

Ageless striker Paul made Luton Town his seventh League club in a career that has seen transfer fees totalling over £4 million changing hands for his services.

Starting at non-League Enfield, Paul was picked up by Coventry in 1991 before switching to Watford where his goalscoring abilities came to the fore leading to big money moves to Chelsea and Birmingham.

At 34, Paul moved on a free transfer to QPR where he still netted a goal every other game and the Rangers fans were disappointed when he was allowed to join Luton in the summer of 2007. Still remarkably fit and a credit to his profession, Paul moved on to Southend in July 2008.

■ Paul FUTCHER

After only 20 games for his home town club Chester, 17 year old Paul was snapped up by Luton manager Harry Haslam for £100,000 in June 1974 just as the Hatters were about to embark on an ill-fated season in Division One.

Making his Hatters debut earlier than the fans expected, Paul proved a revelation playing without fear in the heart of the defence. An international career beckoned but a couple of major road accidents seemed to take the edge off his play although he still commanded a large fee when transferred to Manchester City in 1978.

Paul played League football until nearly 40 and then went on to manage a variety of non-League clubs and took Southport to the F.A.Trophy final in 1998. Now living in Holmfirth, Paul is a sports coach at a Huddersfield college.

■ Ronald (Ron) FUTCHER

Older by 20 minutes than twin Paul, Ron was signed by Luton at the same time as his brother. Unfairly regarded as a makeweight, Ron actually made his Hatters debut before Paul, coming on as a substitute against Sheffield United in November 1974.

His full debut is written in Luton folklore though, as he scored the only goal at table toppers Ipswich and followed it up with a hat-trick against Wolves two days later.

Telepathy with Paul meant that he was always on the end of his long balls out of defence and the Futcher double act graced Kenilworth Road until Ron joined his brother at Maine Road in 1978.

Ron then enjoyed a long League career and is still involved in the game having recently taken up a coaching post in Tampa Bay.

■ Horace Edwin GAGER

London born but Luton raised, Horace was picked up by the Hatters in 1937 after he had earned rave reviews playing for Vauxhall Motors. Finally making his Luton debut on the opening day of the1939/40 season, Horace was ever present until war broke out after only three games.

Horace kept playing during the war years, turning out for Glentoran for a while, but was back at Kenilworth Road when hostilities ended and was virtually ever present until a surprise move to Nottingham Forest in 1948.

A commanding centre-half, Horace made up for the lost years of the war by playing at the City Ground until he was 38. Horace sadly died in 1994.

■ Douglas (Doug) GARDINER

Another Luton player to span the war years, Doug was signed from Scottish junior side Auchinleck Talbot in 1938. Spending three years as a prisoner of war after being shot down over Germany, Doug finally made his Hatters League debut mid-way through the 1946/47 season in a 1-2 defeat at Chesterfield.

A hard working, tenacious wing-half and occasional skipper, Doug gave the Town tremendous service over the next five years before being transferred to Bedford in 1951 where he gave equally loyal help and assistance in a variety of roles.

Doug continued to live in Bedford until his death.

■ Alan Henry GARNER

Although signing for Millwall in 1969, Alan was frustrated to make only two League appearances for the Lions in two years.

A skilful central defender with a tremendous long throw, Alan was trailed by Luton scout Harry Haslam who was surprised to get his man for free in 1971. Alan, though, had to wait patiently until Chris Nicholl was transferred to Aston Villa the following March.

Ever present during the Hatters promotion season of 1973/74, Alan was unfortunate to lose his place to the young Paul Futcher during the following campaign and moved to Watford where he made 200 appearances in a Hornets side moving up through the divisions.

After spells at Portsmouth, Chesham, Barnet and Barton Rovers, Alan now runs a local window business.

■ David GEDDIS

David was part of the highly successful youth set up at Ipswich and was sent out on loan as a 19 year old to Second Division Luton in 1977 to gain experience. He scored some vital goals as the Hatters attempted to win promotion back to the top flight and his speed, power and enthusiasm encouraged Luton manager Harry Haslam to try to sign him.

Ipswich manager Bobby Robson had other ideas though and David won an F.A.Cup winners medal the following season before being transferred to Aston Villa in 1979.

At Villa, David found it difficult to oust Peter Withe or Garry Shaw so he started drifting down the divisions where his strike rate was always excellent.

David has recently left his job as reserve team coach at Leeds.

■ Liam Brendan GEORGE

Joining his home town club Luton from school, Liam signed professional forms for the Hatters in January 1997.

After making his League debut in 1997/98 the tricky and quick forward became first choice at the start of the following campaign but a broken ankle suffered at Wigan cut short his season.

He returned in triumph though, and top scored for the Hatters in each of the next two seasons and added Eire under-21 caps to his collection before falling out with manager Joe Kinnear and drifting down through the divisions.

Liam then turned out for Eastleigh, Hyde and FC United of Manchester and is currently at Barton Rovers.

■ James (Jimmy) GIBSON

Signed by Newcastle United from Linfield in 1959, great things were expected of the big, raw boned forward but he found difficulty in earning a regular first team spot at St James Park making only two appearances in two seasons.

In those days you could earn more money playing non-League than in the wage restricted Football League and so Jimmy joined Cambridge United in 1961 with a club house an added incentive!

Jimmy became a goal machine at the Abbey, netting 65 goals in 145 Southern League appearances, before Luton stepped in to sign him in February 1965 as they attempted to escape relegation to Division Four.

Strangely, the Hatters played Jimmy at wing-half and he failed to score in 32 appearances. He left Luton in 1966 to coach in the USA and still lives there.

Daniel (Don) Joseph GIVENS

Limerick born Don was one of the many boys who travelled over the Irish Sea to join Manchester United but despite making his Eire debut before reaching the United first team it soon became clear that the sheer size of the squad at Old Trafford would make a regular place difficult to achieve.

Luton scout Harry Haslam, using his United connections, managed to entice Don plus three other players to Kenilworth Road in 1970 just as the Hatters were promoted to Division Two. Don proved an excellent foil to the more forceful Malcolm Macdonald and it was a sad day when the clever inside-forward moved to QPR in 1972.

Don finally finished his football career with Neuchatel in Switzerland well into his 30's and is now manager of the Eire under-21 squad.

■ Alexander (Alec) GLOVER

Partick Thistle accepted a big fee from Bradford Park Avenue for their home grown right winger in 1948 and Alec made an instant impact in Division Two terrorising defences with his clever ball play.

Having witnessed his ability at first hand, Luton Town manager Dally Duncan paid £8,000 for his services in September 1949 which was a lot of money at the time. Unfortunately, the Town were struggling at that point and Hatters supporters were rarely able to see Alec in full flow as defensive duties were required of him. He moved on to Blackburn in 1951 and then transferred to Barrow three years later.

After retiring from the game, Alec settled in the Barrow area and died in Ulverston in 2000.

■ Edward Lee (Lee) GLOVER

Joining Nottingham Forest from school, the Kettering born forward won Scotland youth and under-21 caps but could never quite gain a regular place at the City Ground mainly because of serious injury problems.

When Luton Town sold Kingsley Black to Forest in 1991, Lee came in the opposite direction initially on loan. Sadly, his only Hatters appearance, against Southampton at Kenilworth Road, ended in injury and the deal was off.

Lee moved on to Port Vale in 1994 but enjoyed his greatest success at Rotherham where he was a consistent goalscorer.

Lee was recently sacked as player-manager of Grantham Town.

■ Anthony (Tony) Leonard GODDEN

Gillingham born Tony was picked up by West Brom from Ashford Town in 1975 and, after breaking into the first team 18 months later, the safe and agile goalkeeper went on to smash the Baggies record for consecutive appearances.

After eventually losing his place he accepted a loan move to Luton in March 1983 to replace the injured Jake Findlay and remained ever present until the end of that campaign and starred in the magical 1-0 win at Maine Road on the final day to ensure Division One survival.

Tony finished his League career at Peterborough at the age of 35 and after managing several non-League sides is now goalkeeping coach at Rushden & Diamonds.

■ James (Jim) GOLDIE

Scottish forward Jim impressed in junior football with Gairdoch United and briefly joined Aston Villa in 1957 before returning to Scotland with Falkirk and Kilsyth Rangers. It was from this latter club that he was spotted by Luton manager Sam Bartram leading to him moving to Kenilworth Road in 1962.

Although scoring twice in seven Division Two games for the Hatters he was playing in a side doomed to relegation and joined York the following summer where he was relatively successful.

Joining the Metropolitan Police in 1966, Jim turned out for their Southern League side and also made his way up to Detective Sergeant. Now retired, Jim lives in New Malden.

■ Alan Jeffrey GOODALL

Although born in Birkenhead, Alan started his football career with Welsh club Bangor City. Spending four years at Farrar Road, the left sided defender played in the Welsh Cup final, picking up a runners-up medal in a defeat at the hands of Barry Town, and also tasted European football being part of the Bangor side that lost to Serbian side FK Smederevo in the UEFA Cup in 2002/03.

Switching to Rochdale in July 2004, Alan soon became a fans favourite at Spotland because of his all-action style and his ability to also play in central defence when asked.

Alan joined Luton in the summer of 2007 and continued his remarkable injury free run which started at Rochdale before signing for Chesterfield in July 2008.

■ Kenneth (Ken) George Alfred GOODEVE

Manchester born Ken joined United from school but after signing professional forms in 1967 found it impossible to win a first team spot at Old Trafford and instead became one of four Red Devils to sign for Luton Town in April 1970.

At Kenilworth Road, defender Ken skippered the reserve side but with only 15 League appearances in three seasons he wanted regular first team football and became Brian Clough's first permanent signing for Brighton in December 1973.

After only six games at the Goldstone, Ken was sold to Watford, then managed by old Hatters playing colleague Mike Keen, and made 69 consecutive appearances before a groin injury ended his full-time career.

Ken continued to play football until he was 47 though, and is now Customer Care manager for Galliard Homes in London and commutes from Wootton every day!

■ Clive GOODYEAR

After signing for Luton Town as a 17 year old from Lincoln United in 1978, tall and powerful central defender Clive was happy to learn his trade as understudy to Mike Saxby.

A bad knee injury suffered by Saxby early in the 1981/82 season gave Clive his big chance and he was awarded with a medal at the campaign's end as the Hatters won the championship of the old Division Two.

Never looking out of place in the top flight, Clive was eventually sold to Plymouth where he made over 100 appearances before moving to Wimbledon in time to pick up an F.A.Cup winners medal in 1988.

A qualified physiotherapist, Clive worked for a number of League clubs, including the Town, but after leaving Chester is now concentrating on his practice in Bletchley.

■ George William GOODYEAR

Luton boy George was picked up by the Hatters in October 1938 after starring as a fast and clever wing-half for Hitchin Town but had to wait until the end of the war before making his League debut.

George made ten appearances during the 1946/47 season but was always competing against the likes of ex-England international Frank Soo and was transferred to Southend in July 1947.

At Grainger Road, George had an altogether more successful time making 59 League appearances in two seasons before moving on to Crystal Palace where he failed to make the first team due to an immediate change of manager.

After a spell at Biggleswade, George hung up his boots and settled in Sandy before sadly passing away in 2001.

■ Anthony Paul Shaun Andrew Daure GRANT

Defensive midfielder Anthony joined Chelsea at the age of nine and after working his way up through the ranks made his Premiership debut in May 2005, coming on as a late substitute for Joe Cole in a 3-1 win over Manchester United at Stamford Bridge.

In order to gain experience, the England youth international was firstly loaned to Oldham before spending the whole of the 2006/07 season at Wycombe.

Showing terrific commitment rare among loanees, Anthony picked up two red cards and seventeen yellows during his stay at Adams Park, mostly for mistimed tackles, leading to five separate suspensions.

Anthony joined Luton on loan in November 2007 and gave four wholehearted League appearances in his spell at Kenilworth Road, although he did end his time with the club being red carded at Bristol Rovers. Anthony was then loaned out to Southend who were hoping to make the move permanent.

■ Kimberley (Kim) Tyrone GRANT

Born in Ghana but brought up in Brighton, Kim joined Charlton from school where he made a name for himself as a pacy forward scoring 18 goals in 123 League appearances for the Addicks.

Ex-Charlton boss Lennie Lawrence, by now at Luton, paid £250,000 for his services in March 1996 hoping that his goals would help the Hatters avoid relegation but he failed to settle at Kenilworth Road and moved to Millwall for £185,000 a little over a year later.

Spells in Belgium and Portugal then followed for the Ghana international before he returned to this country with Yeovil. Kim then put in some appearances for AFC Wimbledon and has recently been appointed boss of Conference side Woking.

■ Robert Paul (Paul) GRAY

Signed by Luton on youth trainee forms, the Portsmouth born forward was offered a professional contract in June 1988 four months after making his first team debut in a Simod Cup win at Everton.

Paul eventually made his League debut, coming on as substitute in a 2-3 defeat at Arsenal in December 1989, before netting on his home debut against Coventry three months later.

Finding it difficult to win a regular place in the side, the Northern Ireland under-21 international went to Wigan in 1991 but failed to make the grade at Springfield Park and drifted out of the game after appearing for Bangor and Ards in Ireland.

■ Philip (Phil) GRAY

After joining Tottenham from school, Belfast born Phil made his Spurs debut as an 18 year old but a series of injuries meant that he was not able to stake a regular claim and he moved to Luton in 1991 for £275,000 where he teamed up with his old boss David Pleat.

A consistent goalscorer at Kenilworth Road it came as a major disappointment when the stocky forward moved to Sunderland for £775,000 in 1993. By now a Northern Ireland international, Phil top scored for Sunderland in each of his first two seasons at Roker Park but left to join French club Nancy under freedom of contract. A big money transfer to Fortuna Sittard followed and it was then back to Luton in 1997 to renew acquaintances.

Phil is still turning out in a Hatters shirt, guesting for the Trust in Luton fundraising side.

■ Anthony (Tony) Patrick GREALISH

Although born in West London, Tony was proud of his Irish roots and went on to make 44 appearances for Eire as a dogged midfielder.

Joining Orient from school, Tony had five years at Brisbane Road before moving to Luton in 1979 in one of the first 'transfer tribunals'. The eventual fee of £150,000 was money well spent as he enjoyed two good seasons in the Luton midfield making 78 League appearances and scoring two goals, including a blinder at Chelsea.

Surprisingly transferred to Brighton in an exchange deal involving Brian Horton, Tony skippered the Seagulls in the 1983 F.A.Cup final before working his way down through the divisions.

Tony worked in insurance for many years before becoming involved in a scrap metal business.

■ Harry Rodney (Rodney) GREEN

A prolific scorer wherever he went, Rodney first caught the eye with Bradford City in 1963 which led to a £9,000 move to Gillingham a year later. After falling out with the management he was sold to Grimsby where he formed a productive partnership with future Hatter Matt Tees.

The pair were sold to Charlton for £23,000 but Rodney never settled and instead jumped at the chance to join Allan Brown's revolution at Kenilworth Road as the Hatters were about to embark on a memorable 1967/68 campaign.

After scoring on his Luton debut, Rodney injured his knee and by the time he returned the forward line had a settled look and he became a peripheral figure and moved on to Watford before ending his career in South Africa.

Rodney now owns a business selling reproduction furniture near his home town of Halifax.

■ David Michael GREENE

Luton born David joined his local club from school before making his debut for the Hatters in a 1-3 defeat at Grimsby in March 1993 as a 19 year old.

A reliable and tough centre-half, David seemed to have forced his way into a regular place in the side at the end of the following campaign in the absence of the injured Trevor Peake and starred in the F.A.Cup quarter-final draw at West Ham.

Sadly, David was hit by injuries and was unable to force his way back into the side and instead reluctantly accepted a move to Colchester.

David enjoyed four successful years at Layer Road before transferring in quick succession to Cardiff and then Cambridge after which he retired from the game.

David still lives in Luton.

■ Anthony (Tony) Charles GREGORY

Luton Grammar School student Tony was a teenage wonderkid playing for England schoolboys at Wembley as well as the successful Bedfordshire Youth side that won the national championship.

Not surprisingly he was snapped up by the Hatters in 1955 and such was his progress that he made his League debut less than a year later. After dropping out after this sensational start he made only sporadic appearances over the next two years before winning a place on the left wing in the Town's F.A Cup side in 1959, a team that was kept intact all the way through to the final.

A two year stint in the National Service followed, as well as a move to Watford, which preceded a tour of the non-League sides in the south combined with a career in marketing.

■ Carl Brian GRIFFITHS

Sadly, Luton Town supporters never saw the best of Carl as he suffered a stress fracture after only ten appearances, and seven goals, into the Hatters successful 2001/02 promotion winning side. Many Town supporters felt that the championship of Division Three would have been won had Carl remained fit alongside Steve Howard with whom he had started to enjoy a sound partnership.

A prolific goalscorer for seven clubs before joining Luton, the talented Welshman attracted over £1 million in transfer fees but his injury effectively ended his League career although he was still banging in goals for Brentwood Town until recently and has now been appointed manager of the Essex Ryman League side.

■ Augustine Ashley (Ashley) GRIMES

Manchester United invited Dubliner Ashley over for a trial in 1972 but rejected him only to pay Bohemians £20,000 for his services five years later!

Although never a regular at Old Trafford he did manage nearly 100 League appearances in six years before moving to Coventry in 1983 and then transferring to Luton a year later in a swap deal involving Kirk Stephens.

At Kenilworth Road, Ashley added to his Eire international caps and put on many cultured displays at left back or left midfield. Totally left footed, Ashley provided the awkward cross from the right that enabled Brian Stein to score the winner in the 1988 Littlewoods Cup final.

After a spell in Spain, Ashley saw out his career with Stoke before joining old colleague Lou Macari at several clubs as coach.

Ashley's son is now on the books at Millwall.

■ Ernest William (Bill) GRIPTON

Cool and commanding centre-half Bill signed on with his local side West Brom before the war and although he held the record for the most war-time appearances for the Baggies he could not hold a regular spot in the side once hostilities finished.

Instead, he moved to Luton for £3,000 in 1948 but could not displace Syd Owen or his deputy Les Hall at the heart of the Hatters defence but had much more luck at his next club, Bournemouth.

Bill joined Worcester City in 1952 and became their groundsman. Motor Neurone disease forced his early retirement and he sadly died in 1980.

■ John GROVES

Son of pre-War Derby star Arthur who played alongside Luton manager Dally Duncan at the Baseball Ground, it was pre-ordained that young John should sign on for the Hatters just before his 16th birthday.

After National Service, John made his Luton debut as an inside forward before reverting to his favoured wing-half position and going on to make over 250 appearances with the highlight of his Hatters career coming in the 1959 F.A.Cup final.

A move to Bournemouth followed in 1963 but after two seasons he had to retire due to a back injury. He then settled back in his native Derby where he worked for Courtaulds for 30 years and although now retired is still an occasional visitor to Kenilworth Road.

■ Bontcho Lubomisov GUENTCHEV

Experienced, skilful, two-footed Bulgarian international Bontcho signed for Ipswich from Sporting Lisbon for £250,000 to a great fanfare in 1992. He became a cult hero at Portman Road due to his heroics in helping Bulgaria through to the 1994 World Cup semi-finals but often flattered to deceive in the blood and thunder of English football.

Moving to Terry Westley's Luton in 1995 he played in a side doomed to relegation and was often asked to turn out up front when his best position was out wide. He failed to make an impact in Division Two and was handed a free transfer in 1997.

After moving around the London non-League circuit Bontcho is now coach at Hendon and runs a coffee bar in Kensington.

■ Alan Nicoll GUILD

Alan combined studying for an eventual first class honours degree in political economy at St Andrews University with appearances as an amateur for East Fife.

Once his studies were completed the giant centre-half accepted an offer to join Luton in 1969 but he found his chances limited to one League appearance, at home to Middlesbrough in 1970.

One of four Luton players to join Cambridge United over the summer of 1971, Alan had a better time at the Abbey and was a regular for three seasons before moving to Cambridge City and St Neots and then drifting back to Scotland.

■ Robert (Bob) Edward HACKING

An amateur with Blackburn during the War, Bob was later in the R.A.F. stationed in the south and guested for the Hatters for whom he signed professional forms in April 1945 at the age of 27.

He managed only one League appearance for the Town before being recruited by Brighton for £500 in 1947 and then on to Southport a year later.

At Haig Avenue he moved back to wing-half from inside-forward and quickly became a crowd favourite due to his clever ball skills and managed to play on until 1954 before retiring from the game to become a market gardener.

Bob continued to live in the Southport area until his death in 2001.

■ William (Billy) HAILS

Durham born Billy started off his career at Lincoln in 1953 but moved on to non-League Peterborough where he earned a reputation as a talented right winger, helping his side to five Midland League titles, election to the Football League followed by the championship of Division Four.

Billy finally left London Road in 1962 to join Northampton who he immediately assisted to the Third Division championship but his run of success ended when he moved to Luton in 1964 in exchange for Harry Walden.

Playing only three times for a relegation bound Hatters he went on a free transfer to Nuneaton then coached and managed Peterborough before acting as physiotherapist for Watford.

Billy is now retired and living in Hemel Hempstead.

■ Derek David HALES

Derek came to the attention of Luton when banging in the goals for Dartford and although he had a good job as a qualified Post Office engineer he took the plunge and joined the professional ranks at Kenilworth Road in March 1972.

Even though he scored on his full debut for the Hatters in a 1-1 home draw with Cardiff in February 1973 he was not given much of a chance at Kenilworth Road and went to Charlton for £4,000 that summer.

The rest is history, as the predatory goalscorer, in two spells at the Valley, netted a goal every other game as well as enjoying big money moves to Derby and West Ham in a long career!

Derek now lives in Sittingbourne and coaches at his old school in Rainham.

■ Leslie (Les) Frederick HALL

Les was on the books of Luton for 13 years, making 79 League appearances, but never signed a full-time professional contract, preferring to play part-time whilst retaining a job in his native St Albans.

Starting out with St Albans City, where he continued to train throughout his career, Les turned out for Luton during the war years but was overlooked on resumption of peace-time football until called up to replace the injured Horace Gager in a cup-tie at Plymouth in 1948.

Such was his display at centre-half that Gager was unable to regain his place and was eventually transferred. Les was eventually replaced by Syd Owen but continued to give sterling service to the reserve side as well as bringing on the young players in the 'A' team.

Les continues to retain a keen interest in the Hatters.

■ Victor (Vic) Lewis HALOM

Although born in Swadlincote, the burly striker made a name for himself with a trio of London clubs, starting with Charlton as an apprentice, and then moving on to Orient and Fulham.

It was from the latter club that Luton manager Alec Stock signed him as a replacement for Malcolm Macdonald in September 1971 for £35,000 but he was not a prolific goalscorer at Kenilworth Road and new boss Harry Haslam allowed him to move to Sunderland after signing Barry Butlin.

At Sunderland, Vic picked up an F.A.Cup winners medal within three months of joining them and became part of Roker Park folklore. After finishing with League football, Vic managed Barrow, Rochdale and Burton Albion and is now a Customer Manager based in Manchester.

■ William (Billy) Hudson HARBER

Billy was picked up by the extensive early 1960's Swindon scouting system while playing for East London boys and signed on for the Wiltshire side in December 1961.

After only two League games for the Robins, and with his new wife homesick for London, he accepted a move to Luton in 1964 where he soon gained a reputation as a terrier like winger setting up chances for the prolific John O'Rourke.

A knee injury cut down his appearances in 1965/66 but it was still a surprise when he was released at the end of that season. Billy then played for several Southern League clubs before hanging up his boots and spending many years as a football coach in Tower Hamlets.

Billy now lives in Woodford Green where he cares for his wife.

■ Thomas (Tommy) HARE

A small but uncompromising full-back, Motherwell born Tommy joined Southampton as an 18 year old and made 13 appearances in the Saints promotion winning side of 1965/66.

The signing of David Webb put paid to his Southampton career and he moved to Luton on a free transfer in the summer of 1967. He was the regular right back at the start of the following campaign but a bad injury sustained at Doncaster effectively ended his League career as by the time of his return the Town had a settled team that would go on to win the championship of Division Four.

Tommy moved back to Southampton, where he still lives, and played for a succession of local sides.

■ Leslie (Les) Philip HARFIELD

Les joined his local side, Southampton, from school signing professional terms in November 1969. He made two League appearances for the Saints, scoring in the second, but found first team appearances hard to come by with the top flight side and agreed to step down a level by joining Harry Haslam's new look team in the summer of 1972.

Sadly, the quick striker fared little better at Kenilworth Road and made only a cameo appearance coming on as substitute for Gordon Hindson in a 1-2 home defeat at the hands of Hull in October 1972. His ten minutes of glory remain the second shortest League career in the history of the Hatters.

Les eventually moved back to Southampton and took up a job on the docks.

■ Michael (Mick) Gordon HARFORD

One of the most popular players to have pulled on a shirt for Luton Town, Mick was the perfect centre-forward combining power in the air with a perfect touch on the deck. It is crying shame that he did not earn more than two England caps, both won while he was at Kenilworth Road, which he may have done were he to have been plying his trade at a more 'fashionable' club.

Sunderland born, Mick turned out for ten clubs in a long career but he enjoyed his best spell whilst at Luton, forming a tremendous partnership with Brian Stein, and was virtually unstoppable on his day with no defender relishing playing against him.

Mick is, of course, now manager of the Hatters.

■ Alan HARPER

Liverpool born Alan started off as an apprentice with the Reds but made his League debut for the Blues and earning two League championship medals and an F.A Cup winner's medal whilst at Goodison Park.

The steady and unspectacular right back or right midfielder then made big money moves to Sheffield Wednesday and Manchester City before returning to Everton and then on to Luton on a free transfer in 1993.

His calm influence and experience proved a godsend to a young Luton side which won through to the F.A.Cup semi-final in 1994 but Alan wished to return north and joined Burnley that summer.

After finishing on the playing side, Alan coached at Burnley before going back to Everton in a similar capacity. Alan retired from his position at Goodison Park in 2005 due to injury and now scouts for Bolton.

■ Gerald (Gerry) Randall HARRISON

Starting off as youth trainee at Watford, Gerry made his League debut as a 17 year old for the Hornets but it was while at Bristol City and then Burnley that he earned regular football.

A move to Luton on a 'Bosman' free transfer in 1998 was virtually agreed until Sunderland stepped in but Gerry contracted hepatitis soon after relocating to the North-East and found his chances limited. Luton got their man on loan later that season and he put in several all-action displays in midfield as well as taking over in goal on one occasion whilst at Kenilworth Road.

The Town could not afford to keep him and he eventually finished his League career at Halifax. Gerry was still turning out for Hyde United in 2007/08.

■ Michael (Mike) John HARRISON

One of the many products of the Chelsea youth system of the 1950's, Mike made his debut for the Blues as a 16 year old but in five years at Stamford Bridge never really established himself despite winning England u-23 caps.

An £18,000 move to Blackburn in 1962 was the making of him as he earned a regular place there as an immensely powerful and quick winger. A transfer to Plymouth in 1967 was quickly followed by a move to Luton a year later when he helped the Hatters win promotion to Division Two with a tremendous penalty kick routine his party piece.

Mike is now settled back in Plymouth and was a representative for a medical firm.

■ Andrew (Andy) HARROW

With Luton Town struggling for goals at the start of the 1980/81 campaign, manager David Pleat made a rare dip into the Scottish transfer market and bought Raith Rovers marksman Andy for £50,000.

Sadly, Andy did not fit in at Kenilworth Road and his three full League appearances all ended in defeat for the Hatters and in each he did not get a sniff of a goal. Pleat engineered a swift return to Scotland for the disillusioned Andy with Aberdeen boss Alex Ferguson glad to pay £50,000 for his services.

He did not last long at Pittodrie and moved swiftly on to Motherwell, Raith and East Fife before settling down in Kirkcaldy.

■ John HARTSON

Luton Town scout Cyril Beach recommended several Welsh youngsters to the Hatters with Hartson another one off the conveyor belt signing professional terms in December 1992.

Scoring on his League debut at the start of the following campaign, John's precocious talents came to the fore during the famous televised win over Newcastle in the F.A.Cup in February 1994.

The big clubs came sniffing around and Arsenal paid a record fee for a teenager of £2.5 million for the powerful striker in 1995 and since then he has become a regular for Wales and enjoyed several big money moves in both this country and Scotland.

John announced his retirement from the game in February 2008.

■ Richard George HARVEY

England Schoolboy and Youth international Richard worked his way up through the ranks at Luton before making his League debut as a 17 year old in November 1986 in a 1-0 home win over QPR . A strong, fast left back or left sided player with a powerful shot he eventually became a regular member of the Hatters top flight side.

Richard then began to have appalling luck with injuries which left him missing the best part of three seasons before he fought his way back into contention with the Town now drifting down through the divisions.

Eventually leaving Luton to join Aylesbury in 1998, Richard is now a postman in his home town of Letchworth.

■ Robert (Bob) James HATTON

'Have boots will travel' seemed to be the motto of Bob who never seemed to hang about very long at most of his nine League clubs but such was his prowess in front of goal that there were never any shortage of takers no matter how brief his stay was likely to be.

Bob was just the sort of experienced player that rookie Luton manager David Pleat needed in the summer of 1978 and although the wily striker stayed only the statutory two seasons he took the young Brian Stein under his wing along the way and becoming a crowd favourite at Kenilworth Road.

After leaving the game, Bob worked in insurance and for the PFA as a financial adviser before retiring at 55. Bob now dabbles in property.

■ William (Willie) Stephanus HAVENGA

South African born Willie came over to this country to join Birmingham City having been spotted playing for Bremner OB in his home country.

Due to the size of the squad at St Andrews he made only one League start in two years and accepted a move to Luton in May 1950 where he was given more of a chance. In his first season at Kenilworth Road he enjoyed a sixteen game run in the side and netted a hat-trick against Swansea on Boxing Day 1950 but a broken wrist then hindered his progress.

The tiny winger with the fierce shot then moved on to Ipswich and had spells at Kettering, Worcester and Hinckley before returning to South Africa.

■ Barry HAWKES

Barry followed big brother Ken down from the north-east, signing on for Luton in 1955 but then had to wait almost four years, with National Service getting in the way, before winning his first team debut on the left wing against Manchester United in 1959.

Better known as a ball playing inside forward, Barry managed eight first team starts before being allowed to move to Darlington in 1960 and then to Hartlepools a year later.

After a broken leg ended his professional career he worked for a wholesale greengrocery company for many years. Now retired, Barry lives in Peterlee.

■ Kenneth (Ken) Kilby HAWKES

Spotted by Luton's north-east scout Dick Trembath while playing for Shotton Colliery Welfare, Ken joined the Hatters in 1951 but his career at Kenilworth Road was put on hold when he was called up for National Service.

Ken finally broke into the Luton first team in 1957 and was then almost ever present until the relegation season of 1959/60 and played for the Hatters in the 1959 F.A.Cup final.

A rugged left-back, Ken was part of new manager Sam Bartram's cull in 1961 and he moved on to Peterborough, followed by Bedford and St Neots.

After hanging up his boots, Ken then worked for Walter Clarke and Co for 28 years and received a whole bottle of sherry on retirement! Ken is still a welcome regular at Kenilworth Road.

■ Gary John HEALE

Signed from Canvey Island by Luton Town in 1976 as an 18 year old, Gary had an unbelievable start to his Hatters career, scoring on his debut during the 7-1 thrashing of Charlton in September 1977 and then netting twice in a League Cup second replay against Manchester City two months later.

That was as good as it got for the skilful winger as he fell out of favour under new manager David Pleat and was sold to Reading for £40,000 which was a record for the Royals at the time.

A regular in the Reading side for three years, Gary was then surprisingly sold to Sparta Rotterdam and then moved to the States with his American wife where he still coaches.

■ Markus HEIKKINEN

Although born in Sweden, due to his Finnish parents working there at the time, Markus regarded himself as a Finn becoming a regular for the national team.

After playing for MyPa and HJK Helsinki he wanted to try his luck in England and joined Portsmouth where he was not given a fair crack of the whip and so headed north to Aberdeen where he became a favourite.

Determined to play in England, Markus came to Mike Newell's Luton in 2005 and did not look back despite playing in an unfamiliar central defensive position as opposed to midfield where he appeared for his country.

Markus was rightly voted Luton's 'Player of the Season' in 2005/06 but sadly left for Rapid Vienna a year later.

■ Petri Juhani HELIN

A month after appearing for Finland against England in a World Cup qualifier, tough midfielder or wing-back Petri was signing for Ricky Hill's Luton as they battled against the drop to the football basement.

Regarded as a major coup at the time, the ex-F.C.Jokerit and HJK Helsinki stalwart scored on his Hatters debut in a 1-1 draw at Bury but following the dismissal of Hill his form went into decline and he left for Stockport in the summer of 2001.

At Edgeley Park another change of manager saw him moved on to Turkish side Denizlispor on loan, after which he retired from the game and returned to his former club, F.C. Jokerit, where he took up the position of managing director.

■ Vince Mark HILAIRE

Tricky winger Vince joined Crystal Palace from school, making over 250 League appearances for the South London club and seemingly set to stay there for the rest of his career until a call came from Luton manager David Pleat in July 1984.

The chance of Division One football was too good to turn down but, beset with injuries, Vince managed only nine games at Kenilworth Road before he was on his way again with Portsmouth paying £100,000 for his services. He enjoyed four successful years at Fratton Park followed by spells at Leeds, Stoke and Exeter before becoming player/manager at Waterlooville.

Vince now coaches junior football in the Portsmouth area.

■ Ricky Anthony HILL

Luton Town legend Ricky burst onto the scene as a 17 year old coming on as substitute in a dull end of season game against Bristol Rovers in 1976 and immediately lit up proceedings by laying on a goal with his first touch and scoring with his second.

After twelve months of being nurtured gently in the reserves, Ricky eventually won a regular place which, barring injury, he kept for the next twelve years picking up a promotion to the top flight and England caps along the way.

One of the finest midfielders in the Hatter's history, combining skill, strength and speed, Ricky left Luton in 1989 to seize a chance of French football with Le Havre.

After taking up coaching posts on both sides of the Atlantic, Ricky answered the call to pick up the reins at Kenilworth Road in 2000. Sadly, the job he craved turned sour which was a great shame for the supporters who all badly wanted him to succeed.

All at Luton were pleased to see Ricky turn out for the Town in a re-run of the 1988 Littlewoods Cup final win in May 2008.

■ Ian Michael HILLIER

Welsh under-21 international Ian signed on as a youth trainee at Tottenham but could not make the breakthrough into the first team in three years at White Hart Lane.

Ian then decided to try his luck at Joe Kinnear's Luton in 2001 and in his first campaign at Kenilworth Road he enjoyed an extended run and scored one of the goals of the season during a 2-1 win at York.

Extremely versatile, Ian could play almost anywhere in defence or midfield which became his undoing as he could not nail down a regular place in a set position after his bright start.

Following a loan spell at Chester, Ian joined Newport County in 2005 and has now completed three seasons in Nationwide Conference South.

■ Gordon HINDSON

Gordon was a player who had all the attributes necessary to become a top quality midfielder or winger, possessing speed, ball control and a fierce shot but he rarely grabbed a game by the scruff of the neck.

Allowed to leave by first club Newcastle, Gordon signed for Luton in 1971 for £27,500 but was never a true regular at Kenilworth Road despite making 68 League appearances in just under four years.

After a loan spell at Carlisle, Gordon signed for Blackburn but a broken ankle ended his League career and he returned to the north-east where he played for and coached a variety of non-League clubs while embarking on a career in Sports and Leisure Centre management.

■ Lars HIRSCHFELD

Canadian international goalkeeper Lars started his career playing indoor football with Edmonton Drillers before having a spell in Germany.

It was while playing for his country though, that he was spotted by Tottenham and he moved to North London in 2002 but found it difficult to win a first team spot and gladly accepted a loan move to Luton playing five League games for the Hatters in February and March 2003.

Moves to Dundee United and Leicester followed before he threw in his lot with Norwegian side Tromso where he was quickly voted the best goalkeeper in their history. Moving to Rosenborg in 2005, Lars helped his new side to the championship the following year.

A big money transfer then took Lars to Romanian side CFR Cluj in January 2008.

■ Peter James HOLMES

A product of the F.A.School of Excellence as well as an England schoolboy and Youth international, Peter was signed on by Sheffield Wednesday where he was coached by ex-Luton hero Ricky Hill.

When Hill became manager of the Hatters in 2000, Peter became one of his first signings and the talented midfielder went on to stay seven seasons at Kenilworth Road although never able to carve out a regular place in the side.

Never letting the side down and banging in some vital goals in over 100 League appearances for the Town, Peter was allowed to go to Chesterfield and Lincoln on loan in 2006/07 before joining Rotherham on a permanent basis.

■ William (Billy) Gerald HOLMES

Balham born Billy played for almost ten seasons in the Football League but only managed 63 games in that time.

In three years at first club Millwall, Billy mustered only one substitute appearance as he did at his next port of call, Luton, coming on in a 3-0 home win over Blackpool in 1973. A move to Barnet followed and then on to Wimbledon where his goals helped fire them into the Football League in 1977 but he then swiftly left in an £8,000 transfer to Hereford.

Billy's League career finished at Brentford before he spent time at Aylesbury. Billy sadly died at the tragically young age of 37 in 1988.

■ Paul HOLSGROVE

Son of the Wolves and Sheffield Wednesday stalwart John, young Paul started off as a youth trainee at Aldershot but after only three substitute appearances in two years moved to non-League Wokingham where he started to make a name for himself.

Paul then, famously, became Luton manager Jimmy Ryan's only purchase during his 16 months in charge at Kenilworth Road but the tall elegant midfielder only turned out twice for the Hatters before moving on to Heracles in Holland.

Back in the U.K, Paul had some success at Reading before continuing his nomadic existence through six further League clubs in England and Scotland and then on to non-League Hayes. Paul was last at Windsor and Eton but went back to Hayes as assistant manager in 2006.

■ Graham Roy HORN

Giant goalkeeper Graham was another nomadic footballer who plied his trade with eight League clubs as well as enjoying a long stay with LA Aztecs in the USA.

Joining Arsenal from school, Graham found it impossible to break through at Highbury and so went on a year long loan to Portsmouth but mid-way through his time there Luton put in a straight bid for him which Pompey could not match.

At Kenilworth Road, Graham helped the Hatters win promotion to the top flight in 1974 with a series of brave displays but was always competing for a first team spot with Keith Barber which he eventually lost.

Graham finished his League career with Torquay and settled in the West Country where he still plays village cricket.

■ Brian HORTON

Hednesford born Brian was a late starter in League football and was 21 before making his debut for Port Vale. Making up for lost time, Brian went on to make over 200 appearances for Vale before moving to Brighton in 1976 where he also broke the double century barrier at the same time helping the Seagulls into Division One for the first time.

Brian was 32 when he moved to Luton in exchange for Tony Grealish in 1981 but he proved to be David Pleat's final piece in the jigsaw and oversaw the Hatter's rise to the top flight as an inspirational skipper and combative midfielder.

After retiring from the playing side, Brian has become a high profile manager at Manchester City amongst others and is currently assistant at Premiership new boys Hull City.

■ Scott Aaron HOUGHTON

Hitchin born Scott was an England schoolboy international and attended the F.A. School of Excellence before signing on for Tottenham where a glittering career was promised.

Apart from scoring two goals against the Hatters in 1991, Scott was sadly unable to make a name for himself at White Hart Lane and moved to David Pleat's Luton in 1993 where he was a little more successful.

A year later, though, the little midfielder or winger with a blistering shot was on his way to Walsall where he probably found his level and from there he moved to Peterborough, Southend and Leyton Orient before finishing his League career with Halifax.

Scott subsequently made a tour of the non-League clubs in Beds, Herts and Cambs before becoming manager of St Neots.

■ Steven (Steve) John HOWARD

Big, strong target man with no little skill on the ground, Steve has scored goals wherever he has been and is currently helping Leicester to win back their Premiership place.

Born in Durham, Steve was spotted by Hartlepool while playing for Tow Law Town and was thrust straight into the first team where, as a 19 year old, he finished joint top scorer in his first season.

Bigger clubs showed interest and a £120,000 bid took him to Northampton in 1999 but, despite being successful at Sixfields, he was surprisingly allowed to move to Luton for £50,000 two years later.

At Kenilworth Road he became the club's third highest post-war goalscorer and top-scored in each of his five seasons with the club before a £1 million move to Derby in 2006.

■ Jake Thomas HOWELLS

Hemel Hempstead born Jake played for his town at youth level and was on the books at Watford for a period before being picked up by Luton for whom he starred at under-15 level.

A skilful, left-sided defender, Jake turned in some mature performances for the Hatters reserve side before earning a surprise first team spot on the bench on the final day of the 2007/08 campaign against Huddersfield at Kenilworth Road. Jake came on to replace Sol Davis and acquitted himself well as the Hatters suffered a narrow defeat.

Regarded as one for the future by all at Kenilworth Road.

■ Roger Ernest HOY

Roger joined his boyhood favourites Tottenham from school, signing professional forms in 1964 and making his League bow two years later.

In an out of the side at White Hart Lane, Roger was guaranteed first team football at Crystal Palace and stepped down a division just in time to see his new team win promotion to the top flight for the first time in their history.

A bid from newly promoted Luton in 1970 was accepted and Roger enjoyed 12 months at Kenilworth Road before falling out with the Hatter's management and moving on to Cardiff where his League career was effectively ended by a bad knee injury.

Roger then emigrated to Australia where he played and coached for a while before working for a transport group.

For the last 18 years, though, this mid-field enforcer who took no prisoners on the playing field has become a full time church minister!

■ Ceri Morgan HUGHES

A product of Luton Town's extensive scouting network in South Wales, Ceri was just 19 when he made his Hatters debut in the top flight and within a few months was a regular first team member.

An aggressive, two footed attacking midfielder, Ceri was sadly dogged by long term injuries that held back his progress and the team was back in Division Two before he enjoyed a virtually injury free 1996/97 campaign which saw the Town reach the play-offs.

A dream move to Premiership Wimbledon followed for the Welsh international but a further stream of injuries cut back his appearances. A final transfer, this time to Portsmouth in 2000 ended with more wretched luck with injury, leaving Ceri no choice but to call it a day.

■ Iorwerth HUGHES

After refusing to sign professional forms for Luton until he had won a couple of promised amateur caps for Wales, goalkeeper Iorwerth eventually came to Kenilworth Road in 1949, initially as understudy to England international Bernard Streten.

He was happy to bide his time but finally won a first team spot playing 36 League games over two seasons and picking up four Welsh caps along the way.

A record fee for a goalkeeper of £15,000 was agreed between the Hatters and Cardiff in 1951 but Iorwerth did not have a happy time at Ninian Park and so moved on to non-League Worcester, to replace Luton bound Ron Baynham, as the Bluebirds refused to release his registration.

Iorwerth, in due course, moved back into the Football League spending four years with Newport before turning out briefly for Hastings. Iorwerth lived in Stopsley at the time of his death in 1993.

■ John Paul (Paul) HUGHES

England schoolboy international midfielder Paul had a promising career mapped out when he worked his way up through the ranks from youth trainee to the Premiership with Chelsea, taking in loan spells at Stockport and Norwich to expand his knowledge along the way.

When his former boss, Glenn Hoddle, became manager at Southampton he soon recruited Paul but a serious groin injury put him out of the game for almost a year. By the time of his return to fitness a new manager was in situ leading to the creative midfielder being allowed to move to Luton in August 2001.

When fully fit, Paul proved a vital member of the Luton squad but he suffered a series of niggling injuries that cut back his appearances. Sadly a long, debilitating virus eventually ended his playing career and Paul has now set up his own web-site business.

Luton Town Team Line-ups

1946/47
Back row (left to right): Pembleton (trainer), Soo, Lake, Bywater, Cooke, Gardiner, Duggan.
Front row (left to right): Waugh, Daniel, Billington, Driver, Duncan, Gager.

1947/48
Back row (left to right): Garner, Bywater, Morton, Palmer, Hughes.
Second row (left to right): Walker, Mackey (trainer), Ruffett, Gardiner, Sanderson, Duncan (manager), Driver, Mitchell (director), Soo, Duggan, Lake, Hall, Kettley, Hann (trainer), Cooke.
Third row (left to right): Hewson (director), Daniel, Wright (director), Billington, Jeyes (chairman), Gager, England (director), Connelly, Woods (director), Richardson (director).
Front row (left to right): High, Warner, Shanks, Thompson, Waugh, Owen, Wallbanks.

1948/49

Back row (left to right): Pemberton, Wilson, Cooke, Daniel, Eames.
Middle row (left to right): Mulvaney, Gripton, Shanks, Streten, Duke, Arnison, Small, Ruffett.
Front row (left to right): C Burtenshaw, O'Brien, Duggan, Collins, Gardiner, Lake, Waugh, Brennan, W Burtenshaw.

1949/50

Back row (left to right): Hann (trainer), Watkins, Cooke, Streten, Aherne, Gardiner, Wilson.
Front row (left to right): Small, Shanks, Arnison, Duncan (manager), Taylor, C Burtenshaw, Owen.

1950/51

Back row (left to right): Pemberton, Morton, Cooke, Hughes, Lake, Watkins.
Front row (left to right): Havenga, Shanks, Whent, Owen, Taylor, Wyldes.

1951/52

Back row (left to right): Hann (trainer), Arnison, Wyldes, Hawkes, Morton, Groves, Davies, Wheeler,
A Taylor, Havenga, Kelly (coach), Mackey (trainer).
Middle row (left to right): Duncan (manager), Cooke, Shanks, Smith, Pemberton, Stibbards,
Turner, Hall, Dunne, Streten, Davie, Moore, Jones, Sexton, Coley (secretary).
Front row (left to right): Hewson (director), J Taylor, Wright (director), Aherne, Mitchell (director),
Owen, Woods (director), Stobbart, England (director), Watkins, Richardson (director).

1952/53

Back row (left to right): Morton, Smith, Cooke, Streten, Sexton, Baynham, Dallas, Williams, Taylor, Thompson, Allen, Coley (secretary), Crarer (medical officer).
Middle row (left to right): Kelly (assistant manager), Hann (trainer), Mackey (trainer), Aherne, Shanks, Pemberton, Richardson (director), Scott, Hall, Moore, Jones, McJarrow, Davies, Turner, Wright (director), Kelly, Bradley, Duncan (manager).
Front row (left to right): Cullen, Hewson (director), Watkins, England (director), Mitchell, Jeyes (chairman), Owen, Mitchell (director), Pye, Woods (director), Dunne.

1953/54

Back row (left to right): Morton, Dunne, Streten, Jones, Watkins.
Front row (left to right): Turner, Cummins, Owen, Pye, Downie, Mitchell.

1954/55

Back row (left to right): Cummins, Collier, Morton, Streten, Watkins, Baynham, Shanks, Dallas.
Second row (left to right): Mackey (trainer), Taylor, Arnison, Davies, McEwan, Scott, Kelly, Thompson, Wright (trainer), Kelly (assistant manager).
Third row (left to right): Coley (secretary), Cullen, Smith, Adam, Turner, Allen, Dunne, Pemberton, Groves, Duncan (manager).
Front row (left to right): Hodgson (director), Wright (director), Aherne, England (director), Pye, Mitchell (chairman), Owen, Richardson (director), Mitchell, Hewson (director), Crarer (medical officer).

1955/56

Back row (left to right): Smith, Groves, Pearce, Dallas, McLeod, Brown, Jones, Kelly.
Second row (left to right): Coley (secretary), Crarer (medical officer), Taylor, Collier, Baynham, Streten, Pemberton, Mackey (trainer), Wright (trainer), Duncan (manager).
Third row (left to right): Hodgson (director), Wright (director), Dunne, Richardson (director), Aherne, Owen, Mitchell (chairman), Morton, England (director), Hewson (director).
Front row (left to right): Allen, Davies, Turner, Cullen, Cummins, Shanks, Hawkes, Thompson.

1956/57

Back row (left to right): Daniel, Groves, Collier, Streten, Macklin, Baynham, Pearce, Legate, Kelly.
Middle row (left to right): Wright (trainer), Thompson, Davies, Owen, McLeod, Dunne, Pemberton, Cummins, McNally, Mackey (trainer).
Front row (left to right): Adam, Turner, K Hawkes, Smith, Cullen, Shanks, B Hawkes, Pounder, Aherne, Morton.

1957/58

Back row (left to right): Groves, Dunne, Baynham, Jones, Pearce.
Front row (left to right): Cullen, Turner, Owen, Brown, Morton, McLeod.

1958/59

Back row (left to right): Bingham, Hawkes, Morton, Shanks, Dunne, Mackey (trainer), McNally, Adam, Middleton, Cummins.

Second row (left to right): Chambers, Kelly, Smith, Marsh, Owen, Groves, Baynham, McLeod, Folwell, Brown.

Third row (left to right): King (trainer), Duncan (manager), Hodgson (director), Tooley (director), England (director), Mitchell (chairman), Hewson (director), Wright (director), Crarer (medical officer), Coley (secretary).

Front row (left to right): Parrin, Pacey, Legate, Turner, King, Lesnick.

1959/60

Back row (left to right): Dixon, Collins, Brice, Baynham, Collier, Folwell, Kelly.

Second row (left to right): King (trainer), Groves, Morton, Turner, Pacey, Kilgannon, Walker, Raffell, G King, Shanks (coach).

Third row (left to right): K Hawkes, Bingham, Dunne, Owen (manager), Brown, McNally, Cummins.

Front row (left to right): B Hawkes, A McCann, D King, Parrin, Rowlands, H McCann, Lesnick.

1960/61

Back row (left to right): Folwell, Underwood, Groves, Collins, Baynham, Ker, McNally, McCreadie, Tracey.
Second row (left to right): Fielding (coach), Pacey, McCann, Noake, Raffell, Kilgannon, McBride, Brown, Turner, Bingham, Cummins, King (trainer).
Third row (left to right): Lesnick, Spencer, Hawkes, Dunne, Bartram (manager), Morton, Kelly, Imlach, McGuffie.
Front row (left to right): Andrews, Buckland.

1961/62

Back row (left to right): Wilsher, Lornie, Ker, Baynham, O'Hara, Bramwell, Reed.
Second row (left to right): Collins, Morton, Kelly, Pacey, McNally, McGuffie, Groves.
Third row (left to right): Jardine, McKechnie, Fleming, Turner, Fairchild, Walden, Riddick.
Front row (left to right): Daniel, Legate, Ashworth.

1962/63
Back row (left to right): Hargreaves, Lownds, McKechnie, Baynham, Ross, Ker, Turner, Riddick, Lornie, Fairchild, Fleming.
Middle row (left to right): Brennan, Groves, Cope, Pacey, Daniel, Goldie, Caleb, Morton, Scott.
Front row (left to right): Jardine, Walden, Clarke, Reed, Bramwell, McNally, Kelly, McGuffie.

1963/64
Back row (left to right): King (trainer), Daniel, Morton, Baynham, Fincham, Pacey, Bramwell.
Front row (left to right): Walden, Turner, Davies, Salisbury, Jardine.

1964/65

Back row (left to right): Reid, Pacey, Caleb, Fincham, Baynham, Tinsley, Rivers, Bramwell, Riddick, Lownds.

Second row (left to right): King (trainer), Readhead (secretary), Whittaker, O'Rourke, Knights, Martin (scout), Hails, McBain, Riley, Harvey (manager), Bentham (trainer).

Third row (left to right): Crarer (medical officer), Richardson (director), B England (director), A England (director), Hodgson (chairman), Bigg, (director), Hawkins (director), Mitchell (director).

Front row (left to right): McKechnie, Slough, Rioch, Hyde, Long, Forsyth, Jardine.

1965/66

Back row (left to right): Pleat, Slough, Edwards, Fry, Tinsley, Whittaker, O'Rourke, Reid, McKechnie.

Middle row (left to right): Readhead (secretary), Watkins (trainer), Rivers, Caleb, Read, Riddick, Phillips, Gibson, Jardine, Rioch, Moore, Martin (manager), Bentham (trainer).

Front row (left to right): Hyde, England (director), Hawkins (director), Hodgson (chairman), Harris (director), Richardson (director), Long.

1966/67
Back row (left to right): Mooney, Nicholson, Rivers, Read, Thear, Adamson, Moore.
Middle row (left to right): Martin (manager), Jardine, Slough, King, Lamb, Whittaker, N Rioch, B Rioch, Watkins (trainer).
Front row (left to right): Johnson, Pleat, Riddick, Thomson, French.

1967/68
Back row (left to right): Brown (manager), Ryan, Jardine, Slough, Read, Branston Dougan, Moore, Evans (trainer).
Front row (left to right): Hare, French, Buxton, Allen, Rioch, Whittaker, McDerment.

1968/69

Back row (left to right): Brown, Jefferson, McDerment, Starling, Taylor, Read, N Rioch, Potter.
Second row (left to right): Williams, Denton, Ryan, Allen, Slough, Dougan, Branston, Jardine, Moore.
Third row (left to right): Brown (manager), French, Lewis, Sheffield, B Rioch, Whittaker, Harrison, Whitehouse (trainer).
Front row (left to right): Jackett, Sweeney, Wainwright, McDonald, Meldrum, Hodgkinson.

1969/70

Back row (left to right): Stevenson, Jardine, French, Keen, Allen, Phillips.
Middle row (left to right): Ryan, Guild, N Rioch, Davie, Read, Dougan, Branston, Wainwright.
Front row (left to right): Lewis, Slough, Moore, Bannister, Harrison, B Rioch, Sheffield.

1970/71

Back row (left to right): Hoy, Bannister, Court, Ryan, Nicholl, Starling, Read, Branston, Moore, Jardine, Slough.

Front row (left to right): Collins, Tees, Givens, Macdonald, Keen, Phillips, Busby, French.

1971/72

Back row (left to right): Woods, Busby, Garner, Court, Shanks.

Middle row (left to right): Whitfield (trainer), Givens, Nicholl, Read, Wainwright, Anderson, Andrews (coach).

Front row (left to right): Goodeve, Hoy, Moore, John Ryan, Slough, Jim Ryan.

1972/73

Back row (left to right): Robinson, Hales, Harfield, Hindson, Hatch, Halom, Thomson, Faulkner, Price, Anderson, Jim Ryan, Jones, Sparks.
Middle row (left to right): Castiello, Garner, Wainwright, Goodeve, Barber, Carrick, Read, Moore, Slough, Litt, Gilchrist.
Front row (left to right): McCrohan (coach), John Ryan, Aston, Haslam (manager), Fern, Busby, Whitfield (trainer).

1973/74

Back row (left to right): Holmes, Anderson, Horn, Barber, Faulkner, Goodeve.
Middle row (left to right): McCrohan (coach), Cruse, John Ryan, Slough, Price, Moore, Thomson, Hindson, Garner, Game (physiotherapist).
Front row (left to right): French, Busby, Jim Ryan, Butlin, Aston, Fern, Shanks.

1974/75
Back row (left to right): Pollock, Anderson, John Ryan, P Futcher, Price, Husband.
Middle row (left to right): Game (physiotherapist), Thomson, Faulkner, Barber, Horn, Butlin, Garner, Litt, McCrohan (coach).
Front row (left to right): Chambers, West, Haslam (manager), Hindson, Jim Ryan.

1975/76
Back row (left to right): West, Jim Ryan, Aston, Anderson, Chambers.
Second row (left to right): Hindson, R Futcher, Faulkner, Barber, Horn, Buckley, Price, Game (physiotherapist).
Third row (left to right): Thomson, P Futcher, McCrohan (coach), Haslam (manager), Litt, Alston.
Front row (left to right): Spiring, Fuccillo, King, Pollock, Seasman, Husband.

1976/77
Back row (left to right): Gregory, Buckley, Smith, Wassell, Deans, Hill, Simon.
Second row (left to right): Jones, P Futcher, Faulkner, Knight, Barber, John Ryan, Price, McNichol, Game (physiotherapist).
Front row (left to right): Fuccillo, Chambers, Carr, McCrohan (coach), Haslam (manager), Husband, Aston, Mead.

1977/78
Back row (left to right): Game (physiotherapist), Carr, Jones, McNichol, Faulkner, Aleksic, Knight, P Futcher, Price, Buckley, McCrohan (coach).
Front row (left to right): Hill, Husband, Smith, Boersma, Haslam (manager), West, R Futcher, Fuccillo, Heale.

1978/79
Back row (left to right): Ingram, Stephens, Stein, Moss, Carr, Sherlock.
Middle row (left to right): Aizlewood, McNichol, Jones, Aleksic, Turner, Price, Donaghy.
Front row (left to right): Gutteridge (coach), Fuccillo, West, Hatton, Pleat (manager), Hill, Boersma, Johnson (physiotherapist).

1979/80
Back row (left to right): Pearson, Heath, Harriott, Heale, Goodyear, Turner, Sisman, Ollis.
Second row (left to right): Coates (trainer), Donaghy, Aizlewood, Findlay, Jones, Judge, Stephens, Stein, Moore (coach).
Third row (left to right): Fuccillo, Hill, Saxby, Gutteridge (coach), Pleat (manager), Smith (chief executive), Hatton, Price, Birchenall, Moss.
Front row (left to right): Cosby, Johnson, Piotrowski, Murphy, Bunn, Walker, Conquest, Cole, Woodward, Madden, Brammer.

1980/81

Back row (left to right): Pearson, Johnson, Harriott, Small, Walker, Smith, Goodyear, Turner, Heath.

Second row (left to right): Coates (trainer), White, Aizlewood, Findlay, Saxby, Antic, Judge, Donaghy, Ingram, Moore (coach).

Third row (left to right): Stephens, West, Grealish, Stein, Pleat (manager), Price, Smith (chief executive), Moss, Fuccillo, Hill, Sheridan (physiotherapist).

Front row (left to right): Brammer, Cosby, Foote, Phelps, Madden, Woodward, Beasley, Bunn, Cole, Patterson.

1981/82

Back row (left to right); Antic, Stein, White, Bunn, Goodyear, Judge, Saxby, Findlay, Fuccillo, Keys, Donaghy, Horton, Aizlewood.

Front row (left to right): Madden, Johnson, Turner, Brammer, Ingram, Stephens, Heath, Small, Hill.

1982/83
Back row (left to right): Johnson, Turner, North, Small, Goodyear, Bunn, Kellock, Walsh.
Middle row (left to right): Moore (coach), Money, Saxby, Beasley, Findlay, Judge, Aizlewood, Fuccillo, Hartley (coach).
Front row (left to right): Coates (trainer), Hill, Donaghy, Stephens, Horton, Pleat (manager), Moss, Stein, Antic, Sheridan (physiotherapist).

1983/84
Back row (left to right): Johnson, Turner, Daniel, Breacker, Beasley, North, Thomas, Parker, Watts.
Middle row (left to right): Moore (coach), Money, Goodyear, Sealey, Elliott, Saxby, Findlay, Aylott, Bunn, Hartley (coach).
Front row (left to right): Coates (trainer), Stephens, Hill, Donaghy, Moss, Pleat (manager), Horton, Antic, Stein, Walsh, Sheridan (physiotherapist).

1984/85

Back row (left to right): M Stein, Johnson, Breacker, S North, M North, Parker, Turner, Daniel.
Middle row (left to right): Moore (coach), Nwajiobi, Bunn, Findlay, P Elliott, Dibble, Goodyear, Thomas, Coates (trainer).
Front row (left to right): Hartley (coach), S Elliott, Moss, Hill, Donaghy, Pleat (manager), B Stein, Grimes, Hilaire, Sheridan (physiotherapist).

1985/86

Back row (left to right): M Stein, Preece, Nwajiobi, S North, M North, Daniel, Johnson.
Middle row (left to right): Moore (coach), Parker, Sealey, Breacker, Elliott, Harford, Dibble, Thomas, Faulkner (coach).
Front row (left to right): Hartley (coach), Hill, Donaghy, Foster, Pleat (manager), Nicholas, B Stein, Grimes, Sheridan (physiotherapist).

1986/87

Back row (left to right): Tuite, Preece, M Stein, Nwajiobi, M North, McEvoy, Johnson.
Middle row (left to right): Ryan (coach), Breacker, Sealey, M Harford, S North, Dibble, Newell, Faulkner (coach).
Front row (left to right): R Harford (coach), Hill, Donaghy, Foster, Moore (manager), Nicholas, B Stein, Grimes, Kirby (physiotherapist).

1987/88

Back row (left to right): Preece, Nwajiobi, Harvey, North, Cobb, Black, M Stein.
Middle row (left to right): Ryan (coach), Faulkner (coach), Johnson, Grimes, Sealey, M Harford, Dibble, McDonough, R Wilson, Weir, Kirby (physiotherapist).
Front row (left to right): D Wilson, B Stein, Foster, R Harford (manager), Donaghy, Hill, Breacker.

1988/89
Back row (left to right): Preece, M Stein, Cobb, Allinson, Harvey, Black, R Johnson.
Middle row (left to right): Galley (physiotherapist), Faulkner (coach), Wegerle, Dreyer, Oldfield,
Sealey, M Harford, Chamberlain, M Johnson, Grimes, McDonough, Ryan (coach).
Front row (left to right): Williams, Wilson, Foster, R Harford (manager), Donaghy, Hill, Breacker.

1989/90
Back row (left to right): Cooke, O'Brien, James, M Johnson, Harvey, Mead, Black, Gray.
Middle row (left to right): Mancini (coach), Ryan (coach), McDonough, Dowie, Rodger, Sealey,
Chamberlain, M Harford, Beaumont, Dreyer, Faulkner (coach), Galley (physiotherapist).
Front row (left to right): Preece, R Johnson, Wilson, R Harford (manager), Wegerle,
Breacker, Williams.

1990/91

Back row (left to right): Cooke, Gray, Johnson, Nogan, Harvey, Rees.
Middle row (left to right): Ley (coach), Moore (coach), James, Hughes, Dowie, Petterson, Chamberlain, Rodger, McDonough, Faulkner (coach), Galley (physiotherapist).
Front row (left to right): Beaumont, Breacker, Dreyer, Ryan (manager), Preece, Black, Elstrup.

1991/92

Back row (left to right): James, Farrell, Beaumont, Rodger, Chamberlain, McDonough, Johnson, Dreyer, Harvey.
Front row (left to right): Nogan, Hughes, Rees, Preece, Pembridge, Black.

1992/93
Back row (left to right): Salton, Campbell, Linton, Chamberlain, Johnson, Sommer, Greene, Dreyer, Kamara.
Middle row (left to right): Moore (coach), James, Telfer, Allpress, Nogan, Harvey, Peake, Owen (coach).
Front row (left to right): Claridge, Preece, Gray, Pleat (manager), Hughes, Rees, Oakes.

1993/94
Back row (left to right): Moore (coach), Hartson, James, Dixon, Sommer, Greene, Petterson, Dreyer, Linton, Campbell, Pleat (manager).
Front row (left to right): Telfer, Thorpe, Harper, Peake, Preece, Oakes, Hughes.

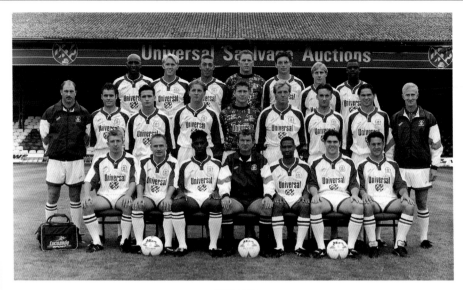

1994/95

Back row (left to right): Thomas, Campbell, Linton, Sommer, Greene, James, Johnson.
Middle row (left to right): Goodyear (physiotherapist), Harvey, Hughes, Hartson, Davis, Dixon, Oakes, Skelton, Moore (coach).
Front row (left to right): Houghton, Preece, Williams, Pleat (manager), Marshall, Thorpe, Telfer.

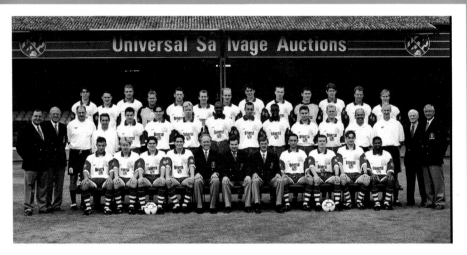

1995/96

Back row (left to right): Chenery, Power, Simpson, Barber, McLaren, Matthews, G Johnson, Greene, S Davis, K Davis, Taylor, Peake, James.
Middle row (left to right): Green (director), Bassett (director), Goodyear (physiotherapist), Lowe (coach), Harvey, Skelton, Oldfield, Thomas, Linton, M Johnson, Guentchev, Woolgar, Turner (coach), Moore (coach), Shannon (scout), Terry (director).
Front row (left to right): Woodsford, Waddock, Thorpe, Hughes, McGiven (assistant manager), Kohler (chairman), Westley (manager), Oakes, Jones, Alexander, Marshall.

1996/97

Back row (left to right): Woodsford, Guentchev, Grant, McLaren, Patterson, Simpson, Taylor, Chenery.

Middle row (left to right): Goodyear (physiotherapist), Oldfield, Linton, Johnson, Feuer, K Davis, Thomas, Alexander, Skelton, Peake (coach).

Front row (left to right): James, Thorpe, S Davis, Lawrence (manager), Kohler (chairman), Turner (coach), Waddock, Marshall, Harvey.

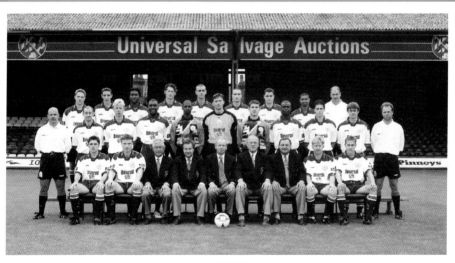

1997/98

Back row (left to right): Kean, Evers, Douglas, McLaren, Davies, Fotiadis, Harvey, Marshall, Goodyear (physiotherapist).

Middle row (left to right): Turner (coach), Showler, Oldfield, Thomas, Abbey, Feuer, K Davis, Johnson, Willmott, Alexander, Peake (coach).

Front row (left to right): Thorpe, S Davis, Terry (director), Kohler (chairman), Lawrence (manager), Bassett (director), Green (director), Waddock, James.

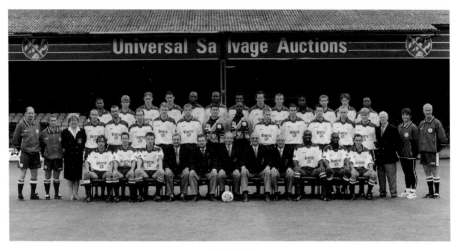

1998/99

Back row (left to right): Marshall, Sweeney, Clarke, Spring, Boyce, Augustine, McGowan, Lawes, Fraser, Douglas, Cox, McIndoe, Scarlett.
Middle row (left to right): Goodyear (physiotherapist), Lowe (coach), Cherry Newbery (secretary), Fotiadis, Davies, Showler, Doherty, White, K Davis, Abbey, James, Willmott, McLaren, Alexander, Lough, Shannon (scout), Mandy Malins (fitness trainer), Moore (coach).
Front row (left to right): George, Gray, S Davis, Green (director), Kohler (chairman), Lawrence (manager), Bassett (director), Terry (director), Thomas, Johnson, Evers.

1999/00

Back row (left to right): Moore (coach), McKinnon, Zahana-Oni, Locke, Sodje, White, Kandol, Doherty, Boyce, Taylor, Goodyear (physiotherapist).
Middle row (left to right): Hartley (coach), Scarlett, McIndoe, McGowan, Abbey, Tate, McLaren, Spring, Fraser, Mandy Malins (fitness trainer).
Front row (left to right): Gray, Fotiadis, Green (director), Bassett (director), Johnson, Lawrence (manager), Terry (director), George, Douglas.

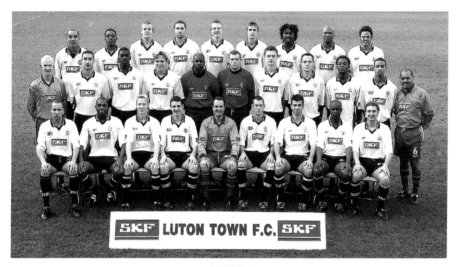

2000/01

Back row (left to right): M Stein, Scarlett, Fraser, Fotiadis, Taylor, Holmes, Douglas, McGowan, Brennan.
Middle row (left to right): Moore (assistant manager), Thompson, Stirling, Karlsen, Abbey, Ovendale, Ayres, Breitenfelder, Kandol, Baptiste, B Stein (coach).
Front row (left to right): George, Boyce, Helin, Spring, Fuccillo (manager), McLaren, Watts, Johnson, Locke.

2001/02

Back row (left to right): Crowe, Valois, Perrett, Ovendale, Emberson, Bayliss, Neilson, Fotiadis.
Middle row (left to right): Sewell (physiotherapist), Harford (coach), Skelton, Coyne, Howard, Holmes, Hughes, Boyce, Kabba, Stein (coach), Cherry Newbery (secretary).
Front row (left to right): Brkovic, Mansell, Spring, Johnson, Kinnear (manager), Watson-Challis (chairman), Nicholls, Forbes, Hillier, Taylor.

2002/03

Back row (left to right): Brkovic, Neilson, Perrett, Ovendale, Berthelin, Emberson, Holmes, Hillier, Bayliss.
Middle row (left to right): Sewell (physiotherapist), Davis, Griffiths, Thorpe, Howard, Coyne, Skelton, Hughes, Fotiadis, Leary, Stein (coach).
Front row (left to right): Boyce, Kimble, Forbes, Nicholls, Harford (coach), Kinnear (manager), Spring, Johnson, Mansell, Robinson.

2003/04

Back row (left to right): Mansell, Hillier, Neilson, Bayliss, Spring, Davis, Boyce, Crowe.
Middle row (left to right): Julie Frost (physiotherapist), Nicholls, Hughes, Beckwith, Howard, Brill, Coyne, Showunmi, Stein (coach).
Front row (left to right): Brkovic, Forbes, Perrett, Newell (manager), Harford (director of football), Robinson, Leary, Foley.

2004/05

Back row (left to right): O'Leary, Bayliss, Neilson, Vine, Leary, Showunmi, Davies, Barnett, Hillier, Mansell.
Middle row (left to right): Coleman (physiotherapist), Blinkhorn, Hughes, Howard, Beckwith, Seremet, Beresford, Brill, Coyne, Underwood, Keane, Bowden (physiotherapist), Stein (coach).
Front row (left to right): Holmes, Brkovic, Nicholls, Newell (manager), Tomlins (chairman), Harford (director of football), Perrett, Robinson, Davis.

2005/06

Back row (left to right): Underwood, Keane, Barnett, Leary, Davies, Vine, Foley, Andrew, Edwards, Stevens.
Middle row (left to right): Murray (physiotherapist), Kharine (coach), Stein (coach), Hughes, O'Leary, Showunmi, Beckwith, Seremet, Brill, Beresford, Howard, Coyne, Heikkinen, Johnson (coach), Bowden (physiotherapist), Catlin (kit man).
Front row (left to right): Morgan, Holmes, Brkovic, Nicholls, Tomlins (chairman), Newell (manager), Perrett, Robinson, Davis, Feeney.

2006/07

Back row (left to right): Bowden (physiotherapist), Andrew, Barnett, Keane, Leary, Foley,
Underwood, Edwards, Stevens, Johnson (coach).
Middle row (left to right): Catlin (kit man), Kharine (coach), Holmes, Vine, O'Leary, Bell, Beresford,
Barrett, Brill, Boyd, Emanuel, Langley, Pendleton, Sedgley (coach), Murray (physiotherapist).
Front row (left to right): Heikkinen, Morgan, Brkovic, Robinson, Newell (manager), Stein (assistant
manager), Coyne, Perrett, Davis, Feeney.

2007/08

Back row (left to right): Asafu-Adjaye, Talbot, Keane, Langley, Andrew, Parkin, Underwood,
Robinson, Brkovic.
Middle row (left to right): Scott-Stackman (physiotherapist), Edmondson (physiotherapist), Bradley
(kit manager), Gargiulo (sports scientist), Goodall, Sinclair, Edwards, O'Leary, Barrett, Brill,
Beresford, Spring, Furlong, Davis, Emanuel, Cummins (director of youth football), Lewis (sports
scientist), Kharine (coach), Carver (coach).
Front row (left to right): Foley, Currie, Hutchison, Coyne, Blackwell (manager), Ellis (assistant
manager), Perry, Morgan, Peschisolido, Bell.

■ William (Billy) Marshall HUGHES

Although Billy lost a large chunk of his playing career due to the war he was still regarded as 'the most polished full-back in the country if not the world' when Second Division Luton paid a record £11,000 to Birmingham for his services in 1947.

New Luton manager Dally Duncan had pulled off a major coup in bringing the Welsh international to Kenilworth Road but after only 31 appearances he was off to Chelsea with centre-forward Hugh Billington for a combined £20,000. Billy left Chelsea in 1951, age 33, for Hereford and then skippered Flint Town United to the Welsh Cup final.

In later life Billy ran a pub and was steward at the Wolseley Cars Social Club before passing away in Birmingham in 1981.

■ James (Jimmy) HUSBAND

Snapped up by Everton as a 15 year old in 1963 from Newcastle junior football, Jimmy became a regular for the Goodison side three years later and earned a League Championship medal in 1970.

The England under-23 international was a fast and skilful forward with an eye for goal and became Luton manager Harry Haslam's final piece in the jigsaw as the Hatters sought successfully to win promotion to the top flight in 1973/74.

Scorer of many vital goals during that season and the next four years for the Town, Jimmy finished his career, along with many others, in the NASL.

On his return, Jimmy settled in mid-Bedfordshire and still lives in Clophill in semi-retirement and was a welcome guest of the club in 2005 for the Kenilworth Road Centenary celebrations.

■ Donald (Don) HUTCHISON

Vastly experienced midfielder Don has turned out for nine clubs in a long career commanding transfer fees in excess of £11 million along the way.

After starting with Hartlepool in 1990, Don soon caught the eye of Liverpool leading to a switch to Anfield whilst still a teenager. Big money moves to West Ham (twice), Sheffield United, Everton and Sunderland followed before Don started to wind down with free transfers to Millwall and Coventry.

Capped 26 times by Scotland, scoring six times, including one strike against England, Don impressed in Luton Town's pre-season tour to Norway in 2007 and was offered a contract when it was hoped that he would be able to pass on some of his skills to the Hatters youngsters.

Don was released by the Hatters in the summer of 2008.

■ Morten Lauridsen HYLDGAARD

Giant goalkeeper Morten was signed by Coventry from Danish side Ikast F.S. for £200,000 in 1999 but had to wait three years before claiming a first team place at Highfield Road.

The Danish Under-21 international became first choice for the Sky Blues in 2002/03 before it was realised that further appearances would trigger an extra payment to his former club. Reluctantly, Morten moved on to Hibernian but was unable to replace Swedish goalkeeper Daniel Andersson, however he was handed a lifeline when Luton manager Mike Newell signed him on a free transfer in January 2004. An adequate shot-stopper, Morten made 18 League appearances over the remainder of that season before returning to Denmark with Brande I.F and then on to Aarhus.

■ Besian IDRIZAJ

Born in Vienna of Kosovan parents, Besian made his debut for Linzer ASK in the Austrian league as a 15 year old. Such was his progress that he was voted Austria's Young Player of the Year in 2004/05 as well as picking up under-21 caps including one against England who were beaten by their Austrian counterparts.

After a trial period, Besian joined his boyhood favourites Liverpool on a two year contract in 2005 where he became a regular in the Anfield reserve side. Sent out to Luton on loan in March 2007 he came to a club in turmoil with manager Mike Newell just departed and it was understandable that he was unable to show his full talents although the tall striker did net a coolly taken goal against Southend as the season drew to a close.

After returning to Liverpool, Besian was loaned out to Wacker Innsbruck during 2007/08 but has now been released by the Reds.

■ Samuel (Sammy) Gary IGOE

Tiny midfielder Sammy made up for his lack of stature with speed and skill and became a regular for Portsmouth, the club he joined from school.

A £200,000 cheque took him to Reading in 2000 where he became a crowd favourite due to his whole hearted attitude. Towards the end of the 2002/03 campaign he found himself out of the side and accepted a loan move to Joe Kinnear's Luton, making a superb debut in a home draw with Tranmere and then following it up with an incisive display at Cheltenham.

Sadly, Sammy then received an injury in training which cut short his stay. He joined Swindon that summer and more recently turned out for Bristol Rovers for whom he scored in the Johnstone's Paint trophy final at Cardiff and then netted the winner in the League Two play-off final at Wembley in 2007. Sammy signed for Bournemouth in July 2008.

■ John James Stewart (Stewart) IMLACH

Lossiemouth born Stewart crossed the border to sign for Bury in 1952 but it was at Nottingham Forest where he made a name for himself as a very fast, skilful winger picking up Scottish international caps along the way.

Starring for Forest in the 1959 F.A.Cup final against Luton it came as a surprise when he joined the freshly relegated Hatters for £8,000 a year later. New manager Sam Bartram followed Stewart into Kenilworth Road and soon carried out a cull of players early in the following campaign which saw the bewildered winger on his way to Coventry after only eight games.

After finishing his playing career, Stewart coached at Everton, Blackpool and Bury before going back to his pre-football job as a joiner. Stewart died in 2001 but his son Gary has recently brought out a book on his dad entitled, 'My father and other working class football heroes' which is highly recommended.

■ Godfrey Patrick INGRAM

Local boy Godfrey was a schoolboy prodigy, starring for England schoolboys and predicted a glittering career after signing on for the Hatters in 1977. Undoubtedly supremely talented, it was a major surprise to see him fail to win a regular place in the side at Kenilworth Road.

Godfrey moved to the USA in 1981 and found the playing style there far more suited to his talents and he enjoyed a ten year stint playing for St Louis Storm and San Jose Earthquakes banging in goals for fun and was at one time voted the 'Most Valuable Player' in the NASL.

Godfrey is, of course, a leading light in the Luton 2020 consortium.

■ Matthew (Matt) Alan JACKSON

Another schoolboy international star, Matt signed on for Luton in July 1990 before making his League debut as a substitute in a 0-2 defeat at Arsenal in August 1991.

Eight games and two months later though, the commanding and intelligent defender was off to Everton for £600,000 where he played for five years picking up an F.A.Cup winners medal in 1995 during his stay there.

A move to Norwich in 1996 followed and then on to Wigan in 2001 where he seemed to get better with age becoming club captain at the JJB Stadium and marshalling his defence against the best the Premiership could throw at it.

A final move, this time to Watford in 2007, has ended with Matt recently deciding to hang up his boots.

■ Richard JACKSON

Whitby born Richard joined his local League side Scarborough from school before signing professional forms in March 1998.

A year later, after making barely 20 League appearances for the Seamer Road side, Richard was on the move with Derby County putting in a £30,000 bid for his services leading to an eight year spell at Pride Park during which time he played 127 first team games for the Rams including some in the Premiership.

Able to play in either full-back role, Richard was the longest serving Derby player when he was given a free-transfer in the summer of 2007 and was quickly signed up by Luton manager Kevin Blackwell.

■ Julian Colin JAMES

Luton coach John Moore first spotted Tring born Julian playing in a county schools match at Hemel Hempstead and he eventually signed professional forms in June 1988.

Julian was dismissed for a supposed professional foul when making his full Hatters debut in a Littlewoods Cup tie at Leeds the following season, but his evening was not completely ruined as the Town did go on to win the tie.

First and foremost a defender, James could play anywhere along the back and his versatility became a godsend to a succession of Luton Town managers. Capped twice for England at under-21 level, he became a regular in the Hatters side in 1991/92 and apart from injuries was a feature in the team until a badly broken leg suffered at Bristol Rovers in April 1998 effectively ended his career.

Julian now runs his own building firm.

■ Percy George Burge JAMES

Rhondda born Percy was 32 when he was picked up by Luton Town from amateur side Oxford City in 1949. The clever left winger made a scoring debut in a 2-5 defeat at Bury in October 1949 and kept his place the following week when leaders Tottenham were held to a 1-1 draw at Kenilworth Road in front of a then record League crowd of 27,319.

The Welsh Amateur international then surprisingly found himself out of the side and, although earning good reviews as part of a strong Hatters reserve side, decided to return to non-League football, joining Worcester City where he eventually became player/manager. Percy died in 1993.

■ Frederick (Fred) JARDINE

It was a surprise in footballing circles when Fred was given a free transfer by Dundee but the Hatters moved swiftly to sign the pacy left winger from under the noses of Wolves in 1961.

Sadly, Fred joined a Luton side that was tumbling through the divisions and it was not until they were in football's basement that he managed to win a regular place in the team by which time he had been converted to full-back.

His surging runs on the overlap and a perfectly executed sliding tackle endeared him to the Luton crowd as the Town won the Division Four championship in 1968. His appearances in the side dwindled after that and after a short spell at Torquay he hung up his boots.

Fred worked at John Pope's gents outfitters in Dunstable Road for many years and still lives in Luton.

■ William (Billy) John JENNINGS

Although born in Hackney and having trials with Tottenham, Billy joined Watford as a 17 year old and soon became known as a predatory goalscorer with the Hornets, leading to a £110,000 switch to West Ham in 1974 where he picked up an F.A.Cup winners medal a year later.

Slight and not particularly tall, Billy was tremendous in the air but a bad Achilles injury saw his effectiveness wane in the top flight and he moved on to Orient in 1979. A short term deal took him to Luton in March 1982 when Hatters manager David Pleat was looking for experienced cover and Billy scored a vital goal against Norwich over Easter which virtually confirmed promotion to Division One.

After a brief tour of non-League clubs Billy then concentrated on his restaurant businesses in London and Brentwood.

■ James (Jimmy) Thomas JINKS

Londoner Jimmy joined Millwall in 1938 and made a scoring League debut for the Lions on the closing day of the 1938/39 season. During the war years he was a prolific scorer, averaging almost a goal a game, and appeared for Millwall at Wembley in the 1945 Football League South Cup final against Joe Payne's Chelsea.

A clever two footed centre forward, Jimmy moved on to Fulham in 1948 and then on to Luton in March 1950. By then he was almost 34 but his experience, in a few cameo appearances, helped keep the threat of relegation at bay.

Following a short stay at Aldershot, Jimmy played for Ashford and Snowdown Colliery Workers before leaving the game. Jimmy died in Eltham in 1981.

■ Brian JOHNSON

Brian starred for the Sunderland youth team which lost to Arsenal in the 1966 Youth Cup final but was not retained at the season's end and was snapped up by Luton along with team mate Terry Adamson.

A speedy and brave winger, Brian made his Hatters debut in a 0-0 draw at Chester in October 1966 and made eight appearances over the course of that campaign including winning a 'man of the match' award when his promptings tore York City apart as the Town won 5-1 at Kenilworth Road on the final day of the season.

With Luton supporters thinking that Brian had done enough to earn a regular spot he was unable to displace Ray Whittaker in 1967/68 as the Hatters walked away with the championship of Division Four.

Brian turned his back on the game after that and returned to his native Newcastle where he joined Royal Mail.

■ Gavin JOHNSON

Stowmarket born Gavin joined Ipswich from school and went on to make over 100 League appearances for the Portman Road side over six seasons despite suffering a succession of serious knee injuries.

Given a free transfer in 1995, Gavin was quickly signed on by Luton manager Terry Westley but could manage only a handful of games as the Town struggled in Division One. By the time the Hatters had recruited Lennie Lawrence to the hot seat, Gavin was on loan at Wigan and a £15,000 cheque eventually took him to Springfield Park permanently.

Considering his early injury record as well as subsequent broken legs, this solid and obviously indestructible left sided midfielder or defender has gone on to enjoy a long career and was still turning out at Conference level with Oxford at the age of 36.

Gavin is now with Bury Town.

■ Marvin Anthony JOHNSON

Picked up by the Hatters from school football in Aylesbury, Marvin was moved into defence for the youth side before signing professional forms in October 1986.

With an established partnership of Steve Foster and Mal Donaghy in the Town's top flight defence at the time, Marvin had to bide his time but once he established himself in the side he was difficult to budge and went on to make 373 League appearances for his only club before hanging up his boots in 2002.

Showing whole hearted effort and a penchant for spectacular own goals, Marvin was a crowd favourite at Kenilworth Road and it was no surprise when he was offered a coaching position with the club when he stopped playing.

Marvin is now manager of St Neots Town.

■ Robert (Rob) Simon JOHNSON

Bedford born Rob turned professional for Luton in August 1979 but his career was almost over before it started as he suffered two serious knee injuries, which he had to get over before making his League debut for Lincoln on loan in August 1983.

The tenacious full-back earned his Hatters debut soon after but further injuries meant that his appearances were only sporadic over the next six years although he did turn out in the magical Littlewoods Cup final win over Arsenal in 1988.

A move to David Pleat's Leicester in 1989 was not a success and after spells at Barnet and Hitchin he turned to physiotherapy which he had studied during his long periods on the sidelines.

Rob is currently a physiotherapist with the English Institute of Sport and has his own practice in Matlock.

■ Graham JONES

Tough, no-nonsense defender Graham came up through the ranks at Kenilworth Road where he learnt his trade under then youth coach David Pleat. After making his League debut on the final day of the 1975/76 campaign, in a 3-0 win over Blackpool, Graham could never stake a regular place in the Luton side and after four years of trying was happy to make a move to Torquay which was far more to his liking, as he missed only one game during his first two seasons at Plainmoor.

Graham moved back to his home town area when joining Stockport in 1983 and from there turned out for Runcorn, Altrincham, Northwich Victoria and finally Colne Dynamoes.

■ Leslie (Les) Clifford JONES

Although born in Wales, Les came to the notice of Luton Town when playing for Luton District and South Beds League side Craig Athletic.

Cool under pressure, too cool some said, and able to play in both full-back positions, Les made his debut at the back end of the 1950/51 season and eventually earned a fairly regular place in the Hatters side despite having to compete against both Seamus Dunne and Bud Aherne.

Often mentioned in dispatches to the Welsh international selectors, Les asked for a transfer after losing his place to Ken Hawkes and moved to Aston Villa where he made only five appearances before signing up with the Army.

On leaving the forces, Les joined Worcester City before hanging his boots up. Les is now back in Luton.

■ Alan Graham JUDGE

Proving that goalkeepers can go on much longer than outfield players, Alan was still pulling on his gloves for Banbury United at the age of 46!

Born in Kingsbury, Alan joined Luton from school and signed professional forms in 1978 before making his debut at Newcastle on the closing day of the 1979/80 season. Regarded as number two to Jake Findlay at Kenilworth Road, Alan nevertheless earned headlines when saving Gerry Gow's penalty at fellow promotion contenders Rotherham during the Hatter's championship winning campaign of 1981/82.

Alan accepted a step-down to Reading in 1982 and was back in the top flight with Oxford three years later where he won a Milk Cup winners medal.

Alan is goalkeeping coach at Oxford City.

■ Matthew Peter JUDGE

Barking born Matthew came to the Hatters from school with his early performances for the youth team, where he scored goals for fun, giving rise to great expectations for the future.

A natural goalscorer, Matthew was used sparingly, appearing in the LDV Vans Trophy and as substitute in the F.A.Cup clash at Wigan in December 2002 before making his League debut coming on as substitute during a 5-0 win at Colchester in April 2003.

Despite a cracking last minute winner at Stevenage in the following season's LDV competition Matthew, by now an Eire youth international, made only one further substitute appearance before being surprisingly released in 2004.

Matthew was recently seen back at Kenilworth Road meeting up with some of his old colleagues and is playing his football in Eire with Sligo.

■ Duncan Alan JUPP

Duncan came up through the youth system at Fulham winning nine Scottish Under-21 caps along the way and his form gave rise to a big money move to Premiership Wimbledon in 1996.

Sadly, Duncan made only 30 League appearances in six years with the Dons and accepted a transfer to Notts County in 2002 closely followed by a further move to Luton in February 2003 where he joined up with his old Wimbledon boss Joe Kinnear.

Released at the end of that campaign, Duncan joined Southend who he helped to win two consecutive promotions with his marauding forays down the wing allied to solid defensive full-back play.

Duncan signed on for Gillingham in the summer of 2006 before recently moving to Bognor.

Luton Town Post-War A to Z

■ Stephen (Steve) KABBA

Lightning quick striker Steve was on the books of Crystal Palace as a youth trainee and as part of his football education was loaned out to Joe Kinnear's Luton in March 2002 just as the Hatters were about to win promotion from Division Three.

Steve came on as substitute in three games where his quality was evident but despite attempts by Kinnear, Palace would not part with him although they had a change of heart a few months later, selling him to Sheffield United for £250,000.

At Bramall Lane a succession of injuries, plus a surfeit of strikers, cut down his appearances and he was pleased to move back nearer to his London birthplace when joining Watford for £500,000 in January 2007.

Steve has recently started a six month loan move to Blackpool.

■ Christopher (Chris) KAMARA

After failing to gain an apprenticeship with home town club Middlesbrough, Chris joined the Navy and while stationed at Portsmouth caught the eye of Pompey scouts leading up to him being bought out by the club and making his League debut against Luton as a 17 year old in 1975.

A tough tackling midfield leader, Chris went through a variety of clubs before joining David Pleat's Luton in November 1991 as the Hatters were clinging on to top flight football. Loaned out to Sheffield United a year later, Chris spoke out in the press against the hierarchy at Luton but was then forced to eat humble pie when the Blades returned him to Kenilworth Road!

Chris finished his playing career at Bradford City before managing the Bantams and is now well known as a pundit on Sky Sports.

■ Tresor Osmar KANDOL

African born Tresor was spotted by Luton Town scouts when playing in London and signed YTS forms for the Hatters in the summer of 1997. He was awarded a full-time contract a year later making his League debut at Bristol Rovers in February 1999.

An undoubtedly talented striker with a languid style, Tresor was also high maintenance and soon fell out with new Luton manager Joe Kinnear who showed him the door.

After brief attempts at reviving his League career failed, Tresor moved around the non-League circuit before re-surfacing at Barnet, who paid Dagenham and Redbridge £50,000 for his services, in January 2006.

At Barnet his goals kept the Bees in the Football League and in a remarkable reversal of fortune he found his way into the Championship with Leeds. Tresor is currently on loan at Millwall.

■ Kent KARLSEN

Looking for strength in the spine of his team, Luton manager Ricky Hill went to Scandinavia for Kent, a centre-half who had served a solid apprenticeship in the Norwegian Premier League.

An Under-21 international, Kent's five years with Valerenga brought considerable success, including a Norwegian F.A. Cup winners medal, and Hill moved swiftly to sign the player in November 2000 after a short trial period.

Sadly, Kent's stay at Kenilworth Road was short as Hill was dismissed shortly after and new boss Joe Kinnear had his own preferences for central defence.

Kent left Luton after only six League appearances and returned to Norway where he was last seen turning out for FK Tonsberg.

■ Robert (Rob) Steven KEAN

At the start of the 1997/98 season, Luton Town manager Lennie Lawrence was suffering a horrendous injury crisis culminating in only 14 players being available for an away trip to Bristol City at the end of September.

Of those 14, four would be making their League debuts including Rob Kean who came on as substitute for skipper Gary Waddock. Luton born, and a member of the successful youth squad at Kenilworth Road which won the South East Counties championship in consecutive seasons, Rob was a promising midfielder but he did not get the opportunity to add to his solitary appearance being released the following summer.

Rob, who still lives in Luton, is now an aircraft engineer and turns out for Barton Rovers.

■ Keith Francis KEANE

Another local boy who rose through the ranks, Keith joined the Hatters from school and signed professional forms in August 2004 by which time he already had 15 League appearances under his belt.

A genuine utility player, 17 year old Keith opened his Hatters account as a full-back at Wycombe in February 2004 where he acquitted himself well against the speedy Jermaine McSporran. It was not long before he scored his first goal, with a last minute winner at home to Bristol City in the following April.

A League One championship medal the following season, Eire Under-21 caps, Young player of the Season in 2005/06, the scorer of the Goal of the Season in a televised clash at West Bromwich in 2006/07 and subsequent captaincy of the team, it is difficult to realise that Keith is still only 21.

■ Michael (Mike) Thomas KEEN

Mike had already enjoyed a footballing career which would have been the envy of most professional players before having a second!

Signing on for Q.P.R. in 1959, Mike soon established himself in the side and oversaw, as skipper, the club's rise from Division Three to Division One as well as picking up the League Cup along the way.

Following ex-manager Alec Stock to Luton in 1969, the cultured midfielder then skippered the Hatters to Division Two and then saw his side narrowly fail to win back to back promotions.

After leaving the Town, Mike had a spell as player and manager at Watford before taking the hot seat at Northampton and Wycombe. After leaving the game Mike has run sports shops in Wycombe and Bicester.

■ William (Billy) KELLOCK

Glaswegian midfielder Billy failed to make the grade at Aston Villa and moved to Cardiff in 1972 where he made his League debut for the Bluebirds as an 18 year old. Short stays at Norwich and Millwall followed before he dropped out of the League to join Kettering,

finally fulfilling his potential as an aggressive, goalscoring midfielder and he continued to shine at Peterborough where he banged in 43 goals in 134 starts.

Luton manager David Pleat paid £30,000 for the talented Billy just as the Hatters were about to enter the top flight in 1982 but his stay was short, presumably because Pleat did not think he could cut it in Division One.

Transfers to Wolves, who he helped to promotion, Southend, Port Vale and Halifax followed before he finished back at Kettering where he managed a Country Club.

■ Terence (Terry) William John KELLY

Local boy Terry signed on for his home town side Luton in 1950 after starring for Vauxhall Motors but had to then spend two years in the RAF on National Service before he could begin to forge a career at Kenilworth Road.

A tall, commanding centre-half, Terry had a problem displacing skipper Syd Owen from that position and made his debut at centre forward at Bristol Rovers in 1954 and scored! Terry had to wait until Syd retired before claiming a regular spot in the Luton side and by the time he left the club to join Cambridge City in 1963 he had racked up 136 League appearances for the Hatters.

After a spell at Dunstable, Terry worked at Vauxhall until retirement and was still living in Luton at the time of his sad, recent death.

■ Michael (Mick) Francis Martin KENNEDY

A true football journeyman, Mick played over 500 League games spanning ten clubs, who paid over £1 million for his services and earned a reputation as a midfield enforcer and self-styled hard man in a long career.

Starting off at Halifax, Mick rarely stayed longer than two years at a club apart from Portsmouth who he helped to the top flight in 1987. The Hatters were one of the sides he stayed with for only twelve months but the 1989/90 season was not without incident as Mick worked under three managers, was sent off twice and made sure that Derby did not score by fair means or foul after coming on as substitute in the final day 3-2 win at the Baseball Ground which saved the Hatters from relegation.

Eire international Mick now runs a 'Soccer School' in Lahinch, Co Clare.

■ Spencer Charles KETTLEY

Welshman Spencer was stationed at Bletchley and was turning out for Newbury Town as the war drew to a close and was picked up by Luton in August 1944 as the club attempted to rebuild.

Despite being regarded as a wing-half, it was at inside-forward that Spencer made his only League appearance for the Hatters in a 1-2 home defeat at the hands of Leicester in October 1946.

Spencer filled a variety of positions for the reserve side over that 1946/47 campaign but 'did not seem to have recovered completely from (war) service in the tropics.' Spencer proved everyone wrong though by continuing to play football at non-League and parks level until he was 54!

After a career in the shoe trade, Spencer lives in retirement in Desborough.

■ Derek Tennyson KEVAN

Derek was nearing the end of an illustrious career by the time he signed for Luton in December 1966 but his transfer was seen as a major coup for a side that was struggling at the wrong end of Division Four.

Born in Ripon, Derek had started out at Bradford PA but it was while at West Brom that he earned 14 caps for England and rattled in 157 goals in 262 League appearances. He continued to score for Chelsea, Manchester City, Crystal Palace and Peterborough before becoming one of Luton manager Allan Brown's first signings.

Although playing only 11 League games for the Hatters before moving to Stockport in exchange for Keith Allen, Derek certainly re-awakened enthusiasm at Kenilworth Road.

Derek now lives in retirement in Spain.

■ Dean Laurence KIELY

Released by both West Brom and Coventry as a boy, Dean made it third time lucky when he signed on for York in May 1990 and within three years was the Minstermen's regular goalkeeper and saving penalties at Wembley to earn his side promotion in the play-offs.

Moving to Bury on a tribunal transfer in 1996, he won a Division Two championship medal in his first season.

By the time of his £1 million move to Charlton in 1999 he was already a Republic of Ireland international, despite having played for England schoolboys in the past. A transfer to Portsmouth in 2006 did not work out and he brought his uncanny shot-stopping skills and defensive organisation to Luton on loan last in 2006/07.

Sadly the Hatters could not afford to keep him and he finished the campaign back full circle at West Brom.

■ Thomas (Tommy) KIERNAN

One of the most skilful inside-forwards of the early post-war years, Tommy had been transferred to Celtic from Albion Rovers for £4,000 in 1945 but was then surprisingly sold to Stoke two years later even though he was a regular and a crowd favourite at Parkhead.

Beset by injury at the Victoria Ground, Tommy was allowed to move to Luton for the then huge fee of £8,500 in November 1948 and he immediately caught the imagination at Kenilworth Road with his displays in the two epic FA cup ties with Leicester in early 1949.

Sadly injury also caught up with him at Luton and he eventually moved back to Scotland with St Mirren as part of the deal that brought Willie Davie to Kenilworth Road and then on to Alloa and back to Albion Rovers where he became coach. Tommy stayed in the Coatbridge area and died in 1991.

■ John KILGANNON

John was watched several times by Luton Town whilst playing for his home town team, Stenhousemuir, in Scottish League Division Two.

Eventually they took the plunge and signed him in April 1959, just before the Town's appearance in the F.A.Cup final, and he made his debut at centre-forward on the closing day of the 1958/59 campaign at home to Blackpool.

The following season turned out to be a disaster for the Hatters, with relegation from Division One, with John, a constructive inside-forward, played mainly on the wing.

John was released in the wake of relegation and returned to Scotland with Stirling but died in a car accident in 1967, aged only 31, leaving a wife and four young daughters.

■ Alan Frank KIMBLE

One half of a set of identical twins, Alan was on the books of Charlton as a youngster but it was only after moving to Cambridge in 1986 that he earned a regular first team place.

In seven years at the Abbey, Alan made almost 300 League appearances and was regarded as the best left-back in the club's history. Quick and a clean tackler, Alan was remarkably consistent and it was no surprise when he earned a move to Premier League side Wimbledon in 1993 for £175,000.

After missing most of the 2001/02 season with a knee injury, Alan was given a free transfer and was quickly pounced on by his old boss Joe Kinnear at Luton. By then 36, Alan could not reproduce his earlier form and after 12 League appearances over the 2002/03 campaign was allowed to move to Dagenham & Redbridge. Alan is now assistant manager at Ebbsfleet.

■ Andrew (Andy) Edward KING

Local boy Andy joined the Hatters from school before making his League debut on the final day of the 1974/75 campaign while still only 18. A quick, two footed midfielder with an eye for goal Andy set Division Two alight in the following season and although the club's parlous financial state was well known it still rankles that only £40,000 was paid by Everton for his services in April 1976.

Andy became a favourite on Merseyside and then spent time with QPR, West Brom and Wolves before eventually returning to Luton for a short spell in 1985 and then finishing his League career with Aldershot.

A time in the commercial department at Kenilworth Road was followed by managerial stints at Mansfield and Swindon amongst others. Andy has recently taken over a pub in Flitwick and scouts for Plymouth.

■ Gerald (Gerry) Henry KING

Welsh schoolboy international Gerry started out with Cardiff, making his debut as a 17 year old, but found it hard to maintain a regular place in the side at Ninian Park and so reluctantly accepted a move to Torquay in 1965.

At Plainmoor, Gerry helped the Gulls to promotion and played a blinder against Luton along the way, something that was remembered by Hatters manager George Martin who was pleased to pick up the left winger on a free transfer over the summer of 1966.

After scoring on his debut, Gerry struggled in a poor Luton side and was probably glad to escape and move back to Wales with Newport. Gerry ran a coal business after retiring from the game and was a drayman for Ansell's Brewery for many years.

Now living in Cwmbran, Gerry works on hospital deliveries.

■ Andrew (Andy) Derek KIWOMYA

An England Youth international, Andy was on the books of Barnsley as a youngster but had managed only 17 League appearances spread over ten years with six clubs before he earned a regular spot with Bradford City after his transfer there in 1995.

With winger Paul Showler on the injured list, Luton manager Lennie Lawrence brought the speedy Andy to Kenilworth Road in March 1997 on loan and he made an immediate impact by starring in a 2-0 win at Burnley on his debut.

He played four more times for the Hatters over the remainder of that season and was then loaned out to Burnley, who had obviously liked what they saw a few months earlier, before he finished his League career at Notts County.

Andy became assistant manager at Worksop Town and was shortlisted for the manager's job at Farsley Celtic in December 2007.

■ Anthony (Tony) KNIGHT

Romford born Tony was spotted by Luton scouts and after serving his apprenticeship signed professional terms for the Hatters in May 1976.

Still only 17, Tony found himself thrust in at the deep end when, with regular goalkeeper Keith Barber going down with a heavy cold, he was forced into the firing line at home to Bristol Rovers in November 1976. He acquitted himself well in a 4-2 win and was credited with some wonder saves as Rovers fought back late in the game.

Sadly, that was as good as it got for Tony as, although he made a further five appearances for the Hatters deputising for the established number one, he was released in 1978 and moved to Dover for one season and then on to Brighton where he failed to make a first team appearance.

■ Anthony (Tony) Frank KNIGHTS

Tony made his League debut for his local side Grimsby Town, who he had joined from school, in December 1959 and although not a regular in the side over his first couple of years at the club he did manage to secure the left-half slot for the Mariners during the second half of the 1961/62 campaign which ended in promotion to Division Two.

The hard working Tony held his place at the higher level but following Grimsby's relegation in 1964 he was surprisingly handed a free transfer and was picked up by Luton.

He fared little better at Kenilworth Road as, after making two League appearances, he injured his back and when fit again could not force his way back into the first team. He was released in 1965, moving to Aldershot and then back to Lincolnshire with Gainsborough. Tony died in 2001 from a heart attack while at Waltham Windmill Golf Club.

■ Leslie (Les) Eric LAKE

Luton boy Les began his football career with local side Holly Rangers and graduated through the Town's Colts team during the early war years. He was playing regular first team football as the war drew to a close and took this through to the 1946/47 season where his ability to play in either full-back position meant that he was one of the first names on the team sheet.

Surprisingly, he lost his place early in the following campaign and was then regarded as a deputy for the remainder of his time at Kenilworth Road. At the end of the 1948/49 season he decided to emigrate to the United States but was back again before Christmas and was taken on again by the Hatters but his appearances were limited due to the form of Billy Cooke and Bud Aherne.

Les died in 1973 at the young age of 53 following a training run.

■ Richard Barrington Michael LANGLEY

Cool and skilful midfielder Richard joined his local side QPR as a youth trainee before making his League debut in an away game at Swindon in 1998. Although beset by injury at Loftus Road he was always on the team sheet when fit and his displays and some vital goals earned his team a place in the Division Two play-off final in 2003 when Rangers lost to Cardiff.

Only two games into the following season Richard moved to Cardiff for £250,000 and enjoyed two years in South Wales before returning to Rangers and from there to Luton in the summer of 2006.

Although playing for England at youth level Richard has now won several caps for Jamaica.

■ David LAWSON

Born in Wallsend it was only natural that David should join his boyhood favourites Newcastle from school but he failed to get a first team game at St James and so moved to lowly Bradford Park Avenue in 1967 where he got a taste of League action.

A safe rather than spectacular goalkeeper with sound positional sense, David made the short move to Huddersfield in 1970 and turned out for the Terriers in the top flight. When Huddersfield were relegated, David commanded the British record fee for a goalkeeper of £85,000 when he went to Everton where he became a crowd favourite.

When he finally lost his place to George Wood, David accepted a free transfer to Luton in 1978 but it did not work for him at Kenilworth Road and he moved to Stockport only five months later, hastened by the Hatters signing of Jake Findlay.

■ Michael Antonio LEARY

Another London born youngster who was spotted by Luton Town scouts and enticed to Kenilworth Road where there was a better than even chance of making an eventual first team appearance.

A strong tackling midfielder, Michael moved up through the ranks and made his League debut in a 1-1 draw at home to QPR in September 2003 and opened his goalscoring account with a brace in a 3-4 defeat at Hartlepool the following April.

Sadly, Michael could not force his way into a regular first team spot with the Hatters and after long loan spells with Bristol Rover, Walsall and Brentford he has now moved to Barnet on a permanent contract.

■ Roland (Roly) Arthur LEGATE

Son of Arlesey, Roland was turning out for his local side in the Parthenon League and attracting scouts from several clubs which meant that Luton Town had to move smartly to sign him on professional terms on his 17th birthday in May 1956.

Five months later Roland was making a goalscoring debut in Division One but after three appearances it was back to the reserves and although National Service took a chunk out of his career it was not until the 1960/61 campaign that the forceful winger earned a recall and scored four goals in five games to answer his doubters.

He was released at the end of the following season but eight goals from 15 starts from the left wing was an eye catching return.

After spells at Yiewsley, Folkestone and Stevenage, Roly returned to Arlesey who he played for and managed for many years.

■ Brian LEWIS

Starting off with Crystal Palace in 1960, Brian soon made a name for himself as a clever midfielder and inside forward and it was not long before he made the step up to Portsmouth in Division Two and then on to Coventry with whom he scored their first goal in the top flight in 1967.

Finding himself out of the Sky Blues side, Brian amazingly accepted a £35,000 move to Luton in 1968 just as the Hatters had won promotion from Division Four. Becoming an instant crowd favourite Brian top scored over the 1968/69 season, won countless penalties through gamesmanship and saw four opposition players sent off for retaliation!

New manager Alec Stock was not so keen and moved him on to Oxford and from there he went to Colchester, with whom he starred in the famous F.A.Cup win over Leeds before finishing his League career back at Portsmouth.

Brian sadly died of cancer at age 55 in 1998.

■ David LINDSAY

Luton paid £8,000 to St Mirren for dour full-back David in the summer of 1948. The Hatters did well to entice the well built Scot to Kenilworth Road as a host of clubs, most notably Middlesbrough from Division One, had seen David build a reputation for himself north of the border and was on the verge of international honours. That he had played for the Town as a war-time guest probably helped to secure his signature.

Unfortunately, David did not last long at Luton for, after only seven games at the start of the 1948/49 campaign, he lost his place and with reserve football not suiting him he accepted a move to Barnsley who happily paid £8,000 so the Hatters were not out of pocket.

David enjoyed four seasons at Oakwell before taking up with Wisbech Town where he became player/manager. David died in 1992.

■ Desmond (Des) Martin LINTON

Although born in Birmingham, Des joined Leicester from school and was voted their Young Player of the Year in 1990. Having broken into the Foxes League side it came as a surprise when he was allowed to move to Luton as part of the deal that took Steve Thompson to Filbert Street.

A tall, fast defender who liked to push forward down the flanks, Des was injured almost as soon as he started his Luton career and it was not until the 1992/93 season that he won a regular place in the Hatters side mainly at right back.

After he lost his place at Kenilworth Road, Des moved on to Peterborough on transfer deadline day in 1997 and after a short spell with Swindon finished his playing career with Cambridge City.

Des now runs a courier business alongside some of his old Luton playing colleagues.

■ Stephen (Steve) Eric LITT

Steve was turned down by his home town club Carlisle as a youngster but was then taken on as an apprentice at Blackpool only to be released in the summer of 1972.

New Luton manager Harry Haslam, after listening to his old pal Paddy Sowden the youth team manager at Bloomfield Road, decided to give the giant 18 year old centre-half a try and awarded him a contract at Kenilworth Road.

Steve waited patiently for his chance before making his League debut during the 1973/74 season, but as understudy to the consistent and rarely injured John Faulkner his appearances were limited.

A frustrated Steve left these shores in 1976 to join Minnesota Kicks. He returned a year later to enjoy a season with Northampton before emigrating to the States for good.

■ Adam Spencer LOCKE

Adam joined his local side Crystal Palace as a youth trainee but after signing professional forms in 1988 failed to win a first team place and so moved to Southend where he was altogether more successful.

A clever, ball playing midfielder or wing back who liked to get forward, Adam was surprisingly transferred to Colchester in 1994 and then on to Bristol City three years later where he was voted the find of the season in his first year there.

Signed by Luton manager Lennie Lawrence in 1999 to add experience to a young squad, Adam made over 60 League appearances for the Hatters before losing his place when new boss Joe Kinnear swept through the club.

Adam was still turning out for Clanfield (Hants) last season.

■ Christopher (Chris) LONG

After turning out for Hatfield Town as a youngster, Chris was spotted by Luton Town who offered him professional terms in February 1966 on his 18th birthday.

Only two months later he was making his League debut in a patched up Hatters side at Barrow which the Town won 1-0 against the odds. Down to 12 fit men, Luton manager George Martin was forced to pick Chris who acquitted himself well on the left wing 'managing to get across some useful centres.'

Sadly that was as good as it got for Chris who left Kenilworth Road for Stevenage and then back to Hatfield, his home town club. Chris still lives in Hatfield.

■ John (Jack) LORNIE

Scottish Schoolboy international Jack was snapped up by Leicester in March 1958 from junior club Banks O'Dee. Although scoring on his League debut for the Foxes he was always regarded as reserve centre-forward at Filbert Street and made only eight appearances (including one against Luton) in three years before signing for Luton in 1961 for £3,500.

Although never letting the side down, as proved by his six goals in 19 League appearances, he was playing in a side that was slipping down the divisions at Kenilworth Road and he left for Carlisle as the Hatters plunged into Division Three in 1963.

Subsequently turning out for Tranmere and Ross County, Jack is now living back in Aberdeen.

■ Mark Usher LOWNDS

Strong and enthusiastic wing-half Mark was plying his trade with Ryhope Colliery Welfare when he was recommended to Luton by their scout in the north-east.

Mark initially signed for the Hatters as a part-time professional as he wanted to complete his apprenticeship first, but eventually made his League debut playing in an unfamiliar forward role and scoring in a 5-1 trouncing of Swansea in January 1962.

Gaining a regular place in the side in his favoured left-half position following relegation to Division Three in 1963, Mark always gave 100% but was powerless to prevent the slide into Division Four in 1965.

Mark left the club that summer on a free-transfer and has since settled in South Africa.

■ Roy Evan LUNNISS

Roy was picked up by Crystal Palace manager George Smith from Carshalton, signing professional forms in April 1960 and going on to make 25 League appearances as a solid, take no prisoners type of full-back. When he was released in 1963 he turned to Smith, by now manager at Portsmouth, and became a regular member of the Pompey squad over the next three seasons before being released for breach of contract.

Roy had a spell playing in South Africa before returning to England and signing a short term contract with Luton, who were managed by one of his old Portsmouth playing colleagues, Allan Brown. His only League outing for the Hatters came in a 3-0 home win over Brentford on the last day of 1966 but he was 'carrying timber' and looked unfit and was allowed to leave.

Roy joined up with Oakland Clippers and settled in the States although he is now back in London.

■ Malcolm Ian MACDONALD

When Luton signed a little-known full-back from Fulham for £17,500 in the summer of 1969 it raised no more than a couple of column inches in the local press. Within a couple of months, converted to a forward because of injuries, Mac became a goalscoring sensation and in two seasons at Kenilworth Road netted 49 goals in 88 League starts and earned himself a big money move to Newcastle.

On Tyneside, Mac became every bit the hero he had been at Luton only this time he started to pick up England caps along the way, scoring five in one international, before surprisingly accepting a £333,333 transfer to Arsenal in 1976.

Wear and tear to his knees forced him into retirement at the age of 29 and on rejoining Fulham, Mac took over the hot seat in 1980 and guiding the Cottagers to promotion. He resigned after publicity about his private life and is now a radio broadcaster on Tyneside.

■ Malcolm Peter (Peter) MacEWAN

Former Luton favourite Billy Arnison, on returning to South Africa following a career ending injury, became a part-time scout for the Hatters and recommended big centre-forward Peter to his old club.

Peter, who had been turning out for Germiston Callies, swapped the South African summer for the English winter of 1954 and within 24 hours of stepping off the plane was playing first team football for Luton in a friendly against Hajduk Split.

Peter holds the distinction of scoring two goals at Doncaster that helped clinch promotion in 1955 and then scored on the Town's first game in Division One. In the summer of 1956 Peter decided to return to Johannesburg where he became a sportswear rep.

■ Neil MADDEN

Born in Luton in 1962, Neil came up through the ranks at Kenilworth Road and eventually got his first team chance in the final home game of the 1979/80 season against Wrexham.

The Town had just missed out on promotion to the top flight and used the clash with the Robins to blood a couple of youngsters with Neil replacing Alan West in midfield and Clive Goodyear taking the place of centre-half Mike Saxby.

The Hatters won 2-0 with Neil acquitting himself well but that was to be his last chance and he left Kenilworth Road to join Hitchin Town.

Neil still lives in Luton and works at the airport.

■ Lee Richard Samuel MANSELL

Rarely can a player have made such an impact on his first team debut as Lee when he scored for the Hatters 58 seconds into an F.A.Cup replay against QPR at Loftus Road in 2001.

Showing enthusiasm and a good turn of pace from midfield, Lee was virtually ever present for the remainder of that season scoring five goals from 18 League starts as the Town plunged into Division Three.

After starting as first choice the following season, Lee lost his place to Ahmet Brkovic and apart from a reasonable run in 2003/04 he was always on the periphery of the action.

Leaving Luton on a free transfer in 2005, Lee went to Oxford where he was voted 'Player of the Year' as United dropped out of the Football League and sadly the same thing happened with his next club, Torquay.

■ Wilson Edmund (Eddie) MARSH

Although born in Dundee, Eddie moved with his parents to London at the age of ten and was picked up by Charlton from Erith & Belvedere after impressing Addicks manager Jimmy Seed in a representative game.

Because of the form of Charlton goalkeeper, and future Hatters manager, Sam Bartram the patient Eddie had to bide his time and made only 26 League appearances in eight years at the Valley. When Luton goalkeeper Bernard Streten hung up his gloves in 1957, Eddie made the move to Kenilworth Road but frustratingly he found himself second fiddle to the consistent Ron Baynham and made only two appearances in two years.

A final move to Torquay was more to his liking and on retirement he settled in the West Country and worked for Berger Paints.

■ Dwight Wayne MARSHALL

After turning out for several non-League clubs in the London area, big time football seemed to have passed 25 year Dwight by and he looked on an unsuccessful trial at Crystal Palace as the last throw of the dice.

Fortunately, Palace coach Wally Downes recommended him to Plymouth where he made up for lost time by finishing top scorer in his first season. A £150,000 move to David Pleat's Luton in 1994 saw the lightning quick striker top score once more but a badly broken ankle in 1995/96 was blamed for the Hatters sinking to relegation.

Dwight took a long time to recover from the break and then found it difficult to re-establish himself in the side and so moved back to Plymouth in 1998.

Dwight has subsequently played for Kingstonian, Slough and Aylesbury and works for Freedom Finance.

■ Damian MATTHEW

Chelsea prodigy Damian had already starred for the Blues and made nine England Under-21 appearances when he was loaned out to Luton in September 1992 to further his football education.

The Hatters were suffering from an injury crisis at the time and Damian stepped in to help stem the tide without particularly catching the eye.

A big money move to Crystal Palace then followed but it was a subsequent move, to Burnley in 1996, where he finally won a regular first team place in midfield and also showed his shooting prowess with several well taken goals.

Damian's final move came in 1998 when he went to Northampton but after only two appearances in two years at Sixfields he was forced to accept that a back injury had put paid to his football career. After six years working in Chelsea's academy, Damian is now coach to the Charlton Under 18's.

Robert (Rob) David MATTHEWS

Rob first caught the eye of Notts County when turning out for Shepshed Charterhouse while studying for a degree at Loughborough University.

He signed for the Magpies in March 1992 and made his full debut against the Hatters at Meadow Lane on the final day of that season, scoring twice to send the Town down from Division One after ten years at the top.

Injuries cut back his appearances at Meadow Lane but after returning to the side and firing on all cylinders he was snapped up by David Pleat's Luton for £80,000 in March 1995.

Sadly things did not work out at Kenilworth Road and he became York City's record signing six months later. Since then the hard working winger or inside forward has appeared for several League clubs in the north finishing with Hull for whom he scored the only goal here in 2001.

Rob was last at Northwich Victoria.

Patrick (Pat) Comerford McAULEY

"Snake-hipped, a football artist with delightful footwork and great intelligence and a true craftsman", were some of the compliments paid to one of the finest natural footballers to wear a Glasgow Celtic shirt.

Celtic attempted to build their post-war side around the talented Pat but the player suddenly demanded more money or a transfer which caused much anguish at Parkhead.

Luton Town manager Dally Duncan made a cheeky attempt to bring the player back to his struggling Division Two side and succeeded for £4,500 in December 1950. Unfortunately, Pat was not a success in the hurly-burly of English lower League football and moved on to Kettering and then back to Scotland with Albion Rovers.

Pat was a crane operator at Ravenscraig at the time of his death in 1970, aged only 48.

Alan McBAIN

Strong tackling full-back Alan was picked up by Swansea who had seen him play Scottish junior football with Aberdeen. After making no headway at the Vetch he made the move to Carlisle where he settled down to make 70 League appearances in three seasons.

In June 1963, Carlisle made a bid for Luton goalkeeper Alan Ross and forward Jack Lornie but Hatters manager Bill Harvey insisted on McBain being included as part of the deal having already seen him perform.

It took Alan a while to stake a regular place at Kenilworth Road but after doing so he was difficult to dislodge.
Released after the Town plunged into Division Four in 1965, Alan joined Corby for whom he starred in an F.A.Cup upset against the Hatters the following season.
Alan now lives back in Aberdeen in retirement.

Joseph (Joe) McBRIDE

A fee of £12,500 took archetypal centre-forward Joe from Kilmarnock to Wolves in December 1959 but surprisingly his style did not fit in at Molineux and he was allowed to move to Luton only two months later.

It was said that Joe was signed behind manager Syd Owen's back but the bustling striker managed to net six goals in 13 starts in a struggling Luton side that eventually dropped to Division Two at the end of the campaign.

Early in the following season Joe was transferred to Partick Thistle, in exchange for Jim Fleming, where his skill in the air and two footed ability on the deck continued to catch the eye. This led to an eventual move to Celtic where he became Jock Stein's first signing and, but for injury, he would have played in the 1967 European Cup final win over Inter.

Albert McCANN

Maidenhead born Albert was invited to Kenilworth Road along with his brother and initially worked part time in the club's offices before signing professional forms in 1959.

Making a promising debut in April 1960, just as the Hatters were about to be relegated from Division One, Albert seemed set for a long Luton career but was not given a fair crack of the whip and was allowed to move to Coventry in 1961.

After a sound first season at Highfield Road the bandy-legged midfielder fell out of favour with new manager Jimmy Hill and, disillusioned, signed for Portsmouth.

At last his skills were recognised and he went on to make 338 League appearances over 12 years at Fratton Park and also earned a testimonial.

Albert later managed a newsagents in Portsmouth before running a care home on Hayling Island.

William Harvey (Harvey) McCREADIE

After becoming Accrington Stanley's youngest ever League player at the age of 16 in 1959, young Scottish centre-forward Harvey began to attract the scouts with the eventual winners being Luton Town who paid £5,500 for his services in January 1960.

Harvey was given only one chance at Luton, in a 2-3 defeat at Wolves, as the Town slipped out of Division One but by then off field problems were beginning to bite with fines for failure to report for training and going absent without leave.

The final straw came with his arrest following an altercation at the California Ballroom in Dunstable and manager Sam Bartram quickly offloaded him to Wrexham.

He fared little better at the Racecourse and moved swiftly on to Northwich and Mossley before returning to Scotland with Hibs.

■ William (Billy) Stirling McDERMENT

Picked up from Scottish junior football by Leicester in 1961, Billy had difficulty in winning a permanent place in the Foxes line-up and in six years at Filbert Street made only 23 League appearances.

Regarded as a big signing by Luton in 1967, as the Hatters were about to embark on their successful Division Four championship season, Billy was the original utility man at Kenilworth Road appearing in every outfield position apart from inside-left in his two years with the club.

The wholehearted Scot then spent a less than successful spell at Notts County before moving back to Scotland with Morton where he enjoyed an extended run in the top flight.

■ Darron Karl McDONOUGH

Although born in Belgium, Darron was brought up in the Manchester area leading up to joining Oldham straight from school.

After scoring for the Latics on his League debut in 1990, Darron became a crowd favourite at Boundary Park with his bravery and tough tackling, as borne out by his dismissal at Luton in 1982! Although defence was probably his best position, he could play in midfield and attack and Oldham supporters were sad when top flight Luton paid £87,000 for his services in 1986.

Injuries caused more often than not by his bravery meant Darron missed chunks of his four years at Kenilworth Road including the 1988 League Cup final, although he did appear at Wembley in 1989.

After leaving Luton to become Kevin Keegan's first signing at Newcastle, Darron was forced to quit the game due to a snapped Achilles. Darron now lives near Oldham in a house he built himself and has a joinery business.

■ Richard (Ricky) Patrick McEVOY

One of the many Dublin boys that came to Luton Town over the years, Ricky signed professional forms as an 18 year old in August 1985 and soon came to the attention of Town fans when appearing in the reserve side as a skilful midfielder.

Ricky's only first team chance came on Boxing Day 1986 when he replaced the injured Darron McDonough just after half-time in a 0-2 home defeat at the hands of Watford.

Although he gained some experience on loan at Cambridge United later in that season, Ricky decided to return to Dublin on receiving an offer from Shamrock Rovers.

■ Gavin Gregory McGOWAN

England schoolboy and youth international Gavin seemed to have his career mapped out when he made his League debut for Arsenal as a 17 year old in 1993 and then went on to help the Gunners win the F.A.Youth cup a year later.

Sadly, Gavin's early promise at Highbury did not continue and after two loan spells at Luton he joined the Hatters on a free transfer in 1998.

A skilful, attacking full-back Gavin unfortunately played in a Luton team that was eventually destined to be relegated to the football basement and so was not able to see his abilities flourish in a winning side.

After leaving Luton, Gavin turned out for many non-League clubs in the London area and was last at Redhill combining his football with a job as a P.E. teacher in Croydon.

■ Alwyn Scott McGUFFIE

Spotted by ex-Hatter Charlie Watkins, Alwyn was enticed away from Queen of the South as a 16 year old and after initially playing on an amateur basis signed professional forms for the Town in September 1954.

A clever, ball playing wing half of whom great things were expected, Alwyn made a promising League debut in 1956 but never quite fulfilled his early promise due to his perceived lack of defensive qualities.

After National Service in the army and with the Town's fall from the top flight, Alwyn was picked more frequently and when given a place in the forward line showed an eye for goal. Alwyn finally left Kenilworth Road in 1964 and ran a sports/toy shop in Marsh Road for many years but is now back in Scotland.

■ Michael McINDOE

Edinburgh born Michael joined the Hatters from school, signing professional forms in April 1998. After making his League debut, coming on as substitute in a 3-1 win at Wigan, Michael was regularly picked throughout the 1998/99 campaign and into the following season and seemed set for a long Luton career until well documented off-field problems meant him losing his place in the side.

The clever left sided midfielder or winger then made a fresh start at Hereford and from there moved back up through the divisions with Yeovil, Doncaster and Wolves before joining up with his old Glovers manager Gary Johnson at Bristol City in the summer of 2007.

■ Hugh McJARROW

During the war, Hugh worked down the mines as a 'Bevin Boy' before signing on with Chesterfield in peacetime. Hardly a regular in the Spireites side initially, Hugh exploded on to the football stage in 1949/50 when converted to a centre-forward and making goalscoring look easy.

This newly discovered talent led to him being snapped up by Sheffield Wednesday in 1950 who he helped to promotion in his first season. After losing his place to Derek Dooley, Hugh made a £5,000 move to Luton where he scored twice on his debut in a 3-3 home draw with Nottingham Forest in February 1952.

Finishing his first season at Kenilworth Road with five goals from five starts Luton supporters looked forward to more of the same but a succession of injuries cut back his appearances leading to a move to Plymouth where he was no more successful.

Hugh sadly died in 1987, aged only 59.

■ Thomas (Tommy) Sharp McKECHNIE

Brave and tough forward Tommy was playing Scottish junior football for the romantically named Kirkintilloch Rob Roy when he was noted in dispatches by a Luton Town scout, eventually signing for the Hatters in the summer of 1961.

Due to injuries Tommy was pitch-forked into the Luton first team at the start of 1961/62 without even a reserve team appearance under his belt and did remarkably well netting ten goals in 33 starts. As the Town slipped down the divisions so did Tommy's goalscoring prowess although he always gave 100% and his all action style frightened defences.

After short stays at Bournemouth, Colchester and Bury Town, Tommy returned to Scotland and now lives in his birthplace, Milngavie, in retirement.

■ Raymond (Ray) McKINNON

Talented Scottish under-21 midfielder Ray headlined for his local side Dundee United leading to a £750,000 move to Brian Clough's Nottingham Forest in 1992. Sadly it did not work out at the City Ground and he moved back to Scotland with Aberdeen and then full circle to Dundee United.

Fancying another chance in England, Ray transferred to Luton in 1998 and in his first season at Kenilworth Road was ever present barring niggling injuries, gracing the midfield with clever and perceptive football.

Unfortunately, this did not last and he left for Livingston before making a grand tour of several Scottish League clubs. Ray is now an acclaimed restaurateur in Dundee.

■ Paul Andrew McLAREN

High Wycombe born and a Bucks County youth player, Paul joined Luton as a trainee before making his League debut on the final day of the 1993/94 campaign in a 2-2 draw at Stoke.

A strong tackling midfielder, able to make telling forward runs, Paul suffered knee ligament injuries early in his career but bounced back to star in a poor Luton side that eventually dropped to the basement in 2001.

Paul took the opportunity at this point to move to Sheffield Wednesday on a 'Bosman' free transfer where he stayed three years in another struggling side.

Spells at Rotherham and Tranmere followed with Paul signing on for Bradford City in July 2008.

■ Hugh McLEISH

19 year old Scottish inside-forward Hugh was a surprise choice for Luton in a top of the table Division Four clash at Bradford City in December 1967, but he acquitted himself well and hit a post in the closing minutes as the Hatters went down 0-2.

Hugh had played for the Dundee United 'A' team and had just finished a short spell at Sunderland when he won a trial at Luton. He then starred for the reserves in a win over Watford and was picked for the Bradford trip in place of the injured Keith Allen.

Hugh made only one more appearance for the Hatters, bizarrely at Bradford P.A. later that month, before accepting a contract at Stevenage.

Hugh played for several more English non-League clubs, then returned to Scotland and is now in Falkirk.

■ George James McLEOD

Luton Town's Scottish scout was sent to watch young Inverness Clachnacuddin inside-left George McLeod and his instant recommendation led to the 22 year old coming to Kenilworth Road in 1955.

After making his first team debut towards the end of the 1955/56 campaign, George was converted to a left winger where his speed and bravery soon earned him a regular spot in the Luton line-up over the next two seasons.

When the Hatters signed Billy Bingham in 1958, right winger Jim Adam moved to the other side leaving George out in the cold. A £6,000 cheque then took him to Brentford where he became a crowd favourite in over 200 League appearances for the Bees.

After a move to QPR in 1964, in exchange for Mark Lazarus, George emigrated to South Africa where he appeared for Port Elizabeth.

■ John Brendan (Brendan) McNALLY

Upon signing for the Hatters from Shelbourne, Brendan had to wait patiently for his chance but eventually took over at full-back from another ex-Shelbourne player Seamus Dunne, not only at club level but also on the international front.

A strong and powerful performer, Brendan turned out for the Town in the 1959 F.A.Cup final and was involved in the incident that left Forest's Roy Dwight with a broken leg although he was left a limping passenger with a torn cartilage.

After leaving the full-time game in 1963, Brendan played for Cambridge City, Dunstable and Chesham before returning to Dunstable as manager where he was instrumental in signing Kerry Dixon.

Brendan still lives in Cambridgeshire.

■ James (Jim) Anthony McNICHOL

Glaswegian Jim started his career with Ipswich but was unable to make the grade at Portman Road and so moved to Luton in July 1976.

At Kenilworth Road, Jim initially found it difficult to displace regular central defensive partnership John Faulkner and Paul Futcher and then with new manager David Pleat bringing in fresh blood he accepted a move to Brentford for £30,000, which was then a record for the Bees.

At Griffin Park, Jim was a regular for six years and performed so well that he was chosen to play for the Scottish under-21side, before he fell out with the Bees management and moving to Exeter and then Torquay where he was famously bitten by a police dog during a relegation clash. In the time added on for patching up his wound the Gulls scored the goal that kept them in the Football League!

Jim is now a publican in Ashburton.

■ Gary McSHEFFREY

A prolific goalscorer at youth level, Gary became the youngest League debutant for his home team club Coventry as well as the Premiership's youngest ever player when he came on as a late substitute against Aston Villa in 1999.

Gary continued to bang in the goals for the Sky Blues but by 2003 found himself out of favour. A loan spell at Luton followed where he became an instant success with eight goals from 18 League starts, with his speed, close ball control and fierce shooting terrorising Division Two defences.

The loan spell rejuvenated his career at Coventry but by the following season he was back in the reserves. A further loan spell at Luton was not as successful for he encountered difficulty breaking past Steve Howard and Rowan Vine, and this time he returned to Highfield Road determined to succeed.

This he did, with the reward a big money transfer to Birmingham in 2006.

■ Gary John McSWEGAN

Gary had seven years with Glasgow Rangers but made only a handful of appearances being unable to oust the likes of Mark Hateley and Ally McCoist from the side.

A £400,000 move to Notts County saw him, at last, realise his potential and the small, speedy striker rattled in the goals, especially in the 1993/94 campaign although hamstring injuries blighted the latter part of his stay at Meadow Lane.

Moving back to Scotland with Dundee United in 1995, Gary switched to Hearts three years later and then had loan spells at Barnsley and Joe Kinnear's Luton in 2002. After playing only three games at Kenilworth Road during the Hatters promotion season from Division Three, Gary returned to Hearts.

Gary is now Under-19 coach at Inverness Caledonian Thistle.

■ Paul Francis McVEIGH

Clever and skilful Belfast born striker Paul started out at Tottenham but after only three appearances in four years at White Hart Lane moved on a free transfer to Norwich in March 2000.

Paul found Carrow Road much more to his liking and went on to make well over 200 League appearances for the Canaries, netting 36 times and picking up 20 caps for Northern Ireland along the way.

After finding himself out of favour during the 2006/07 season, Paul enjoyed a fruitful loan spell at Burnley where his introduction to the side coincided with the Clarets moving away from the relegation positions.

After being released by Norwich in the summer of 2007, Paul gladly accepted a contract at Luton.

■ Raphael Joseph MEADE

Nomadic striker Raphael started off conventionally with Arsenal and worked his way up through the ranks before making over 40 League appearances for the Gunners as a fleet-footed and powerful striker but he was never able to command a regular place at Highbury and so made the surprise move to Sporting Lisbon in 1985.

He came back to these islands to join Dundee United in 1988 before a £250,000 transfer to Luton in March 1989. He only managed four appearances at Kenilworth Road, without pulling up any trees before being offloaded to Odense as part of the deal that brought Lars Elstrup to Luton.

Since then Raphael has played in Hong Kong, and for several clubs in England finishing up at Sittingbourne.

Neil Alan MIDGLEY

Cambridge born Neil joined Ipswich from school but found the going tough at Portman Road and so was allowed to take a loan spell at Luton in September 1999 to gain League experience.

Neil made ten appearances whilst on loan with the Hatters, scoring three goals, including a brace against a strong Burnley side. Forming a good partnership with Liam George the lively striker looked set to stay at Kenilworth Road but Ipswich recalled him and refused to sell.

After only four League outings with Ipswich, Neil eventually transferred to Barnet in 2001 and since then has turned out for Canvey Island, Kettering and latterly Cambridge City.

Albert (Bert) James MITCHELL

Bert scored 41 goals for Luton in only 106 starts which was remarkable at the time as he was a winger and was meant to set up chances rather than take them.

Starting off with Stoke during the war years, Bert made his League debut for the Potters in peacetime and then moved on through Blackburn and Kettering before making a name for himself at Northampton.

A big fee plus Jim Wilson brought him to Kenilworth Road where he quickly became a crowd favourite with his ability to cut inside and shoot. He also boasted a 100% penalty record during his three years with the club.

After joining his old Northampton manager Bob Dennison at Middlesbrough in 1954, Bert, by now 32, saw his career come to a gentle close.

Bert continued to scout for Northampton in later life and died in 1997.

Richard MONEY

Richard was spotted playing for Lowestoft Town by Scunthorpe who quickly signed the 17 year old in 1973. Able to play across the back four and in midfield the skilful utility man soon had the scouts flocking to the Old Show Ground leading to a £50,000 move to Fulham in 1977.

Less than three years later Liverpool paid a huge £333,333 to take him to Anfield but he found opportunities limited there and took a step down to join the Hatters who were just about to be promoted to the top flight in 1982.

Taking over from Mark Aizlewood, Richard oversaw promotion and then made 31 League appearances the following campaign before moving to Portsmouth and then back to first club Scunthorpe.

After coaching and managerial roles both here and abroad, Richard took over the hot seat at Walsall in 2006 which he left in April 2008. Richard is now Academy Director at Newcastle

Bernard John MOORE

Bernard joined his local side Brighton during the early years of the war and by the end of hostilities was banging in goals for fun. He then had to put in some service in the Far East and on his return found a first team place hard to come but, even so, was surprisingly sold to Hastings in 1948 for £200.

As if to prove the Seagulls wrong, Bernard scored an amazing 138 goals in 121 Southern League starts which prompted Luton to pay £4,500 for his services in January 1951. His goals kept the Town in Division Two that season but after injury cut back his appearances in the following campaign he was back to his best in 1952/53.

Brighton were forced to pay £3,000 to take him back to the Goldstone in 1954 and from there he moved to Bedford's F.A.Cup giant killing team of 1956.

Bernard lives in Putnoe in retirement.

John MOORE

After joining Luton from Motherwell in 1965 on the recommendation of scout and ex-Hatter Davie Hutchinson, John enjoyed almost 40 years at Kenilworth Road in a long, varied and loyal career.

As a tough, no nonsense defender John made 273 League appearances for the Hatters and after spells at Brighton and as manager of Dunstable Town he returned to Kenilworth Road as a coach under David Pleat before stepping up into the hot seat in 1986 and leading the club to its highest ever position of seventh in the top flight in 1986/87.

Not relishing the high profile life of a football manager, John resigned in 1987 but was back at the club as a coach under Jim Ryan four years later.

Serving under several managers, John remained at Kenilworth Road until his 60th birthday and is now involved in schools coaching in Bedford.

Dean Lance MORGAN

Enfield born Dean had early trials at Luton but started his football career at Colchester, signing professional forms in August 2001.

Undoubtedly skilful, quick and two footed Dean was in and out of the side at Layer Road, turning it on one week and becoming virtually anonymous the next. Recommended to Reading by Phil Parkinson, Dean suffered the same inconsistencies at the Madejski although at one stage manager Steve Coppell called the attacking midfielder the 'most skilful player at the club'.

Joining Luton on a free transfer in 2005, Dean scored a stunning winner against Southampton on his home debut before dipping in and out of the side.

■ Murdoch (Murdo) MORRISON

After playing for Clydebank Juniors and Belhaven Star, goalkeeper Murdo was signed on by the Hatters in September 1945, making his Luton debut in the closing matches of the last war-time season of 1945/46.

With the onset of League football once more, Murdo found himself behind George Duke and Les Bywater in the pecking order and made only one appearance – in May 1947 in a 0-4 defeat at Barnsley.

The signing of Bernard Streten became the final straw and Murdo accepted a move to Leyton Orient in 1947 where he made ten League starts before finishing his career at Dunstable amongst others.

Murdo died in 1975 aged only 50.

■ Robert (Bob) Hendy MORTON

Local boy Bob stayed loyal to his roots and ended up spending nearly 20 years with his only Football League side, Luton Town, making 495 League appearances in that time, a club record.

After playing locally for Waterlows, Bob signed amateur forms for the Hatters as the War drew to a close and then signed full-time in 1946. After making his debut in 1948 at centre-forward in a 1-0 win at West Ham, Bob never looked back and the only question mark in his long career was whether he was a better wing-half or forward.

His versatility doubtless cost him senior international honours but whether he was stopping goals as a strong, tough tackling defender or knocking them in at the other end he never gave less that 100% and always played with a smile on his face.

After leaving Luton at the age of 38 in 1964, Bob became player-manager of Bletchley Town before enjoying 16 years with Luton Sports Press. Bob sadly died in 2002.

■ David John MOSS

At the age of 16, Witney born David had the choice of either Oxford or Swindon and opted for the latter who were his boyhood favourites.

He became a regular for the Robins in 1973-74 and over the next four seasons built a growing reputation as a goalscoring winger which led to Luton manager David Pleat nipping in ahead of Stoke to secure his services in 1978.

During his first season at Kenilworth Road, David suffered a recurring pelvic injury but once fully fit he showed his full range of skills with the ability to play on either wing, cross the ball at speed and fierce shooting. He also became the resident dead ball expert in his seven years with the club.

After retiring, he followed his old skipper, Brian Horton, around at various clubs as assistant manager before taking the hot seat at Macclesfield. David is now involved in Youth Development with Liverpool.

■ James (Jim) MULVANEY

Full-back Jim joined Dumbarton in 1941 but also appeared for Wolves, Liverpool, Burnley and York during the war years so a move to Luton in June 1948 did not come as a great culture shock.

Jim had a baptism of fire in an FA Cup replay at Leicester in 1949 when the Hatters went down 3-5 but kept his place in the League team as replacement for the injured Jim Wilson.

When Wilson regained fitness, Jim returned to the reserves but re-surfaced as an emergency centre-forward later on that season scoring twice in a 6-0 mauling of Lincoln!

Jim made three more appearances at centre-forward the following campaign with little success, before moving to Brighton as part of the deal that brought Jack Whent to Luton.

Jim subsequently turned out for Bradford City, Bath and Halifax and passed away in 1993.

■ Alan Bruce NEILSON

Born in Germany while his father was stationed there in the RAF, Alan wrote to Newcastle, his families club, asking for a trial.

The Magpies granted the request, which he successfully came through, but due to the number of big name players being signed by Newcastle at the time, Alan was always on the periphery and accepted a big money move to Southampton in 1995 where he won a regular central defensive place in the Saints Premiership side.

Moneybags Fulham then signed him to play alongside Chris Coleman but he fell out of favour at Craven Cottage and made a move to Grimsby before joining Luton in 2002.

At Kenilworth Road, Welsh international Alan brought experience and versatility to the Luton defence and midfield as the Hatters pushed up through the divisions. Alan is now youth team coach at Kenilworth Road.

■ Samuel (Sammy) Edward NELSON

Sammy first came to the eye of English scouts when playing for Belfast side Linfield Swifts leading to him crossing the Irish Sea and signing for Blackpool in October 1946.

A right winger, Sammy had a good run in Blackpool's Division One side but the signing of the rarely injured Stanley Matthews put paid to his chances at Bloomfield Road.

Disillusioned, Sammy moved to Luton to seek work but it was not long before the Hatters made an offer for his services. He made his Luton debut in a 0-1 home defeat at the hands of Birmingham in January 1948 but did not get another chance that season.

He starred in the pre-season games in 1948-49 and was picked for the first three matches of the new season but was eventually deemed to be too slow for the rigours of Division Two.

Sammy now lives in Belfast in retirement.

■ Michael (Mike) Colin NEWELL

Rejected by home town club Liverpool as a junior, Mike joined Crewe but was allowed to slip away from Gresty Road to Wigan where he enjoyed some success leading to a £90,000 move to David Pleat's top flight Luton in January 1986.

At Kenilworth Road, Mike netted 18 goals in 63 League appearances, including a hat-trick in a 4-1 trouncing of Liverpool, but was then surprisingly moved on to Leicester by new boss Ray Harford who felt the club had an embarrassment of riches up front!

By the time he hung up his boots Mike had notched up over 500 League and Cup appearances for 12 clubs attracting transfer fees of £3.5 million along the way.

After coaching at Tranmere, Mike took Hartlepool to promotion and then did the same for the Hatters in 2005.

■ Peter NICHOLAS

Newport born Peter joined Crystal Palace from school and made his League debut as a 17 year old on the opening day of the 1977-78 campaign. The tough tackling midfielder helped Palace to promotion to Division One in 1979 but managed to win a transfer two years later just before the unfortunately named 'Team of the Eighties' was relegated.

The £400,000 move to Arsenal did not work out and needing to play to keep his place as the Welsh international captain transferred back to Palace before being rescued by Luton's David Pleat in 1985.

He was a revelation at Kenilworth Road with his ball winning skills and it was only the attraction of European football that lured him to Aberdeen in 1987. After spells at Chelsea and Watford, Peter coached at youth level before moving back to Wales where he has managed Barry and Newport and latterly Llanelli.

■ Christopher (Chris) John NICHOLL

Discarded by Burnley as a youngster, Chris was playing for Witton Albion when he was spotted by Halifax who he helped to promotion to Division Three in 1969.

Early in the following campaign, the towering central defender subdued Luton's Malcolm Macdonald leading to a £30,000 move to Kenilworth Road where he eventually became a rock at the heart of the Hatters defence.

Sadly finances dictated Chris's £90,000 move to Aston Villa in 1972 and from there he went to Southampton and finally Grimsby, picking up 51 caps for Northern Ireland during his travels.

Chris received his managerial break at Southampton in 1985 and remained at the Dell until 1991. Since then he has managed Walsall and been assistant manager of Northern Ireland. He is now a local radio commentator at the Bescot Stadium.

■ Kevin John Richard NICHOLLS

Strong tackling midfielder Kevin began his career as a trainee at Charlton and skippered the England youth teams at under-18, under-19 and under-20 levels. After 12 League appearances for the Addicks, and a loan spell at Brighton, a £250,000 move to big spending Wigan in 1999 was not a success but a transfer to Luton two years later proved more to his liking with his enthusiasm and leadership soon making him a firm favourite at Kenilworth Road.

After overseeing two promotions for the Town it came as a disappointment when he moved to Leeds for £700,000 in 2006. From there, Kevin accepted a transfer to Preston but returned to his spiritual home of Kenilworth Road in the summer of 2008.

■ David John NOAKE

Yeovil born David came to the attention of the football world whilst starring for Western League side Dorchester during an epic FA Cup run in 1959. Luton manager Syd Owen made a personal visit to see the strong and speedy winger and agreed a small fee plus a friendly fixture for his services.

David was thrust in at the deep end as the Town were fighting a losing battle to stay in the top flight and his lack of experience told as he fought against Division One defenders.

He fared little better the following season and reluctantly accepted a move to Bristol City in June 1961. At Ashton Gate he had difficulty in ousting Jantzen Derrick and so began a tour of West Country clubs Trowbridge, Frome and Glastonbury.

David now lives in Rochester in retirement.

■ Kurt NOGAN

Kurt was invited to Luton for a trial after being spotted by the Hatters South Wales scout and, after signing professional forms in July 1989, made a dramatic scoring League debut the following February, netting in a 2-2 draw at Liverpool during Jim Ryan's first game in charge of the club.

With a languid style and good positional sense, big things were expected of the Welshman but he was playing in a struggling Hatters side and was released as the Town dropped out of the top flight in 1992.

An invite to Brighton, on an initial three month trial, kick started his career as he netted 49 goals in 97 starts for the Seagulls leading to moves to Burnley and Preston where he was almost as prolific. Finishing his League career with Cardiff, Kurt has since played for Tiverton and is currently with Aberaman.

■ Lee Martin NOGAN

Lee came to Luton on trial as a teenager with his younger brother Kurt but was rejected, leaving him to make a name for himself at Oxford who offered him an apprenticeship and then full time terms.

With Oxford desperate for cash in 1991, a £300,000 bid from Watford was gratefully accepted and the pacy striker earned the first of his two Welsh caps whilst at Vicarage Road after netting several vital goals for the Hornets.

Not relishing a move to the wing at Watford, Lee instead made another big money move this time to Reading followed by subsequent transfers to Grimsby and Darlington from where he came to Lil Fuccillo's Luton in November 2000 but failed to impress in an admittedly poor Hatters side.

Lee finished his Football League career with York, and is now with Whitby Town.

■ Marc Victor NORTH

Ware born Marc joined Luton from school and was the Hatters goalkeeper as they reached the semi-finals of the FA Youth Cup in 1983.

Deciding he preferred the life of a striker, he hung up his gloves with his first taste of League football coming whilst on loan at Lincoln, for whom he later played in the Bradford City fire disaster match.

Back at Kenilworth Road he went on to make 18 League appearances, scoring three goals, before moving to Grimsby in 1987 where he earned a more regular place. After two years at Blundell Park he joined up again with his old Luton boss David Pleat at Leicester.

He later had an unsuccessful trial back at Luton before injury forced his retirement. Marc passed away at the age of 35 in September 2001.

■ Stacey Stewart NORTH

England Youth international centre-half Stacey signed on for his local club Luton from school, but found it difficult to force his way into the Hatters Division One side given the form of firstly Paul Elliott and then Steve Foster.

A firm tackler, good in the air and the possessor of a superb long throw, Stacey made only 25 League appearances in four years at Kenilworth Road before reluctantly moving to West Brom in 1987 for £100,000.

He was altogether more successful at the Hawthorns and after over 100 appearances for the Baggies made a £130,000 switch to Fulham.

Osteoarthritis forced his early retirement from the game and he moved to America where he became involved in a football coaching school.

■ Stanley (Stan) Oswald NORTHOVER

Weymouth born Stan became an artificer in the Royal Navy, turning out for his local side whenever he could. His displays as a sharp, goalscoring inside-forward caught the eye of Luton Town who invited him to Kenilworth Road to appear in a friendly match against Leicester in January 1950 – a game set up as both sides were out of the FA Cup.

Amateur Stan made a huge impression and received permission from his employers to play for the Town again the following Saturday in a Division Two encounter with Swansea at Kenilworth Road.

Sadly, the game ended in defeat and with Stan some years away from discharge from the forces it was decided to part company leaving the player to return to the Navy and enjoy his football with Yeovil and Hastings.

Stan died in 1990.

■ Chukwuemeka (Emeka) NWAJIOBI

Born in Nigeria, Emeka moved to London in 1970 to avoid a civil war that had broken out in his country.

Although invited for trials at Fulham and Millwall, Emeka was made to finish his studies and graduated with a degree in pharmacy before turning out for Dulwich Hamlet.

At Champion Hill, the powerful forward soon had scouts knocking on the door including Luton's John Moore. He decided to come to Kenilworth Road in December 1983, despite persistent efforts from Tottenham, and within weeks was making a scoring League debut against Nottingham Forest.

Emeka became part of David Pleat's so called 'A' team and was an excellent foil to Brian Stein and Mick Harford but persistent injury ended his career prematurely. He has been a pharmacist in North London for many years.

■ Scott John OAKES

After being nursed through the junior sides at his home town club Leicester, Scott was whisked away by Luton manager David Pleat in October 1991 as part of the deal that took Steve Thompson to Filbert Street.

Breaking into the Hatters top flight side almost immediately, Scott put in some mature performances as an attacking midfielder that belied his 19 years. It was two years later, though, that Scott came to national prominence as his goals, which included a hat-trick against West Ham in the 6th round, fired the Town to the FA Cup semi-finals.

With Luton relegated in 1996, Scott was snapped up once more by David Pleat who was now at Sheffield Wednesday but the move proved an injury punctuated mistake leading to spells at Cambridge, Leyton Orient and St Albans.

Scott now runs a courier business with some of his old Luton playing colleagues.

■ Joseph (Joe) O'BRIEN

The Hatters paid £3,000 to League of Ireland club Dundalk for the services of speedy left winger Joe in November 1947. Seen by Luton player/manager Dally Duncan as his replacement on the wing, Joe was thrust into the Town's Division Two side within weeks and although he kept his place for a while it was generally accepted that it was too big a stride and he was put back into the reserves.

In the summer of 1948, during the club's Ireland tour, Joe guested for Dundalk against the Hatters as part of the previous transfer arrangements and was treated as a returning hero. Sadly, this could not be said at Kenilworth Road and after three more appearances he was transferred to Ipswich where he enjoyed a productive first season before injury finished his career.

■ Philip (Phil) O'CONNOR

Discarded by Southend as a youngster, Romford born Phil turned to non-League football with Bexley where the gifted winger caught the eye of Luton manager Harry Haslam who signed him for £2,000 in December 1972.

Phil made his League debut as a substitute at Carlisle later that season and made a full appearance at Oxford on the final day of that campaign. After that he failed to break through again and after a loan spell at Lincoln, where he scored on his debut, he emigrated to Australia.

He found this more to his liking and turned out for several top Australian sides over the next few years and also won caps for his new country including one against England in 1983.

Phil was only 32 when he died in a road accident in 1985.

■ Michael (Mike) John O'HARA

Mike became the Hatter's youngest ever player at 16 years 32 days when he was forced to turn out in goal in a 0-3 defeat at Stoke in October 1960. The Town had lost England international Ron Baynham to a fractured skull the previous week and with reserve Alan Collier recovering from a broken arm there was little choice.

The young Irishman had been playing junior football in Coventry when he asked the Town for a trial, which was successful, and he signed apprentice forms leading up to his sudden elevation.

Mike made one more League appearance plus two in the League Cup before the Town signed the experienced Jim Standen. A move to Swindon saw more first team action before he emigrated to Australia where he still lives.

■ Stephen Michael O'LEARY

Stephen joined Luton Town as a 13 year old after he had been spotted playing for Barnet Schools, and was awarded a Scholarship in the summer of 2001 at the same time as Kevin Foley.

The Hatters had fought off competition from several London clubs for the signature of the Republic of Ireland schoolboy international midfielder, but it was all worthwhile as he made his way up through the ranks before earning his League debut as a substitute in a 4-1 home win over Brentford in February 2004.

Loaned out to Tranmere during the 2005/06 campaign, Stephen earned good reviews at Prenton Park and, bringing this form back to Luton, finally saw him win a meaningful run in the side.

■ John O'ROURKE

England schools and youth international forward John seemed to have lost his way after failing to gain a first team spot at either Arsenal or Chelsea so reluctantly accepted an offer to move to Luton in December 1963.

John became a teenage sensation at Kenilworth Road banging in 22 goals in only 23 appearances in 1963-64 to save the Town from seemingly certain relegation to Division Four. Badly injured on the opening day of the following campaign he was back to his best in 1965-66 netting 32 times before an inevitable big money move to Middlesbrough.

A brilliant header of a ball, John helped the Teesiders to promotion, then did the same for Ipswich, and played for Coventry in their only European season. After finishing his League career with Bournemouth, John became a newsagent in Highcliffe.

■ David Charles OLDFIELD

Although born in Australia, David moved to England as a youngster before being spotted by Luton's John Moore leading to his signing of professional forms for the Hatters in May 1986.

David came to the fore during the 1987-88 campaign, netting twice in a Simod Cup tie at Everton and then scoring the equaliser in a 1-1 draw at Anfield. An unorthodox running style, deceptive pace and the ability to strike from deep led to big money bids being received with a £600,000 offer from Manchester City in March 1989 too good to refuse. He only stayed a year at Maine Road before meeting up with his old mentor David Pleat at Leicester where he enjoyed five good years ahead of a £150,000 bid from Luton's Terry Westley which brought him back to Kenilworth Road.

David was still turning out for Stafford Rangers at the age of 39 and is now manager of Brackley Town.

■ Sidney (Sid) OTTEWELL

Sid had made only three League appearances for Chesterfield before war broke out but as a P. T. instructor during the hostilities he managed to turn out for number of clubs as a guest player.

An aggressive and hard shooting inside-forward, Sid top-scored for Chesterfield in 1946-47 leading to a £5,000 move to Birmingham in June 1947, before moving to Luton six months later.

Despite scoring four goals in 15 League appearances, Sid never settled at Kenilworth Road and he was soon off to Nottingham Forest followed by spells at Mansfield and Scunthorpe.

Sid later played for and managed several non-League outfits in the midlands including Spalding and Lockheed and now lives in retirement in Nottingham.

■ Mark John OVENDALE

Leicester born Mark first caught the eye at Wisbech where his shot stopping abilities led to him joining Northampton in August 1994.

After failing to win a regular place at Sixfields he accepted a free transfer to Barry where he established a League of Wales record by going 1,072 minutes without conceding a goal in 1995-96.

Starring as his side won three consecutive titles, Mark was then subject to a £30,000 move to Bournemouth in 1998 before an amazing £425,000 bid from Ricky Hill's Luton was accepted in August 2000.

Although Mark helped the Hatters to promotion in 2002 he could never claim the number one shirt as his own and was released in 2003.

Since then Mark has appeared for York, Tiverton and Newport but had to retire from the game through injury in June 2007.

■ Sydney (Syd) William OWEN

Syd joined his local club Birmingham on de-mob from the RAF after the war but due to the number of professionals at St Andrews at the time managed only five League appearances with the Blues.

Age 25 and needing to play football, Syd accepted a £1,500 move to Luton which proved money well spent as he went on to make over 400 starts for the Hatters, mainly as a cool, strong centre-half with commanding aerial ability.

Leading the club to promotion to the top flight, playing for England and finally skippering the Town in the 1959 FA Cup final marked a glittering playing career.

Sadly, a spell in the hot seat at Luton was not successful but his next job was - coach at Leeds during their glory years.

Syd retired in 1982 and died in Leeds in 1998.

■ David (Dave) PACEY

After playing for Luton schoolboys, Dave was developed by Hitchin Town where he made their Athenian League side as a wing-half before National Service in the Army.

Hearing that Dave was having trials at Arsenal, Luton director Tom Hodgson travelled to his Army station at Newton Abbot to make sure he signed for the Hatters!

After making his League debut in a 0-3 defeat at Old Trafford on Christmas Day 1957, Dave became a mainstay in the Luton half-back line over the next eight years, injuries permitting.

Scorer of the Town's goal in the 1959 FA Cup final, Dave tried manfully as the Hatters dropped down to Division Four by 1965 but then decided to call it a day before enjoying three years with Kettering.

Dave worked for many years at Electrolux and now lives in Newport Pagnell in retirement.

■ Garry Stuart PARKER

Born in Oxford, cultured midfielder Garry was taken on as an apprentice for the Hatters in 1982 and signed full professional forms a year later. Due to the form of the likes of Ricky Hill and David Preece he failed to earn a regular place at Kenilworth Road and so stepped down a level in 1986, joining Hull who were managed by his old Luton skipper Brian Horton.

Such was his form at Boothferry Park that he was soon back in the top flight with Nottingham Forest where he was on the fringes of the full England side and also starred in the 1989 Littlewoods Cup win against the Hatters!

Further big money moves to Aston Villa and then Leicester followed, much to the disgust of Luton fans, before he brought his career to a close in Oxfordshire non-League circles.

Garry now runs his own building company and manages Kidlington reserves.

■ Samuel (Sam) PARKIN

Roehampton born Sam signed on with Chelsea as a youngster and was sent out to Millwall, Wycombe and Oldham on short loan deals before joining Northampton, where he replaced the Luton bound Steve Howard, on a year long arrangement.

Unable to force his way into the Chelsea first eleven, Sam made a permanent move to Swindon in August 2002 where his career took off with 67 goals in 124 League games for the Robins.

An inevitable big money transfer to Ipswich followed but a broken ankle brought a halt to his career which he hoped to pick up again when moving to Luton in August 2006, but further injuries have blighted his time at Kenilworth Road.

Now back to full fitness, Hatters fans are hoping for a return to the goal standard for the big striker.

■ Darren James PATTERSON

Belfast born Darren was taken on by West Brom from school but after failing to make the grade moved on to Wigan where he first tasted League football. Such was his form at Springfield Park that Crystal Palace put in a £225,000 bid for him in 1992.

Darren finally managed to force his way into the Eagles Premier League side in 1994-95 but as he was now a full Northern Ireland international needed the guarantee of regular first team football.

Turning down the offer of a fresh contract, he instead accepted a £150,000 move to Terry Westley's Luton in 1995 but the strong defender was never truly regarded as a first choice although a succession of injuries did not help his cause.

After spells at Dundee United, York and Oxford an Achilles injury ended his playing career. Darren is now manager at Oxford.

■ Trevor PEAKE

In a long football career, Trevor holds the record as the oldest player in the Hatters history when turning out against Wrexham in 1997 at the age of 40 years 222 days.

Starting off at his home town club Nuneaton, Trevor first tasted League football with Lincoln, who paid £27,500 for his services. After 171 League games for the Imps a £100,000 fee took him to Coventry in 1983 where his displays at centre-half earned him legendary status plus an FA Cup winners medal in 1987.

When Luton manager David Pleat was looking for an experienced head he turned to Trevor who went on to play 179 League games for the Town, picking up several Player of the Year awards along the way.

After taking up a coaching job at Kenilworth Road, Trevor is now an academy coach at Leicester.

■ Reginald (Reg) Stanley PEARCE

Reg was almost 25 when Luton scout George Martin spotted him playing for Winsford in the Cheshire League and encouraged him to sign for the Hatters in 1954.

Although originally signed as an inside-right, Reg played in six positions for the first team before turning out in his rightful position although given the form of Gordon Turner he eventually had to settle for a wing-half slot where he proved a revelation.

Reg was on the verge of international recognition when relegation threatened Sunderland came in for him in February 1958. The Town felt that young Dave Pacey was an adequate replacement and so allowed him to leave, although £20,000 helped!

Sunderland were relegated at the end of that season and Reg failed to hit the high spots again, finishing his career at Cambridge City and Peterborough. Reg lives in Cambridge in retirement.

■ Andrew (Andy) John PEARSON

Andy came up through the ranks at Luton, signing professional forms in November 1978 under the watchful eye of David Pleat.

After earning good reviews in the Hatters reserve side, Andy eventually made his first team debut coming on as substitute for Steve White at QPR in March 1980. The Town were 0-2 down at the time but the substitution worked as Andy's performance on the wing inspired his side to a 2-2 draw in front of the cameras.

He was rewarded with a start at home to Burnley the following week but with mercurial winger David Moss returning from injury that was as good as it got for Andy who left for Hitchin Town the following summer and then on to a career in the police force.

■ James (Jim) Thomas PEMBERTON

Starting out with West Brom during the war years, utility man Jim then stepped down to non-League football with Stourbridge as he could earn far more at that level and it was closer to home.

Missing League football, the lure of an offer from Luton Town in 1947 was too good to refuse and so began a ten year spell at Kenilworth Road where Jim played in every position for the Hatters bar right wing and goalkeeper.

His ability to play almost anywhere meant that he could never claim a regular place in the side but he seemed to get more opportunities as the Town won promotion to the top flight in 1955.

Leaving for Kings Lynn in 1957, Jim then worked at the docks there after hanging up his boots before returning to the midlands where he lives in retirement.

■ Mark Anthony PEMBRIDGE

Mark was one of a procession of players who was spotted by Luton Town's South Wales scout Cyril Beach and went on to join the Hatters, signing professional forms in July 1989.

A left sided midfielder with a vicious shot, Mark made his League debut on New Year's Day 1991 and from then on was ever present in the Town's Division One side, scoring some spectacular goals along the way. Following relegation, a £1.25 million bid from Derby was reluctantly accepted and the Welsh international then went on to carve out a long career for himself at the Baseball Ground then Sheffield Wednesday, Benfica, Everton and, latterly, Fulham. Mark is now on the academy coaching staff at Craven Cottage.

■ Russell (Russ) PERRETT

Russ started his football career with Portsmouth, and was a member of Pompey's acclaimed youth side of the late 1980's, but he was allowed to leave to join Lymington before being given a second chance at Fratton Park which he grasped with both hands.

A tough, brave and clever central defender, Russ made his League debut in 1995-96 but moved to Cardiff four years later after becoming surplus to requirements. At Ninian Park injuries cut back his appearances and he was grateful for a fresh start with Joe Kinnear's Luton in 2001.

Although injury also curtailed his Luton career he never gave less than 100% and was the longest serving player on the club's books by the time he signed for Bournemouth in the summer of 2007. Sadly, Russ has recently been forced to quit the game through injury.

■ Christopher (Chris) John PERRY

Chris joined Wimbledon from school as a youth trainee before signing professional forms in 1991 and making his Premiership debut for the Dons two years later.

Following over 200 first-team appearances for Wimbledon and talk of a call-up for the England squad, Chris moved to Tottenham for £4 million in 1999 where he eventually took Sol Campbell's place in the Spurs central defence.

Losing his place due to injury in early 2003, Chris could not force his way back into the side when fit again and joined Charlton where he became a mainstay in their defence for three years becoming a crowd favourite due to his close marking abilities and his reading of the game.

After a spell at West Brom in 2006/07, Chris moved to Luton on a free transfer in 2007 summer and is now at Southampton following a successful loan spell at St Mary's.

■ Paolo (Paul) Pasquale PESCHISOLIDO

Canadian born striker Paul joined Birmingham from Toronto Blizzard in 1992 and soon earned a reputation as a cool and deadly finisher. His goalscoring prowess saw him become highly sought after and big money moves took him to six League clubs where combined transfer fees totalled almost £3 million.

By now a veteran, Paul helped Derby into the Premiership in 2006/07 having starred in the play-off final victory against one of his old clubs West Brom, before joining Luton on a free-transfer in the summer of 2007. Sadly his time at Kenilworth Road was beset with injury and he managed only two League starts for the Hatters before being forced to hang up his boots.

■ Andrew (Andy) Keith PETTERSON

Australian goalkeeper Andy was so desperate to make a name for himself in the English professional game that he paid his own passage to take up a trial at Luton Town. Fortunately, his gamble paid off as he was offered a contract at Kenilworth Road in 1988 although he had to wait until the start of the 1992-93 season before making his League debut.

Impressing in pre-season with his shot stopping ability and quick reflexes Andy was ever present for the first 14 games but a calamitous performance during a 3-3 draw at Cambridge effectively put paid to his Luton career.

Undeterred by this rejection Andy went to play for 14 clubs in this country in a long career before returning to Australia in 2006 where he has subsequently turned out for Newcastle and ECU Joondalup.

■ Edward (Ted) John PHILLIPS

Leiston born Ted was turning out for his local side when he was plucked by Ipswich in 1953 to start a tremendous rise through the divisions with the Suffolk side.

Starting in Division Three (South), Ted scored 161 goals in 269 League starts for the Blues as they swept all before them, with the crowning pinnacle being the Division One title in 1962.

After a spell at Leyton Orient, Ted moved to Luton in February 1965 as the Hatters fought to keep out of Division Four. Although past his best, Ted showed some glimpses of his previous prowess with frightening shooting and heading power.

Having failed to save the Town from the drop, Ted finished his career with Colchester a town where he still lives in retirement.

■ Peter Stuart PHILLIPS

Peter was a successful England amateur international, combining studies at Cambridge University for an Electronics degree with playing at centre-forward for Bishops Stortford, from where he was persuaded by Luton Town to sign professional forms in 1969.

A fast and tricky forward, Peter made his League debut at Brighton in October 1969 but with Malcolm Macdonald banging in the goals for the Hatters at the time his chances were infrequent and after a loan spell at Torquay he joined Cambridge United where he was altogether more successful.

After 53 League appearances in two years at the Abbey, Peter signed on for Bedford and took up studying again, this time to become a Chartered Accountant. Peter is now based in Finedon.

◼ Forbes Ernest PHILLIPSON-MASTERS

Bournemouth born Forbes joined Southampton from school as a goalkeeper but having failed to make the grade in that position was converted into a centre-half by the Saints coaching staff.

Relishing his new role as a commanding stopper, Forbes was loaned out to, amongst others, Luton who were in desperate need having lost Chris Turner to the lure of the USA. The impressive Forbes played the last ten games of the 1978-79 campaign and helped the Hatters to avoid the drop from Division Two.

His reward was a £50,000 move to Plymouth where he was guaranteed a first team slot and from there he enjoyed a successful spell at Bristol City.

Forbes is now a painter and decorator in Verwood.

◼ Courtney Leon PITT

After working his way up through the youth ranks at Chelsea alongside the likes of John Terry, quicksilver winger Courtney was offered a £200,000 move to Portsmouth in 2001 and was virtually ever-present in his first season there.

New manager Harry Redknapp brought in his own players which left Courtney sidelined, and he jumped at the chance to join Luton on loan at the start of the 2003-4 campaign.

He played reasonably well at Kenilworth Road but was not retained at the end of his loan period and instead went on to sign on for Oxford and then Boston United.

Courtney is now starring for Cambridge United where he is playing as a wing-back.

◼ David John PLEAT

Nottingham born David starred for England Schoolboys before being snapped up by Nottingham Forest at 17. Sadly, his early promise did not fully materialise and he made the move to Luton in 1964.

In a poor team, Pleat was a revelation with his genuine skill on the wing until injuries severely restricted his blistering pace.

David eventually moved into management with Nuneaton before returning to Kenilworth Road, working his way up on the coaching side.

Suddenly catapulted into the hot seat, David justified the Board's faith by winning the championship of the old Division Two in 1982 with an attractive side, but a bid from Tottenham in 1986 was too tempting to refuse and at White Hart Lane, David took Spurs to an F.A.Cup final. David returned to Luton in 1991 and took the club to the F.A.Cup semi-finals three years later.

◼ Maitland (Matt) Alexander Inglis POLLOCK

Scottish Schoolboy international Matt chose Nottingham Forest from a list of suitors but in three years at the City Ground failed to make a first team appearance. After a trial at Walsall he accepted a move to non-League Burton where he was spotted by Luton scout Paddy Sowden who had gone to watch future Hatters star Steve Buckley.

At Kenilworth Road Matt, an industrious midfielder, managed only three League starts in two years and moved on again, this time to Portsmouth in 1976 where he enjoyed a long run in the side.

A spell with Queen of the South followed before he hung up his boots to concentrate on a career as a pharmaceutical buyer.

◼ George Ross POTTER

Tough tackling full-back George had been earning good reviews while turning out for Forfar leading to him being invited for trials at promotion bound Luton in March 1968.

The Hatters liked what they saw when he appeared in a Beds Professional Cup game against Dunstable and offered him a contract and an almost immediate first team call-up in midfield as replacement for the injured Alan Slough.

Although never letting the side down, George found it difficult to win a regular place in a Hatters side moving up through the divisions and so moved to Torquay in 1969 and on to Hartlepool two years later where he went on to make over 200 League appearances.

George emigrated to Australia in 1977 and is now a dollar millionaire, owning three McDonald's restaurants in Brisbane!

◼ John Anthony (Tony) POUNDER

Luton Town scouts took a liking to Atlas Sports (Sheffield) winger Tony and after asking him to Kenilworth Road for trials encouraged him to sign a professional contract at a Sheffield hotel on Boxing Day 1955 just before the Town were due to play at Bramall Lane.

Fast and direct, Tony was given his Division One baptism the following April in a 1-0 home win over Portsmouth and made two further appearances in 1956-57 before moving on to Coventry in search of more regular first-team football.

He did not last long at Highfield Road but made up for it with a long playing career at Crewe, Yeovil, Dorchester and Crewkerne and then watched as his son, also Tony, turned out in almost 200 games for Bristol Rovers and Hereford.

Tony now lives in Yeovil in retirement.

■ Neil Anthony POUTCH

Dublin born Neil joined Luton from school and worked his way up to becoming a regular in the Hatters reserve side as a cultured full-back.

A severe injury crisis at Kenilworth Road, with eight first team regulars out, meant that manager Jim Ryan needed to blood some youngsters for the trip to high flyers Aston Villa in March 1990. This led to full League debuts being awarded to Tim Allpress and Ceri Hughes and a place on the bench for Irish Under-21 international Neil.

Neil got his chance on the hour, replacing Jason Rees, but could do little to affect the game with the Town already two goals down.

That was the only chance that Neil was given and he returned to Ireland with Shamrock Rovers that summer before moving to Drogheda in 1992.

Neil is now involved with property in Spain.

■ David William PREECE

David joined Walsall from school and after signing professional forms for the Saddlers in July 1980 as a 17 year old, enjoyed four years at Fellows Park which included appearances in the semi-finals of the Milk Cup.

A Luton bid of £150,000 plus forward Steve Elliott was accepted by Walsall and David made his way to Kenilworth Road in December 1984. After making his Luton debut in a 1-0 home win over Aston Villa, scoring the only goal, David went on to make 395 first team appearances for the Hatters including one in the Littlewoods Cup Final win over Arsenal in 1988.

The tiny but hugely talented midfielder also won England B honours during his time with the Hatters.

Following his testimonial game against Manchester United at the end of the 1994-95 season he decided to move to Derby before enjoying spells with Cambridge and Torquay.

David sadly passed away recently.

■ Paul Terence PRICE

Paul was a schoolboy prodigy feted by several clubs but the St Albans born defender opted for Luton, making his League debut on the last day of 1972-73.

He had to wait three years, though, before earning a regular place in the side but once established he remained virtually ever-present until a shock, and disappointing, £200,000 move to Tottenham in 1981.

By now a Welsh international, Paul won an F.A.Cup winners medal at White Hart Lane before slipping down the pecking order and trying his luck in the USA. Spells at Swansea and Peterborough followed before moves to non-League Wivenhoe and St Albans.

After a time at Hitchin as joint manager, Paul emigrated to Australia where he has been for the last four years.

■ Jesse PYE

Jesse had already enjoyed a full and successful career when he joined Luton for £9,000 in 1952 but even though he was 32 at the time he was soon regarded as one of the finest players to pull on a Hatters shirt.

Born in Rotherham, Jesse turned out for Sheffield United and Notts County before a big money move to Wolves in 1946 where he scored 95 League goals, two in the 1949 F.A.Cup final as well as an England call-up.

Showing superb ball control for a big man and a fine football brain, Jesse top-scored for Luton in his first season and was instrumental in the training and teaching of future Hatters record scorer Gordon Turner.

Citing the health of his wife, Jesse moved to Derby in 1954 before spending nine years at Wisbech with the last six as manager.

Jesse passed away in 1984.

■ George McIntosh RAMAGE

Brave goalkeeper George started out with the now defunct Third Lanark before being picked up by Colchester in August 1961.

George had to wait 18 months before being given the chance to replace the popular Percy Ames in the 'U's goal but, once established, he was given a good run in the side. Joining Leyton Orient in 1964 turned out to be mistake as a change of manager meant that his appearances were limited and a move to Luton a year later was no more successful as he made only seven League appearances at Kenilworth Road as understudy to Colin Tinsley.

George emigrated to Australia in 1967 and after finally hanging up his gloves became an electrician for the council in Woonona near Sydney.

■ John Anthony (Tony) READ

After failing to make the grade at both Sheffield Wednesday and Peterborough, goalkeeper Tony joined Luton in March 1965, but such was the malaise sweeping through Kenilworth Road at the time it was a while before it was discovered that the new signing had arrived with a broken bone in his foot!

Tony always fancied himself as a striker and got his chance the following season netting twelve goals in only twenty starts including a hat-trick against Notts County at Kenilworth Road.

The rich vein of form did not last and it was back in goal for Tony who became a firm fans favourite over the next six years while seeing off several pretenders to his throne with his spectacular shot stopping and athleticism.

Tony is now retired in Dersingham where he continues to practice his golf swing.

■ Barry Reginald Frank REED

Peterborough born Barry started his footballing career at St Neots before being spotted by Leicester who he joined in 1955.

A cool full-back with good distribution, Barry became a mainstay in the Foxes Football Combination side but was never able to earn a first team chance. After six years at Filbert Street he accepted a free-transfer to Luton but such was the form of Brendan McNally that he made only one Football League appearance for the Hatters in a 1-4 home defeat at the hands of Southampton in September 1961 where he acquitted himself 'moderately well.'

Barry is perhaps better known for managing Barton Rovers to the FA Vase final in 1978.

Now retired, Barry still lives in Luton.

■ Jason Mark REES

Jason was yet another youth player who came off the production line at Kenilworth Road following the recommendation of legendary scout Cyril Beech.

Born in Aberdare, Jason signed on for the Hatters in 1988 before making his League debut as a substitute in a 1-2 defeat at Everton on New Year's Day 1990. A busy, aggressive midfielder, Jason did not earn a regular place in the Luton side until the Town were relegated from the top flight in 1992.

When he found himself out of the side once more Jason, by now a Welsh international, moved to Portsmouth for first team football in 1994 and finished his League career with a tour of West Country clubs Exeter and Torquay.

After spells at Tiverton and Taunton, Jason managed Cullompton Rangers in 2007/08.

■ John REID

Fleet footed inside-forward John started his professional football career with Hamilton Academical from where he joined Bradford City in 1957.

Becoming a crowd favourite at Valley Parade it needed a big bid to prise him away but upwardly mobile Northampton paid £5,000 in 1961 which proved money well spent as John helped them to promotion two years later.

Luton, newly relegated to Division Three, paid a massive £13,000 for his services in November 1963 but he was continually playing in a poor Hatters side although he always showed 100% commitment and flashes of ability.

Spells at Torquay and Rochdale followed as well as a managerial appointment at Market Rasen Town before he became a newsagent in Bradford. John now lives in Keighley in retirement.

■ Gordon George RIDDICK

Watford born Gordon came to Luton as a 17 year old and worked his way up through the ranks at Kenilworth Road before making his League debut in a 1-2 defeat at Rotherham in December 1962.

Gordon made over 100 first team appearances for the Hatters over the next five years but the crowd never warmed to him despite his whole-hearted effort and some vital goals.

Gillingham paid a record fee to take him to Priestfield in 1967 and from there he played for a further four clubs in fairly quick succession, finishing with Brentford.

A minor counties cricketer of note, Gordon ran his own building firm as well as working behind the scenes on Sky TV sports events.

■ Bruce David RIOCH

Born in Aldershot but raised in Luton, Bruce made his League debut as a 17 year old for the Hatters in November 1964 and soon had the scouts flocking to Kenilworth Road where they admired his pace, power and fierce shooting.

After helping the Town to the championship of Division Four in 1968, and seeing his colleagues narrowly miss out the following year, Bruce accepted a record fee move to Aston Villa.

Further big money moves to Derby and Everton followed as well as the honour of skippering Scotland, the country of his father.

Bruce then entered into a second career, managing amongst others, Middlesbrough, Bolton, Arsenal and Norwich with some success and is now with Aalborg.

■ Vidar RISETH

Luton manager Terry Westley paid £110,000 to bring Vidar from Norwegian club Kongsvinger in October 1995 but within weeks the manager had gone leaving the tall striker floundering in a Hatters side destined for relegation.

Town fans never saw the best of Vidar, who left for Linz the following summer on a free transfer, but other clubs certainly have with Celtic, TSV Munich and Rosenborg paying large fees for his services.

With over 50 caps for Norway under his belt, Vidar, now a steadying influence in midfield, caught the eye in a Champions League tie at Chelsea last season where he helped Rosenborg to a 1-1 draw.

■ Alan Desmond RIVERS

Big, no-nonsense centre-half Alan joined Luton from school before signing professional forms for the Hatters on his 18th birthday in January 1964.

Alan made his League debut, deputising for the injured Matt Woods, in a 2-1 home victory over Newport in September 1965, before going on to make 30 appearances for the Town over the next two seasons.

With new manager Allan Brown wishing to bring in his own players, Alan moved on to Watford in 1967 but managed only two games as substitute for the Hornets before a spell at Rangers in South Africa and then a short stay at Crewe.

Alan is now back in South Africa where he watches the career of his son Mark, of Crewe and Norwich fame, from afar.

■ Benjamin (Ben) James ROBERTS

Goalkeeper Ben holds an unwanted record having conceded the fastest ever goal in an F.A.Cup final when Chelsea's Roberto Di Matteo scored after only 42 seconds against his Middlesbrough side.

Joining Boro as a Youth Trainee, Ben found it difficult to earn a regular spot between the sticks at Ayresome Park and was farmed out to five clubs on loan including the Hatters for whom he turned in 14 assured appearances at the end of the1999-2000 campaign.

Transferred to Charlton in the summer of 2000, Ben fared little better at the Valley leading up to more loan moves including a shorter spell at Luton in 2002.

Ben finally earned a permanent goalkeeping spot at Brighton in 2003 but sadly had to retire from the game at 29 following a persistent back injury.

■ Stephen (Steve) ROBINSON

Northern Ireland schoolboy international Steve signed on for Tottenham as a youth trainee but failed to make the breakthrough at White Hart Lane, making only two Premiership appearances.

A busy midfielder, Steve joined Bournemouth on a free transfer in October 1994 and went on to become virtually ever present in the Cherries team for six seasons, picking up full international caps for his country along the way.

A £375,000 move to Preston in 2000 did not work out and, after a loan spell at Bristol City, Steve found a permanent transfer to Joe Kinnear's Luton in 2002 much more to his liking.

Able to play anywhere in midfield, Steve remained a regular in the Hatters side and had made over 200 first team appearances in his six years at Kenilworth Road before being released in July 2008.

■ Graham RODGER

Graham made his League debut for Wolves but due to the financial problems at Molineux was allowed to move to Coventry in February 1984.

At Highfield Road, Graham had difficulty in breaking the central defensive partnership of Brian Kilcline and Trevor Peake but he did manage to win an F.A Cup winners medal there, coming on as substitute as the Sky Blues beat Tottenham in the 1987 final.

In order to gain a regular first team place, Graham accepted a tribunal set £200,000 move to Luton in 1989 which turned out to be a disaster. A succession of injuries severely cut back his appearances and he was probably glad when Grimsby rescued him from his nightmare in 1992.

With the Mariners, Graham enjoyed a far more injury free playing career and was subsequently appointed coach and then manager at the club. Graham is now Football in the Community officer at Blundell Park.

■ David Charles ROWLAND

Stotfold born David first caught the eye while forming a left wing partnership with future Hatter, Roland Legate, at Arlesey Town.

West Ham were quickest off the blocks for his signature but he failed to make the breakthrough at Upton Park and so accepted the chance to join Luton, signing professional forms in January 1958.

David made a League debut for the Hatters as a 17 year old in a 1-2 home defeat at the hands of Manchester City in March 1958 but that was as good as it got for the ball playing inside-left who returned to the 'A' team.

Going on to play for Bedford after leaving Kenilworth Road, David now lives in Potton in retirement.

■ Keith ROWLAND

Northern Ireland international Keith joined Bournemouth as a youngster and soon impressed as a tireless left back or left sided midfielder leading to a big money move to West Ham in 1993.

At Upton Park, Keith became a favourite, despite injuries punctuating his appearances, but after being kept on the sidelines by Julian Dicks moved to QPR along with ex-Hatter Iain Dowie in an exchange deal which took Trevor Sinclair to the Hammers.

Further injury problems hindered his time at Loftus Road and he moved to Joe Kinnear's Luton on loan in 2001to get some match practice. Playing 12 games in a relegation threatened side, Keith made a positive contribution in midfield scoring two important goals along the way.

Spells at Chesterfield, Barnet, Hornchurch, Dublin City and Dagenham then followed and Keith was last at Welling.

Luton Town Post-War A to Z

■ Simon Ernest ROYCE

Veteran goalkeeper Simon is now with his seventh club after joining Gillingham during the summer of 2007 following a loan spell from QPR.

Starting off with Heybridge Swifts, Simon then enjoyed seven years at Southend where his shot stopping abilities eventually earned a move to Charlton in 1998. A transfer to Leicester then followed, loan spells at Brighton and QPR and then back to Charlton.

After falling down the pecking order at the Valley, Simon accepted an SOS call from Luton in October 2004 and came on loan for two games where he had little to do as the Hatters rattled in nine goals against Bradford City and Wrexham.

■ Raymond (Ray) Douglas RUFFETT

Local boy Ray turned out for Christ Church and then Luton Town during the war years and on de-mob from the services in 1947 was offered full-time terms by the Hatters.

A ball playing wing-half, Ray waited patiently for his first team chance which finally came in a 1-3 defeat at Bury in April 1949. Sadly, Ray was injured in the game and his chance was gone.

Ray remained at Kenilworth Road for a further twelve months before joining Abbey United who changed their name to Cambridge United whilst he was there. Ray now lives in Luton in retirement.

■ Bjorn RUNSTROM

Big Swede Bjorn was snapped up early in his football career by Italian side Bologna and from there moved swiftly on to Chievo and Fiorentina without earning a regular place in Serie A.

Still only 19, the talented striker moved back to Sweden with Hammarby and at last was able to show his goalscoring abilities leading to Fulham paying £700,000 for his services in August 2006.

After one substitute appearance for the Cottagers in the Premier League, Bjorn was allowed to move to Luton on loan in 2006/07 where he made seven appearances, netting twice before returning to West London.

Bjorn moved on to Kaiserslautern on loan last season and, after being released by Fulham, has signed permanently for Danish side OB.

■ James (Jimmy) RYAN

Spotted as a youngster while playing junior football in Stirling, Jim joined Manchester United at 17 but, although an extremely clever winger, was always on the fringes at Old Trafford due to the talents of George Best and John Connelly.

Jim became one of four United players who moved to Luton en bloc in April 1970, just as the Hatters won promotion from Division Three, and he went on to make almost 200 remarkably consistent League appearances over the next seven years at Kenilworth Road.

After a spell with Dallas Tornado, Jim returned to Luton initially as a coach before being thrust into the hot seat in January 1990. Despite overseeing two fights against relegation from the top flight with minimal funds, Jim was harshly sacked in May 1991.

Jim found work back at Old Trafford almost immediately and still remains on the Reds coaching staff.

■ John Gilbert RYAN

After failing to make the grade at Arsenal and Fulham, John probably thought it was the end of the line when he joined Division Three side Luton on a free transfer in 1969.

Full-back John soon became a crowd favourite at Kenilworth Road though, with his swashbuckling runs down the wing and fierce shooting and it was a sad day when he left for Norwich in 1976 for £60,000.

At Carrow Road he was moved to midfield and became a consistent goalscorer before spells with Seattle Sounders, Sheffield United and Manchester City. Player/coach roles at Stockport and Chester followed before John was appointed player/manager of a very poor Cambridge United side in 1984. John showed his frustrations by being sent off three times in his five League outings at the Abbey!

John is now Director of Youth Development for the Thailand Football Association.

■ John Oliver RYAN

Liverpool born John was with Bill Shankly's Reds as a teenager but frustrated by the lack of opportunities moved on to Tranmere.

It was at non-League Wigan though, under the tutelage of ex-Hatters favourite Allan Brown, that John finally came to prominence and when Brown moved to Luton as manager he returned for the tricky winger who made a dream League debut, setting up the first three goals in a 5-0 win at Exeter in October 1967.

Despite this great start John only played "when they could not get Graham French out of bed" and after two years and 18 League appearances he transferred to Notts County where an injury finished his full-time career.

John continued to play in non-League circles for several years and is now in charge of Health & Safety for a new construction company following 20 years with Costains.

■ Gareth SALISBURY

Welsh Youth international Gareth started his Football League career with Wrexham, making his debut for the Robins in 1960.

After flitting in and out of the side Gareth made a surprise move to Norwich in July 1962 but could not make the breakthrough and transferred to Luton a year later.

A strongly built inside forward, Gareth netted twice in 12 starts but an Achilles tear lost him his place and a move to Colchester also ended in injury.

Gareth was luckier at Chesterfield, who he joined in 1965, but was even more successful during a three year stint in Australia where he was voted 'Player of the Year' for Victoria State in his second year there.

Upon returning to North Wales, Gareth became a computer specialist for the Health Authority before chronic asthma forced his early retirement. Gareth now lives on Anglesey.

■ Darren Brian SALTON

Darren came to Luton Town as a Youth Trainee in 1988, along with his Edinburgh youth club playing colleague Paul Telfer, before signing professional forms in March 1989. A Scottish Schoolboy and Youth international, Darren was destined for great things after making his League debut for the Hatters at Leeds in 1992.

After earning Scotland Under-21 caps the cool and commanding central defender became a fixture in the Luton side as the 1992/93 campaign progressed but it all ended suddenly when he was severely injured in a fatal road accident in November 1992.

Despite brave thoughts of a comeback it was sadly not to be, but Darren is still involved in football in his role as assistant manager of Hemel Hempstead Town.

■ John Robert McDevitt SANDERSON

Carlisle born John signed on for his local side in May 1938 and such were his performances at Brunton Park that a big money move to Wolves was secured the following February.

Unfortunately, the cultured full-back did not manage to force his way into the first team before war broke out and at the end of the hostilities he was subject to another big transfer, this time to Luton.

John was only able to make six League appearances in 1946/47 before a severe knee injury finished his playing career but as he wanted to remain involved in football the Town offered him the position of groundsman. He picked up the rudiments of the job very quickly and combined this with Honorary Secretary of the Bobbers Stand Club for many years.

John was still living in Luton at the time of his death in 1993.

■ Michael (Mike) William SAXBY

Big, commanding centre-half Mick made his League debut as an 18 year old for his local side, Mansfield, and soon became a cult hero at Field Mill.

Looking for a replacement for Chris Turner, Luton manager David Pleat paid a massive £200,000 to bring him to Kenilworth Road in 1979 where he soon formed a solid defensive partnership with Paul Price and later Mal Donaghy.

With the Hatters walking away with the championship of Division Two in 1981/82 Mike hurt his knee when turning in the area during a home clash with Crystal Palace, an injury which effectively ended his playing career at Luton.

Attempts at a comeback with Newport and Middlesbrough failed, leaving Mike to forge a career with the Nottingham Evening Post and as a radio match summariser at Mansfield.

■ Andre Pierre SCARLETT

Tiny right-sided midfielder Andre joined Luton from school and after working up through the ranks made a dream League debut when coming on as a substitute in a dour home game against Oldham in October 1998 and scoring a match clinching goal in stoppage time.

Sadly this did not preface a long and successful career at Kenilworth Road for the tenacious and skilful Andre as, although always on the fringes of the first team over the next three years, his chances were sporadic and he was never given a long run in the side.

Andre eventually left for Wealdstone and is currently starring for Staines.

■ Joseph (Joe) Cumpson SCOTT

After failing to make the grade at home town club Newcastle, Joe dropped down to non-League football with Spennymoor where he was spotted by Luton Town's scout in the north-east and brought back to Kenilworth Road.

Although he scored on his League debut in a 2-4 defeat at Swansea in September 1952, National Service and injuries meant that it was while before Hatters fans saw the clever inside-forward get an extended run in the side.

When he did get in the team it was invariably out of position so he was pleased to go to Middlesbrough for £5,000 in 1954 where he became a consistent goalscorer.

Joe now lives in Acklam in retirement.

■ Leslie (Les) Jessie SEALEY

A marvellous goalkeeper for nine different League clubs over a twenty year playing career, Les is warmly remembered at Luton where he made over 200 appearances in undoubtedly the best ever Hatters side in the club's history.

Although a Londoner, the brave, positive and loud goalkeeper started his career as an apprentice at Coventry before moving to Luton in 1983 for £120,000. He missed out on the 1988 Littlewoods Cup triumph through injury but was between the sticks for the Town at Wembley twelve months later.

After leaving Luton for Manchester United he added both an FA Cup winners medal and a European Cup Winners Cup medal to his collection.

Les finished his playing career back home at West Ham but sadly died in 2001 at the young age of 43.

■ John SEASMAN

With everyone at Tranmere thinking that Luton scouts were watching winger Steve Coppell they were mildly surprised when a £14,000 bid came in for midfielder John Seasman.

John made his full League debut for the Hatters at Wolves in March 1975, scoring in a 2-5 defeat, but although highly rated by the fans and the local press he was often overlooked by the Luton management until he was told that the cash-strapped Town would have to pay Tranmere an extra £10,000 once he had made ten appearances!

At his next stop, Millwall, John became a crowd favourite helping the Lions to promotion, a feat he also achieved at Rotherham.

After drifting down through the divisions, John became chief scout at Blackburn before working for football agents Base Soccer.

■ Dino SEREMET

Slovenian goalkeeper Dino was plying his trade with NK Maribor in his home country when he was invited over to Luton for trials in the summer of 2004 which proved successful.

As understudy to Marlon Beresford, Dino made six League appearances during the Hatters League One championship winning season of 2004-05 to cover for injury to the number one, plus one in the final game of the season 3-3 extravaganza at Doncaster. In the following campaign Dino could not force his way into the side and was allowed to move to Doncaster and then Tranmere on loan.

Dino left Luton in 2006 for Greek side Kerkyra who play on Corfu.

■ David (Dave) John SEXTON

Although Dave turned out for five clubs over an eleven year period taking in almost 200 League games along the way, his playing career pales into insignificance compared to his coaching and managerial career afterwards.

Dave's playing career started at Newmarket Town before he was snapped up by Luton from Chelmsford in June 1951. After only nine first team starts in two years the bustling inside-forward moved to West Ham before eventually hanging up his boots while at Crystal Palace in 1962.

It was as a coach and manager that Dave came to the fore, though, leading Chelsea and Manchester United, amongst others, to glory before he became part of the England set-up in 1983 and was last assisting Sven-Goran Eriksson as a scout.

■ Donald (Don) SHANKS

An England Youth international defender, Don was surprisingly released by Fulham at 17 in 1970 but was instantly signed by Luton who had been following his progress via scout Harry Haslam. Don won the 'Little World Cup' with England Youth the following year before making his League debut for the Hatters in August 1971.

A tough tackling marauding full-back, Don helped the Town to promotion to the top flight in 1974 but was then surprisingly sold to QPR for £35,000 in November of that year.

Don enjoyed a successful seven years at Loftus Road before a period at Brighton followed by football in Hong Kong, USA and Malta.

With a reputation as a playboy in London gambling circles and a former Miss World as a previous girlfriend, Don now lives in South London.

■ Walter (Wally) George SHANKS

Although born in Malta, Wally was raised in Scotland and was on the point of joining Aberdeen when war broke out. At the end of hostilities he followed his pal, Scottish international Tommy Walker, to Chelsea but with 70 professionals on their books at the time he decided to drop down a division and joined Luton in October 1946.

After biding his time with only an occasional first team game, Wally made the breakthrough in 1949 in his favoured defensive wing half position and apart from injury was an automatic choice until 1957 when he joined the Town's coaching staff.

Following relegation from Division One in 1960, Wally left Kenilworth Road and then concentrated on his sports shop that he ran with record Luton goalscorer Gordon Turner. Wally later ran the 'Brown Owl' shop and now lives in Luton in retirement.

■ Laurence (Laurie) Joseph SHEFFIELD

Much travelled Welsh striker Laurie was not kept on as a youngster at Bristol Rovers so moved on to non-League Barry from where he was brought back into the Football League by Newport, making his debut in 1962.

A prolific goalscorer who was good in the air for a relatively short man, Laurie was in much demand and moved around frequently. A £10,000 cheque brought him to Luton in 1968 and he scored 12 goals in 29 starts alongside Bruce Rioch and Brian Lewis in the Hatters forward line in his first season.

The discovery of Malcolm Macdonald and the signing of Matt Tees spelled the end for him at Kenilworth Road and he was on his way again. A broken ankle eventually finishing his career while he was with Peterborough .

Subsequently Laurie has been a coach with Doncaster, a mortgage adviser and now lives on the golf course.

■ Paul David SHEPHERD

Joining his local club Leeds United from school, full-back Paul won England Youth caps but managed only one League appearance which came in a 0-3 defeat at Arsenal in October 1996.

Loan spells at Ayr and Tranmere then followed leading to a permanent transfer to the former club after which Paul threw in his lot with Keflavik in Iceland.

With Luton needing full-back cover as they fought to avoid the drop to the football basement in 2001, Paul was picked up on a short term contract by Hatters manager Joe Kinnear and played the last seven games of a disastrous campaign.

Paul was released that summer and has since turned out for Scarborough, Leigh RMI and Harrogate and was last at Stalybridge.

■ Steven (Steve) Edward SHERLOCK

After serving his apprenticeship with Manchester City, Birmingham born Steve could not find a way past consistent Scottish international full-back Willie Donachie at Maine Road so jumped at the chance to join David Pleat's Luton over the summer of 1978.

Making his debut, along with six others, on the opening day of the 1978-79 campaign Steve had little to do in the Hatters defence as the forwards went rampant, banging in six second half goals against luckless Oldham.

Steve unfortunately lost his place to Mark Aizlewood after the Town's second game, a 1-3 defeat at Crystal Palace, and he eventually joined Stockport the following summer where he became a terrace favourite making nearly 250 League appearances before moving to Cardiff and finally Newport.

Steve still lives in South Wales.

■ Paul SHOWLER

Paul started in football with Altrincham where he combined his part-time playing career with that of a part-time policeman.

A move to the full-time ranks with Barry Fry's Barnet followed for the left sided-midfielder but with cash restraints biting at Underhill, Paul was granted a technical free transfer and was snapped up by Bradford City, where he became a crowd favourite, leading to a £50,000 move to Lennie Lawrences's Luton in 1996.

At Kenilworth Road Paul was initially a regular in the side, well regarded as a maker and taker of goals, but then a series of injuries, some bizarre, led to him making only four appearances in two years.

Given his injury problems it came as no surprise when Paul was appointed physiotherapist at Peterborough.

■ Enoch Olusesan SHOWUNMI

Kilburn born Enoch was playing for Willesden Constantine when he came to Luton on trial. Sadly, as the Hatters were in administrative receivership at the time, they were not able to pay for an addition to the squad leaving Enoch to offer to play for nothing.

When the club's transfer embargo was lifted, Enoch was given a contract and the big and pacy striker soon became a regular name on the Kenilworth Road teamsheet. He scored a hat-trick against Brentford during his first season and then netted some vital late goals, notably at Bristol City and Bournemouth, during the club's promotion season to the Championship in 2004/05.

After becoming known for coming off the bench Enoch decided to seek pastures new and departed for Bristol City in 2006. Enoch signed for Leeds in July 2008.

■ Barry SILKMAN

Much travelled midfielder Barry turned out for ten League clubs in a long career starting at Hereford in 1974 who he joined from then non-League Barnet.

A talented and flamboyant individual, Barry played most of his football in the London area although it was from Plymouth that he came to Luton on loan in February 1979 when Hatters manager David Pleat was looking for recruits to help his injury stricken side. Barry was unstoppable in his first game, a 2-1 home win over Blackburn, but less so in his next two and he left Kenilworth Road for Manchester City soon afterwards.

Barry, by now a greyhound trainer and players agent, became the oldest player to turn out in the FA Cup since the days of Stanley Matthews when he made a cameo appearance for Harrow Borough in 2000, aged 48.

John SIMS

Burly striker John failed to make the grade at his local club Derby but in one of his few appearances for the Rams he came on as substitute in a European Cup tie against Juventus in 1972.

One of the three clubs that John was loaned out to, before moving permanently to Notts County, was Luton in November 1973 where he made a dream home debut scoring a goal in a 2-1 win over Sheffield Wednesday as the Town sought an ultimately successful promotion to the top flight.

After three years at Meadow Lane, John became one of only a handful of players to appear for all three Devon sides, Plymouth, Exeter and Torquay proving an excellent target man at each.

John managed the Gulls briefly before becoming a licensee in Torquay.

Aaron Matthew SKELTON

After working his way up through the ranks at Luton, great things were expected of Aaron but a succession of injuries, including a particularly nasty torn thigh muscle, sidelined him for long periods and meant that Hatters fans were rarely able to see the talented midfielder at his best.

A change of club, a free transfer to Colchester in 1997, saw his luck turn and he became a big favourite at Layer Road but he was quick to move back to Luton four years later on a 'Bosman'.

Sadly, the injury jinx struck again and he made only 17 League appearances in two years back at Kenilworth Road before moving on to Havant & Waterlooville in 2003.

Aaron is currently turning out for Poole in the Western Premier League.

Leslie (Les) Arthur Heber SLATTER

After playing in a Boys Club international trial at Luton in February 1949 the Hatters were quick to sign the ball-playing inside forward leading to a sensational Football League debut as a 17 year old in a 0-0 home draw with Grimsby the following September.

'An old head on young shoulders' said the report at the time but Les did not get any further chances at Kenilworth Road and drifted off to Kettering. After moving to Belfast Crusaders he was invited back to England, with Aston Villa keen on his services.

He did not make a first team appearance at Villa Park and finished his League career at York in 1954/55 before returning to live in Dunstable and turning out for Bedford amongst others.

Les, who still lives in Dunstable in retirement, was playing local football until he suffered a stroke at the age of 56.

Alan Peter SLOUGH

Luton born and bred, Alan had trials for Watford before the Hatters saw sense and in his eight years as a professional at Kenilworth Road he saw the Town rise from Division Four to knocking on the door of Division One.

A cultured but tough tackling midfielder, who also scored his fair share of goals, Alan moved on to Fulham in 1973 when Luton manager Harry Haslam made it clear he wanted his own players in the side. With Fulham, Alan played in the 1975 FA Cup final alongside Bobby Moore before transferring to Peterborough two years later where his main claim to fame was scoring a hat-trick of penalties in an away game at Chester – a Football League record.

Alan joined up with his old school pal Bruce Rioch as a coach at Torquay United and still remains in the area with his own coaching school.

Bryan SMALL

Quick and tenacious full-back Bryan started off as a Youth Trainee at Aston Villa before eventually making his League debut for the Villains at Everton in October 1991 and going on to win 12 England Under-21 caps whilst at Villa Park.

Eventually Bryan found his first team chances dwindling and so transferred to Bolton to help them rise to the Premiership, before finding his appearances limited once more, leading to a three month loan move to injury struck Luton in September 1997 to cover for long term absentee Mitchell Thomas.

Bryan acquitted himself well at Luton with his foraging runs down the left wing but finances dictated that he could not stay. He signed for Bury in January 1998 and finished his career at Stoke.

Bryan still turns out for the Aston Villa Old Boys team.

Michael (Mike) Anthony SMALL

On leaving school Mike signed on for Bromsgrove Rovers and from there was picked up by Luton Town as a 17 year old.

At Kenilworth Road, Mike gained England Youth honours but could only make four substitute appearances for the first team in three seasons so decided to try his luck abroad and played in the Netherlands, Belgium and Greece over the next seven years before coming back to this country and asking for a trial at Brighton.

At the Goldstone, the now experienced striker was a goalscoring sensation which led to a £400,000 move to West Ham in 1991 where he made his debut against the Hatters.

After scoring 13 goals in 20 starts for the Hammers Mike's status began to wane, not helped by a back injury, and it was not long before he was playing non-League football finally ending up at Baldock Town.

Peter Victor SMALL

Compact, strong and pacy winger Peter was recommended to Luton by ace Hatters marksman Hugh Billington after they had served together in the R.A.S.C. during the war.

Peter met with only limited success at Kenilworth Road but did play particularly well during two epic F.A.Cup ties against Leicester in 1949 leading to a move to the Filbert Street club for £6,000 a year later.

After helping the Foxes to Division One, he did the same for Nottingham Forest and made it a triple when he assisted Brighton to the Division Three title in 1958.

Peter joined the Goldstone Ground coaching staff after hanging up his boots and now lives in Elsworth, Cambridgeshire in retirement.

Harold Raymond (Ray) SMITH

Hull born Ray joined his local side from school before signing professional forms in August 1952.

A speedy winger or inside-forward, Ray made only 23 League appearances in four years at Boothferry Park before dropping down to then non-League Peterborough for regular first team football.

At Posh, Ray helped the club to four Midland League titles before the inevitable elevation to the Football League in 1960. He continued to star as Peterborough swept all before them but was then surprisingly transferred to Northampton in 1962 where he was less successful.

His last move was to Luton in October 1963 but he could manage only ten starts in a poor Hatters side. Ray now lives back in Hull in retirement.

Raymond (Ray) Scorer SMITH

With a middle name such as this, Ray could only have been a footballer but perversely only netted once during his Football League career!

After turning out for Evenwood Town, Ray was spotted by Luton and came to Kenilworth Road in 1950. A rugged, tough tackling wing-half, Ray made his League debut at Doncaster in 1951/52 and made his second appearance for the Hatters a year later on the same ground.

After only 12 appearances in seven years, Ray accepted a move to Southend in 1957 where he earned a regular place in the side. A spell at Hastings followed before he hung up his boots.

Ray worked in Luton until retirement and still lives in the town.

Timothy (Tim) Carl SMITH

Spotted by Luton while playing schoolboy football in his home town of Gloucester, Tim signed apprentice forms for the Hatters before being offered a full-time contract in May 1976.

An enthusiastic midfielder, 17 year old Tim won his first taste of League football when coming on as substitute for Ricky Hill during a 1-3 defeat at Hull in August 1976. He did not disgrace himself but had to wait until the opening day of the following season for his second chance, at home to Orient.

The Town were struggling for bodies with several established first teamers still playing in the USA's extended season. This gave Tim his opportunity but when the missing players returned he was relegated back to the reserves.

Tim returned to Gloucester in 1978 and is still living in the city.

Efetobore (Efe) SODJE

Quick and powerful defender Efe first came to prominence at Stevenage before moving to Macclesfield for a fee of £30,000 in 1997. He scored on his debut for his new club, in a game which marked the Silkmen's first in the Football League.

Famous for wearing a bandana bearing the words 'Against All Odds', Nigerian international Efe subsequently turned out for seven League clubs and was on the books of Gillingham in 2007/08.

During his travels around the Football League, Efe joined the Hatters in 1999 but quickly incurred the wrath of manager Lennie Lawrence after failing to keep in touch whilst away with his country for the African Cup of Nations.

Juergen Peterson SOMMER

Son of a former SV Hamburg player, giant goalkeeper Juergen was brought up in the USA before approaching Luton Town for a successful trial in 1991.

After biding his time behind Alec Chamberlain and Andy Petterson, and moving out on loan to Brighton and Torquay, Juergen finally made his Luton debut on the opening day of the 1993/94 campaign. He was then virtually ever present over the next two seasons as well as making his USA international debut, against England, along the way.

With Kelvin Davis waiting in the wings the Hatters felt able to accept a £600,000 bid from Premier League QPR in 1995 and while at Loftus Road he was able to add to his international caps given his higher profile.

After returning to the States in 1998, Juergen played for Columbus Crew and New England Revolution and is now goalkeeping coach for the national team.

■ Hong Ying (Frank) SOO

One of the finest players of his generation Frank, of Chinese extraction, was playing for Prescot Cables when he was snapped up by Stoke who signed him in 1933. Playing alongside the mercurial Stanley Matthews, the ball playing wing-half was on the verge of full international recognition when war broke out.

Throughout the war, Frank was a regular for England in unofficial internationals and guested for a variety of top clubs. When hostilities ceased he signed for Leicester but never settled, leading to Luton paying a record £4,000 for his services in July 1946.

A class act, Frank graced Kenilworth Road for two years before taking up a host of managerial and coaching positions in England, Italy, Sweden and Denmark.

Frank passed away in 1991 aged 76.

■ Leslie (Les) SPENCER

Les was working in a newspaper office in his native Manchester when he pestered one of the sports reporters to get him a trial at Rochdale. After a few reserve outings, Les was plunged into the Rochdale first team and finished up as top scorer in his first full season.

Spotted by Luton scout George Martin when playing for Rochdale at Watford, Les signed on for the Hatters in 1960 in exchange for £4,000.

After a promising start at Kenilworth Road the talented inside-forward suffered a groin injury which was mis-diagnosed leading to septicaemia and 18 months in plaster from neck to ankle and an abrupt end to his playing career.

After a testimonial game, which was the least the Town could do in the circumstances, Les returned to the newspaper office from where he started and still lives in Manchester.

■ Martin Robin SPERRIN

Son of ex-Brentford star Billy, Martin was plying his trade with Edgware Town when Luton scouts invited him and team mate Brian Stein to Kenilworth Road.

A matter of weeks later, inside-forward Martin was appearing at Old Trafford in a League Cup second replay against Manchester City. His League debut came later in that 1977/78 season in a home clash with Sunderland but by that time manager Harry Haslam had been replaced by David Pleat who wanted his own men in the side.

Martin left Luton for Barry Fry's Barnet before working his way through Hertfordshire sides Bishops Stortford, Hertford and Ware.

A resident of Sawbridgeworth, Martin has been running a kitchen showroom for many years and includes Paul Price as one of his satisfied clients!

■ Peter John SPIRING

After joining Bristol City from school, quick and powerful attacking midfielder Peter soon had the scouts flocking to Ashton Gate when he was moved up front and scored five goals in as many games.

This led to a £65,000 move to Bill Shankly's Liverpool in 1973 but the dream turned to disaster when a series of injuries left him waiting for a League start. Luton manager Harry Haslam then rescued him in November 1974, but five games into his Hatters career he broke a toe when winning a penalty against future champions Derby which opened a space in the side for teenager Ron Futcher.

Unable to win back a regular spot in the Luton side, Peter moved to Hereford where he made over 200 League appearances in a long and successful career. Peter still lives in Hereford where he is an electrical contractor.

■ Matthew John SPRING

Matthew joined Luton as a schoolboy and starred for the Hatters in their epic run to the F.A.Youth cup semi-finals in 1997.

It was not long before the talented midfielder made his League debut, coming on as a substitute in a 0-3 defeat at Bristol City in the same year whilst still only seventeen, and soon earning a regular place in the side clocking up his 100th first team appearance while still barely twenty.

Matthew was tempted away from Kenilworth Road in 2004 but his twelve months at Leeds were ruined by injury although a subsequent move to Watford saw him help the Hornets into the Premiership.

Going full circle, Matthew rejoined Luton in January 2007 before moving on to Sheffield United on a year long loan in July 2008.

■ James (Jim) Alfred STANDEN

After joining Arsenal from Rickmansworth Town as a teenager in 1953, Jim had to wait patiently behind the consistent and injury free Welsh international Jack Kelsey in the Gunners goal.

A goalkeeping crisis at Luton led to the athletic shot-stopper moving to Kenilworth Road in 1960 but once England international Ron Baynham was fit again it was back to the reserves once more for a frustrated Jim.

A move to West Ham, again to cover for injury, was more to his liking as this time he kept his place and picked up FA Cup and European Cup-Winners Cup medals during his stay at Upton Park.

An accomplished county cricketer, Jim emigrated to the USA once he quit first-class sport and worked for a Honda car leasing firm in California until retirement.

■ William (Billy) Reid STARK

Scottish centre-forward Billy was one of that rare breed who played for both Glasgow sides, Rangers and Celtic, although his appearances for each were limited to the reserve team. He did, though, boast an excellent strike rate with all his six League clubs, starting with Crewe in 1960, showing pace as well as good heading ability for someone who was not particularly tall.

Billy moved to Luton from Colchester in September 1965 in exchange for Ted Phillips but after nine League appearances and three goals he was surprisingly loaned out to Corby.

He was back in the Football League the following season with Chesterfield before finishing up at Newport a year later.

Billy now lives in Chesterfield and is a retired project manager for an opencast mining company.

■ Alan William STARLING

Although he was born in Barking, goalkeeper Alan was raised in Luton and joined the Hatters from school, signing professional forms in April 1969.

As a 17 year old, Alan was given his League debut on Good Friday 1970 in a home clash with Rotherham, replacing the out of form Sandy Davie, and after a nervous start won the Kenilworth crowd over and kept his place for six games before being injured.

Alan was handed the shirt on the opening day of the following season but was partly at fault for the 0-4 defeat at Bolton and did not appear for the Town again.

This snub did not affect Alan overmuch as he went on to make 350 League appearances for Northampton and Huddersfield and even managed a goal from the penalty spot for the former.

Alan now lives in Mount near Huddersfield.

■ Alan William STEEN

Alan made a scoring debut for Wolves as a 16 year old in 1939 and was looked on as one for the future but the outbreak of war obviously halted his progress.

Reported as missing during the war, after a bombing raid over Germany in 1943, it subsequently transpired that he had been captured and had spent the rest of the hostilities as a POW.

A speedy winger, Alan signed for Luton in exchange for a 'four figure fee' in 1946 and played ten of the first eleven games of 1946/47 on the wing for the Hatters before losing his place to new signing Dally Duncan.

Alan later went on to give good service to Aldershot, Rochdale and Carlisle and now lives on the Wirral in retirement.

■ Brian STEIN

One of Luton Town's favourite sons, Brian is second only to Gordon Turner in the post-war scoring charts and formed magical partnerships with the likes of Bob Hatton and Mick Harford during his long stay at Kenilworth Road.

Born in South Africa in 1957, Brian was brought to England as a seven year old when his family fled the apartheid regime and was playing for Edgware from where he was recommended to the Hatters in 1977.

Possibly the best finisher the club has ever seen, Brian helped the Town to the top flight in 1982, picked up an England cap and scored twice in the magical Littlewoods Cup final win over Arsenal in 1988.

Surprisingly allowed to move to France that summer, Brian did return to Luton in 1991 before finishing his first class playing career at Barnet.

Brian left Kenilworth Road in the summer of 2007 for the third time after a spell as Mike Newell's assistant.

■ Earl Mark (Mark) Sean STEIN

Brian's younger brother Mark joined Luton as a junior before signing professional forms in January 1984.

After making his Hatters debut in 1984, Mark had to wait until the 1986/87 campaign before earning a regular place in the side when he showed speed off the mark, excellent ball control and an eye for goal.

A bid of £300,000 from QPR in 1988 was too good to turn down and the tiny striker than began a tour around the country taking in spells at Oxford, Stoke, Chelsea, Ipswich and Bournemouth scoring regularly wherever he went before returning to Kenilworth Road in 2000.

The Town turned out to be his last League club and after studying for the necessary qualifications, Mark is now physiotherapist at Barnet.

■ Kirk William STEPHENS

Following four years on the books of his local side Coventry as a schoolboy, Kirk was told he was not good enough and joined non-League side Nuneaton who were then managed by David Pleat.

When Pleat took over the hot seat at Luton one of his first signings was all-action overlapping full-back Kirk, who was soon nicknamed 'Basher' by the Kenilworth Road faithful.

After making his League debut on the opening day of the 1978/79 campaign, Kirk was virtually ever present over the next six seasons before returning to his first love Coventry and then having to quit the game through injury two years later.

Kirk still lives in Nuneaton working in the family business and also helps on Coventry City match day radio.

■ Danny Robert STEVENS

Enfield born Danny joined Tottenham as a trainee from school but failed to make the grade at White Hart Lane and was glad to accept an offer from Luton to move to Kenilworth Road in March 2005.

Only 5'4", Danny makes up for his lack of height with excellent ball control, speed and no little bravery and after some excellent displays in midfield for the Luton reserve team he was handed his League debut, coming on as substitute at Burnley in the final game of the 2005/06 season.

Sadly, Danny was not given any further chances for the Hatters and joined Torquay in the summer of 2007 where he was hoping to help his new side to promotion back to the Football League.

■ Morris John STEVENSON

When Luton Town entertained Morton in a friendly in October 1968 it transpired that all the Scottish team members were in the shop window. The Hatters were impressed with inside-forward Morris leading to him signing for £5,000 a month later.

Morris made his League debut in a 0-1 defeat at Hartlepool in December 1968 but the following week manager Allan Brown was dismissed with the new man at the helm, Alec Stock, wanting his own men at the club.

Morris remained at Kenilworth Road as a squad player until 1970 when he joined Dundee United. He enjoyed three years at Tannadice before ligament damage left him on crutches for nine months and with it the end of his playing career.

After working as a driver for a Tranent, East Lothian candle firm for 30 years, Morris took early retirement in 2006 due to ill health.

■ Jude Barrington STIRLING

After joining Luton from school, Jude signed professional forms for the Hatters in July 1999.

A tall central defender or defensive midfielder, with a huge long throw, Jude was unfortunate to be dismissed on his League debut at Swansea in September 2000 but went on to make a further eight appearances that season as the Hatters were relegated to the football basement.

When it became obvious that new manager Joe Kinnear wanted a complete shake up of playing personnel at Kenilworth Road, Jude joined Stevenage in February 2002 and then went on to play for several non-League clubs before re-entering the Football League with Oxford and subsequently Lincoln and Peterborough.

Jude is now a mainstay in the MK Dons defence.

■ George Campbell STOBBART

Strong, stocky striker George joined Middlesbrough from Netherton in 1939

and banged in a remarkable 125 goals in 168 games for Boro during the war years.

In peacetime, George moved to Newcastle for £4,650 in 1946 and assisted the Magpies to promotion to the top flight two years later before Luton broke their transfer record to take him to Kenilworth Road for £11,500 in October 1949.

A month after joining the Hatters he scored four goals in eight minutes during a 5-2 home win over Blackburn. His experience then helped the Town get through a couple of sticky seasons as they built for the future.

Job done, George transferred to Millwall in 1952 before moving across London to Brentford two years later. He finished his playing career at Bedford before going back to Newcastle where he lived until passing away in 1995.

■ Peter James STONE

Peter was almost 30 when he was thrust in to the Luton Town first team for his one and only Football League appearance in February 1952.

Signed as an amateur for the Hatters from Oxford City, Peter made several impressive appearances for the reserve side before being given the opportunity at centre-half replacing the injured Syd Owen in a home Division Two clash with Hull which finished 1-1.

With Owen fit to return the following week it was back to the reserves for Peter who eventually moved on to Worcester and then back to Oxford City.

Peter lives in Oxford in retirement.

■ Kevin STREET

Crewe born Kevin joined his local side from school and worked his way up through Dario Gradi's academy at Gresty Road before making his League debut during the 1997/98 campaign.

A hard working, attacking right-sided midfielder, Kevin became a valuable squad player but when he found first team starts drying up he accepted a loan move to Joe Kinnear's Luton in 2001.

At Kenilworth Road, Kevin was injured in his first full game, a 1-4 defeat at Macclesfield, and so returned to Crewe before joining non-League Northwich Victoria

and then bouncing back to turn out for Bristol Rovers and finally Shrewsbury.

Kevin is now on the books of Altrincham and combines football with studying for a degree in Theology, with a view to becoming a priest in the future.

Bernard Reginald STRETEN

Before becoming one of the all-time favourites at Kenilworth Road, Bernard was a well regarded amateur international goalkeeper plying his trade with Shrewsbury. He was enticed to Luton by an old team-mate, Frank Soo, in 1947 and was soon the Hatters first choice.

Although not very tall, Bernard made up for his lack of inches with agility and bravery as well as a certain amount of showmanship and went on to make 276 League appearances at a time when the Town boasted Welsh international Iorwerth Hughes and fellow England international Ron Baynham as goalkeeping opponents.

After retiring from the game in 1957, and taking over a business in Mundesley, Bernard was tempted back between the posts by Kings Lynn!

A publican in Bacton in later life, Bernard passed away in Norwich in 1994.

Stephen (Steve) John SUTTON

Goalkeeper Steve began his career at Nottingham Forest, working his way up to become understudy to Peter Shilton. After Shilton left, Steve eventually made the position his own and was a regular for five years, a period at the City Ground that took in two League Cup final wins, one of which was against the Hatters in 1989.

On losing his place to Mark Crossley, Steve went out on loan and in a short spell at Luton in 1992 he was inspirational.

Sadly the Hatters, who were struggling against relegation from the top flight, could not afford to sign him permanently and the superb shot-stopper went to Derby instead.

After spells at Reading, Birmingham, Notts County and Grantham, Steve went back to Forest in 2006, joining the coaching staff.

Ronald (Ron) McDonald SWAN

Scotsman Ron began his football career as a centre-half and during his four years with East Stirling also turned out at centre-forward, scoring twice against Dundee. He was in goal, though, when East Stirling won promotion to Division One in 1963.

Signed by Oldham a year later, Ron enjoyed a couple of good seasons at Boundary Park before losing his place in the 1966/67 campaign. The call from new Luton manager Allan Brown in January 1967 therefore came as a relief but soon turned out to be a disaster as the Hatters were enduring the worst season in their history.

Ron managed 14 consecutive Division Four League games before handing the shirt back to Tony Read.

After many years in the Greater Manchester Police, Ron retired in 1999 and is now a security man on the Oldham Athletic players' tunnel.

Andrew (Drew) TALBOT

Barnsley born Drew signed on with his local club from school but drifted out of the game after a succession of injuries. He came back into professional football, joining Sheffield Wednesday's academy in 2003, before making an impact in the Owls promotion winning side in 2004/05 and scoring in the play-off final win over Hartlepool.

A bad back injury ruled him out of contention for twelve months at Hillsborough and then when fit he moved to Scunthorpe on loan before signing a £250,000 deal with Luton in January 2007.

Drew certainly made his mark at Kenilworth Road when he scored on his home debut against his old side Sheffield Wednesday!

Arthur Alexander TAYLOR

Rarely can a player have made such an impact on his first-team debut as Arthur, who netted in the first minute of an F.A.Cup Third Round tie for the Hatters against Blackburn in January 1953 and scored again a few minutes later in an eventual 5-1 romp.

Poached from Glentoran as a teenager by the Town, Arthur was made to bide his time in the reserve side, playing mainly on the wing, before his amazing debut. Arthur was used again in the Hatters' Division Two side the week after the cup-tie but then had to wait until the start of the following campaign for his next chance.

After only five League games in three seasons Arthur was surprisingly handed the number 11 shirt as the Town entered Division One in 1955 but after only three starts he was not given a further opportunity and returned to his home city of Belfast where he still lives.

John (Jack) Ephraim TAYLOR

Spotted by Luton scout Dick Trembath while playing for Stockton, Hatters officials needed to move quickly, and pay £2,100, to secure the services of the powerful inside-forward in February 1949.

After scoring on his League debut for the Town during a 6-0 hammering of Lincoln, two months after moving to Kenilworth Road, Jack did not seem to make the required progress over the next couple of seasons although a succession of injuries did not help.

In 1951/52, though, he banged in 20 League goals, won an England 'B' cap, and was then sensationally transferred to Wolves for £16,000 where he was disappointed to become merely an understudy.

Jack finished his career with spells at Notts County and Bradford PA before looking after his General Stores in Beechwood Road and breeding poodles for display. Jack sadly passed away whilst still in his 40's.

John Patrick TAYLOR

After being made surplus to requirements at first club Colchester, John worked as a shipping clerk while playing part-time for Sudbury. Spotted by Cambridge United's Gary Johnson he went back into the Football League in 1988 and was a member of John Beck's successful 'U's side where he formed part of a powerful spearhead with Dion Dublin.

Surprisingly transferred to Bristol Rovers in 1992, John continued to bang in the goals leading to a £300,000 move to Bradford City followed by a £200,000 transfer to Luton in 1995. Sadly, a back injury cut short his appearances at Kenilworth Road just as he seemed to be setting up a good understanding with Dwight Marshall.

John went back to Cambridge where he achieved 'Legend' status before becoming manager at the Abbey for two years.

Bad back or not, John was still playing for Mildenhall Town at 43 in 2007/08!

Matthew Simon TAYLOR

Rejected by his home town club Oxford United, Matthew joined Luton as a Youth Trainee before making his League debut for the Hatters on the opening day of the 1999/00 season at Notts County.

With the Town in receivership at the time, promising young talent needed to be pitched in perhaps before they were ready but 17 year old Matthew looked like he had been playing in the first-team for years such was his maturity.

A left sided midfielder or attacking full-back Matthew possessed both pace and a fierce shot and quickly picked up a host of 'Player of the Year' awards at Kenilworth Road. After helping the Hatters to promotion in 2002 it came as no real surprise when Portsmouth stepped in with a bid and the England Under-21 international began parading his talents at Premiership level. Matthew joined Bolton in 2007/08.

Steven (Steve) John TAYLOR

Born in Royton, hard-running and strong forward Steve played for a host of League clubs in the Greater Manchester area, netting regularly for each, but he was unable to reproduce his goalscoring abilities whenever he moved south.

With Luton struggling with major injury problems in January 1979, Steve was brought to Kenilworth Road by Hatters manager David Pleat for £50,000 on the back of previous performances against the Town while he was with Bolton and Oldham.

Steve sadly failed to settle, managing only one goal in 20 appearances, before becoming part of the deal that brought Mike Saxby to Luton from Mansfield. He was not a success at Field Mill either, but later spells at Burnley and Rochdale saw him back to his predatory best.

Steve later managed Mossley and was on the coaching staff at Oldham.

William (Billy) Donnachie TAYLOR

Billy started out his goalkeeping career with St Johnstone in 1958 and won a Scottish Second Division championship medal with them in 1963. Two years later he won another Second Division medal, this time with Stirling Albion, before joining Partick Thistle.

Luton manager Allan Brown was desperate to sign another goalkeeper, preferably Scottish, to provide competition for Tony Read and with Taylor out of favour at Partick following an injury, the big shot-stopper signed for the Hatters in December 1967.

An injury to Read gave Taylor an immediate chance in the Town's Division Four side but he was never able to win a permanent place in the team and after six appearances in two years he joined Epping Town.

Billy worked at Luton Airport for many years until retirement.

Matthew (Matt) TEES

Matt Tees did not look like a 'goal machine', as he was called on the terraces, being slight and not particularly tall but he was tremendously brave, very strong and phenomenal in the air.

Joining Grimsby from Airdrie in 1963, Matt soon formed a prolific partnership with future Hatter Rodney Green leading to the pair of them moving to Charlton for a joint fee of £23,000 in 1967.

Luton manager Alec Stock, looking for a partner for his young striker Malcolm Macdonald, managed to prise Matt from Charlton for £25,000 in 1969 and he proved a wonderful tutor as well as weighing in with his share of goals as the Town won promotion from Division Three in 1970.

Job done, Matt moved back to Grimsby, where he had earned legend status, to finish his playing career and he still lives in the area in retirement.

Paul Norman TELFER

Paul came to Luton Town as a Youth Trainee in 1988, along with his Edinburgh youth club playing colleague Darren Salton, before signing professional forms in November of that year.

A genuine utility player, Paul made his League debut for the Hatters in a 0-1 defeat at Everton in May 1991 and soon made a first team spot his own, usually playing on the right side of midfield and regularly getting on the goalscoring charts.

It was with great regret that the Town sold the remarkably consistent and popular performer to Coventry for £1.5 million in 1995 and since that time the Scottish international has continued to play top flight football in England and Scotland until 2007/08 when he signed on for Bournemouth. Paul is now on non-contract terms with Leeds.

■ Anthony (Tony) Charles THEAR

After failing to make the grade at Arsenal, the Edmonton born striker was snapped up by Fourth Division Luton in 1966 as a hoped for replacement for the recently departed John O'Rourke.

Tony burst on the Kenilworth Road scene in remarkable fashion scoring twice on his full League debut during a 4-0 win over Aldershot in September 1966 and followed it up with another pair in his next game when Rochdale were seen off 3-1.

Sadly that was as good as it got for Tony who scored only once more before losing his place in the aftermath of the horrendous 1-8 thrashing at Lincoln in December 1966. New manager Allan Brown then brought in ex-England international Derek Kevan and allowed Tony to move on to Gillingham in February 1967.

Finding it tough at Priestfield, Tony moved on to Bedford and Folkestone before becoming player-manager of Dunstable. Tony now lives in Ascot.

■ Mitchell Anthony THOMAS

Local boy Mitchell joined Luton Town from school and made his League debut at 18 in a 3-2 win at West Ham in December 1982. Upon earning a regular place in the Hatters top flight side during the following campaign the tall and elegant full back was looked on as a future England international and his standing was enhanced further when Steve Foster joined the Town and bullied him into even greater efforts.

Mitchell controversially left Luton in 1986 to join ex-manager David Pleat at Tottenham but came back to Kenilworth Road seven years later, via West Ham, this time in the Foster role!

After finishing his first class career at Burnley, Mitchell became a players agent.

■ Alan THOMPSON

Although born in Goole, Alan was brought up in Luton and came to the attention of the Hatters when starring for West Park Juniors, a local youth side.

Initially signing on for the Town as an amateur, Alan eventually signed professional forms in December 1949 but two years on National Service, a broken leg and severe competition for places meant that the quick-tackling full-back had to wait until March 1957 before making his League bow.

Playing at left back in a 0-2 defeat at Preston turned out to be Alan's only first team game and he joined Bedford in July 1957 before working for many years at Whitbread.

■ Steven (Steve) Anthony THOMPSON

Following ten years at Bolton, who at the time yo-yoed between Divisions Three and Four, cultured midfielder Steve probably thought that his chances of playing in the top flight had passed him by until Luton manager David Pleat stepped in with a bid of £180,000 in August 1991.

It soon became apparent that he lacked pace at the top level, and so after five games Steve was swiftly off-loaded to Leicester in exchange for Des Linton and Scott Oakes. At Filbert Street Steve helped the Foxes to three successive play-offs with the third successful, at which time he moved on to Burnley!

Steve finished his playing career with spells at Rotherham and Halifax.

■ Peter David THOMSON

Rejected by his home town club Bury, tall striker Peter drifted into non-League football with Chorley and then Lancaster before a bizarre £25,000 move to Dutch club NAC Breda.

He got over a broken leg to score goals in the Dutch Eredivisie before Luton manager Ricky Hill paid £100,000 for his services in September 2000. Playing in a poor Hatters side, Peter sadly did not look the part and his only League goals for the club came in a shock 3-1 victory at Stoke in December 2000.

After being sent out on loan to Rushden, new Luton boss Joe Kinnear allowed him to leave and he later turned out for Southport and Altrincham. Peter is currently with FC United of Manchester.

■ Robert (Bobby) THOMSON

Menstrie born Bobby started his playing career with Partick Thistle before winning a dream move to Bill Shankly's Liverpool in December 1962.

A teak tough full-back, Bobby made only six Division One appearances for the Anfield club so was glad to accept a move to Luton in August 1965 to gain regular first-team football.

The Hatters had been relegated to Division Four that summer but made a brave, albeit ultimately unsuccessful, bid for immediate promotion aided by the uncompromising right-back play of Bobby.

Season 1966/67 proved to be the Town's worst in their history and although Bobby performed well he became part of the major cull at the club in the summer of 1967 and emigrated to Australia where he still lives in retirement.

■ Robert (Bobby) Anthony THOMSON

Classy full-back Bobby joined Wolves from school in 1961 and went on to make 278 League appearances at Molineux in a long career as well as pick up a host of representative honours including eight caps for England.

Bobby moved on a £40,000 transfer to Birmingham in 1969 but within two years was a forgotten man in Blues reserves until he was rescued by Luton manager Harry Haslam in 1972.

Enjoying a new lease of life, Bobby was ever-present during his first two seasons at Kenilworth Road as an overlapping left back, during which time the Hatters won promotion to the top flight and it was only the increasingly loud claims from the talented Steve Buckley that eventually saw him lose his place.

After leaving Luton, Bobby had some success in the USA, was player manager of Stafford Rangers and ran a sports shop in Sedgley

■ Anthony (Tony) Lee THORPE

A Youth Trainee at his local club Leicester, Tony was picked up by Hatters manager David Pleat in 1992 having remembered him from his days at Filbert Street.

He had to bide his time at Luton before coming on during a 6-2 home win over Stoke in November 1993, but hit the headlines when scoring at Premiership Newcastle in the FA Cup two months later.

A natural goalscorer with quick feet, Tony came to the fore when netting 28 goals in 1996/97 and it was no surprise when he moved to Fulham for £800,000 in February 1998. He lasted four months at Craven Cottage before a £1 million move to Bristol City where he was in and out of favour. He enjoyed two loan spells back at Luton before re-signing in 2002 and leaving again in controversial circumstances a year later to join QPR.

■ Colin TINSLEY

Born at Redcar, Colin was an amateur goalkeeper for Redcar Boys Club, and an apprentice bricklayer, when he was picked up by Grimsby in 1954. Although initially deemed too lightweight for Football League goalkeeping duties, two years of National Service bulked him up and after rejecting a new contract at Blundell Park he became a regular at Darlington before accepting a move to Exeter in 1961.

Colin came to Kenilworth Road in 1963 as understudy to Ron Baynham, and when the England international retired he became a mainstay in a poor Hatters side with a succession of brave performances.

After leaving in 1966, Colin played at Kettering for a season but came back to Luton on a short term contract in 1967 for a swansong performance at Southend in an emergency.

Colin still lives in Dunstable after retiring from Tarmac.

■ Colin TODD

A magnificent central defender or defensive midfield player, Colin was lighting quick with a cool football brain and after first catching the eye with Sunderland moved to Derby for a massive £170,000 in 1971.

A regular in the Rams side that won the Division One championship in 1972 and 1975, Colin was surprisingly sold to Everton in 1978 before helping Birmingham into the top flight and Oxford out of Division Three.

The England international had been out of the UK for a year, playing in Canada, when Luton manager David Pleat invited him to help his inexperienced and injury hit side in October 1984. Sadly, he only lasted two games before an injury effectively put paid to his playing career.

Colin later managed Middlesbrough, Bolton and Derby amongst others and is currently in the hot seat at Randers FC in the Danish Superliga..

■ Graeme Murdoch TOMLINSON

A Youth Trainee at Bradford City, Watford born Graham burst onto the scene in 1993/94 scoring six goals in only two months leading to a dream £100,000 move to Manchester United.

At Old Trafford, he was limited to a couple of League Cup appearances and was allowed out on loan to relegation threatened Luton in March 1996. A quick and clever striker Graeme was initially used as a substitute at Kenilworth Road but on his full Hatters debut, at Port Vale, he badly broke a leg.

Taking a long time to get over the injury, Graeme was eventually released by Manchester United and moved to firstly Macclesfield and then Exeter before hanging up his boots to become an Estate Agent.

■ Michael (Mike) George TRACEY

A qualified solicitor, Mike was playing amateur football for Crook Town, with whom he earned an Amateur Cup winners medal, when he was persuaded to turn full-time with Luton in November 1959.

After getting used to the training, Mike made his debut at centre-forward during a home defeat at the hands of Sheffield Wednesday in February 1960 but the rest of his Hatters appearances were in his favoured position on the wing.

After failing to become a regular at Kenilworth Road, Mike moved to Lincoln before turning out for Worksop and Grantham whilst practising once more as a solicitor.

Mike became a partner in a Lincoln firm of solicitors before retiring to a farm in Ireland.

■ Christopher (Chris) James TURNER

Uncompromising centre-half Chris had made over 300 League appearances for Peterborough when Luton manager David Pleat, building his first Hatters side, talked him into moving to Kenilworth Road.

Doubtless a quality defender, Chris soon made it known that he hankered after a return to the New England Teamen in the USA, where he had been playing the previous summer, and a reluctant Pleat let him go after only 30 League games for the Town.

After getting the USA out of his system, Chris turned out for Cambridge and Southend before moving back to Cambridge United as manager where he built up the squad that would be so successful under John Beck.

Chris later managed and then owned Peterborough and has recently been seen taking up a temporary coaching role at Cambridge United.

■ Gordon Reginald TURNER

The Hatter's all-time record goalscorer, with 243 to his credit, was seeing out his National Service in the Navy when he was recommended to Luton manager Dally Duncan by two Lutonian Petty Officers.

Gordon had to wait until 1950/51 before making his League debut and after being mentored by the wily centre-forward Jesse Pye, Gordon struck out on his own in 1954/55 and top scored as the Hatters won promotion to Division One for the first time.

A dead shot and ice cool, Gordon regularly topped 30 goals in the top flight and it was criminal that he was never capped.

After leaving Luton, his only League club, in 1964, Gordon had spells at Wisbech and Kettering before concentrating on the sports shop he owned with another ex-Hatter Wally Shanks.

Gordon tragically died in 1976 at 46 after suffering from Motor Neurone disease.

■ Wayne Leslie TURNER

Luton born Wayne signed on for the Hatters in April 1978 before making his League debut a year later at Wrexham.

A ball winning midfielder, Wayne never won a regular spot in the Hatters side, much to his disappointment, as he always gave 100% effort.

The signing of Peter Nicholas was the final straw and Wayne accepted a move to Coventry in 1985 where he was immediately made captain. Injuries cut back his appearances at Highfield Road and he moved on to Brentford where he was again in the wars.

A move to Conference side Barnet was more to his liking and after four years there he took up a coaching role at Underhill followed by a long stint on the coaching staff back at Luton.

After leaving Kenilworth Road, Wayne later managed Stevenage before focussing his attentions on his property business.

■ Paul Victor UNDERWOOD

Paul started out at Enfield before joining Rushden and Diamonds, then also non-League, for £50,000 in 1997.

This marked the start of an amazing six years at Nene Park with Paul, initially playing as a winger before moving to left-back, skippering the side into the Football League and then overseeing promotion to Division Two.

Cash problems at Rushden saw Paul sign for Luton on a free-transfer in March 2004 but as he suffered a hamstring injury on his Hatters debut it was not until the following campaign that Town fans saw the best of him. Forming a formidable left-sided partnership with Sol Davis, Paul helped the Hatters to promotion from League One in 2005 and then settled effortlessly into the Championship.

Sadly, Paul has not played a League game for Luton since March 2006 due to a series of injuries followed by serious illness.

■ Matthew James UPSON

After being rejected by both Norwich and Ipswich as a boy, Matthew was taken on at Luton who he skippered to the semi-finals of the F.A.Youth cup.

After only one substitute appearance in the Football League for the Hatters the composed central defender was snapped up by Arsenal in May 1997 for an eventual £2 million as 'one for the future'.

Sadly, Matthew's Highbury stay was beset with major injury problems and he decided to make a big money move to Birmingham in 2003 in order to resurrect his career in the Premiership.

Matthew is now at West Ham after a £6 million move in January 2007, is back to his best, and tipped to add to his England caps.

■ Jean-Louis VALOIS

After beginning his professional career at Auxerre, Jean-Louis moved on to Gueugnon and then Lille before making an unexpected diversion to Joe Kinnear's Luton in September 2001.

Rarely can a player have made such an impact on his debut with the Frenchman tearing poor Torquay apart and capping a virtuoso performance with a wonder goal in a 5-1 home win.

Although the hustle and bustle of Division Three football sometimes passed him by, on his day Jean-Louis could win a game on his own and it was sad when, after helping the Hatters to promotion, a dispute with Joe Kinnear saw him move to Hearts.

After wowing the Tynecastle crowd in his early days, Jean-Louis moved on Almeria in Spain before returning to Scotland with Clyde and then playing for Burnley in the Championship.

Jean-Louis was last at United Arab Emirates side Al-Khaleej.

■ Imre VARADI

The product of a Hungarian refugee father and an Italian mother, Imre was born in Paddington but brought up in a charitable institution. Turned down by various League clubs, he joined Letchworth and was training at Luton two evenings a week when he was invited to Sheffield United by ex-Hatters manager Harry Haslam.

This was the start of a long footballing career that took the quick and deadly striker to 12 Football League clubs and seven non-League before he finally finished playing just short of his 40th birthday.

Scoring goals wherever he went, Imre had a brief spell on loan at David Pleat's Luton in March 1992 and scored on his debut in a 2-1 home win over Wimbledon.

Imre now lives in Sheffield and is a players agent.

■ Johnny Pederson VILSTRUP

Johnny had played 150 games for Danish top division side Lyngby, helping them to two titles, when Luton manager Terry Westley was alerted to his availability.

Despite competition from Premiership clubs, Westley got his man for £205,000 in September 1995. A goalscoring midfielder with the reputation of having the hardest shot in Danish football, Johnny failed to enhance his reputation at Kenilworth Road, albeit in a poor Luton side destined for relegation.

A change of manager saw him out of favour and after six months he was back in Denmark with AGF of Aarhus, initially on loan, who he immediately helped to the Danish Cup final earning rave reviews along the way!

Johnny now owns a massage and acupuncture clinic in Copenhagen.

■ Rowan Lewis VINE

Born in Basingstoke, Rowan joined Portsmouth from school but found it hard to win a regular place at Fratton Park leading to season long loans at Brentford and Colchester before moving to Luton on a similar basis in August 2004.

Virtually ever present as the Hatters won the championship of League One in 2004/05 the fleet footed and unselfish striker weighed in with some vital goals leading to him signing permanently.

When his strike partner Steve Howard was sold in 2006, Rowan blossomed as a striker in his own right which alerted scouts and led to the inevitable big bid from Birmingham in January 2007 which was accepted much to the disappointment of the Luton supporters.

Rowan is now with QPR, following his recent move to West London, and is recovering from a broken leg.

■ Gary Patrick WADDOCK

After joining QPR as an apprentice defensive midfielder Gary made over 200 League appearances for the West London club, becoming a crowd favourite for his hard work and tough tackling.

It all came to a grinding halt in November 1985 when Gary received a career threatening injury leading to an insurance pay-out. Gary refused to accept the medical diagnosis and fought back to fitness although he had to play his football for Charleroi in Belgium while the insurance problem was sorted out.

Back in this country, Gary enjoyed spells at Millwall and Bristol Rovers before joining Luton in September 1994 and eventually becoming club captain following many superb displays leading by example.

When Gary eventually retired he returned to QPR as academy coach which led to him taking over the manager's job in 2006. Gary is now in charge at Aldershot.

■ Robin Keith WAINWRIGHT

Local boy Robin signed for Luton as a professional in December 1968 having joined the apprentice ranks a year before.

A skilful midfielder with a languid style, Robin made his League debut while on loan at Cambridge in March 1971 and had to wait until the following campaign before making his first start for the Hatters in a home clash with Preston in Division Two.

Robin went on to make 16 appearances that season but found himself out of favour under new manager Harry Haslam and so moved to Millwall, where he was again in the reserves, and finally to Northampton.

After finishing with League football, Robin played for John Moore's Dunstable and Barry Fry's Hillingdon before spending many years at Wealdstone who awarded him a testimonial against Luton in 1985.

Robin works for Active Luton.

■ Harold (Harry) Bertram WALDEN

Fast and clever winger Harry came to the attention of Luton when he was starring for Southern League Kettering Town.

After signing for the Hatters in January 1961 he was thrust into the first team almost immediately but an elbow injury cut back his appearances that season. Harry was back with a bang in 1961/62 and was regarded as the Town's regular right winger with this form following into the next campaign when many said that a bad injury suffered in March 1963 was a major contributing factor to the Hatter's relegation from Division Two.

Harry moved on to Northampton in 1964 in exchange for Billy Hails plus £3,000 and helped the Cobblers into the top flight a year later. After finishing his career back at Kettering, Harry, who still has an unofficial fan club at Kenilworth Road, became a school caretaker in Northampton.

■ Dennis George WALKER

Spennymoor born Dennis was picked up by West Ham as a youngster and after serving his apprenticeship signed professional forms in May 1966.

After failing to make the breakthrough at Upton Park, Dennis was released a year later and signed a short term contract at Luton just as the Hatters were about to embark on their record breaking Division Four championship winning campaign.

Dennis' twelve minutes of fame came during the Town's first home game of the season, against Barnsley, when he replaced injured full-back Fred Jardine, but he was not tested as the Hatters ran out comfortable winners.

Dennis moved on to Stevenage Town, Cambridge City, Dunstable, Corby and Lockheed Leamington in a long career in non-League and was, for a time, manager of Rothwell Town.

■ William Horace (Horace) WALLBANKS

Horace came from a footballing family with four of his brothers turning out in the Football League at one time or another.

Starting off his own career with Northfleet, the Tottenham nursery team, he moved on to Carlisle as war broke out and then guested for Aberdeen, Luton and Grimsby before signing permanently for the Mariners in 1946.

In need of a right winger, Luton remembered their war-time guest player and signed Horace in May 1947 just in time for him to play, and score, in the final day 6-3 win over Newport.

Horace could not repeat that feat and made only three League appearances in 1947/48 before signing for Weymouth. Horace finished his career at Bedford and then settled in Hull.

■ Paul Anthony WALSH

Plumstead born Paul joined Charlton from school and was only 17 when he became the youngest player to net a hat-trick for the Addicks in a senior game.

Hard-up Charlton were forced to accept a £250,000 bid, plus Steve White, from top flight new boys Luton in 1982 and the seriously talented forward soon became a terrace hero at Kenilworth Road with his twisting runs, close control and goalscoring ability.

Sadly, a bid of £700,000 from Liverpool was accepted for the, by now, England international in 1984 and he went on to grace Anfield for almost four years during which time he picked up a League championship medal. Moving on to Tottenham where he won an FA Cup winners medal, he then signed twice for Portsmouth with a spell at Manchester City sandwiched in between.

Paul's playing career ended with a knee injury in 1996 and he is now a pundit on Sky TV.

■ Peter WALSH

Signed by Luton from Dundalk in August 1949, after appearing against the Hatters in a friendly the previous year, Peter came to Kenilworth Road with a sound reputation as a centre-forward who knew where the goal was.

After being carefully nurtured in the Hatter's reserve side, Dublin born Peter made a dream League debut, alongside another debutant George Stobbart, when he scored the only goal of the game in a Division Two home clash with Leicester in October 1949.

Keeping his place, the quick striker seemed set fair for a long Luton career but lost his position following a 0-3 home defeat at the hands of Hull six weeks later.

At the end of that season Peter drifted off to Brighton, where he failed to win a first team spot, before finishing his career at Hastings United and then returning to his home city of Dublin where he died in 2007.

■ Scott WARD

Harrow born Scott came up through the ranks at Luton before signing professional forms in October 1998 and becoming highly regarded at Kenilworth Road as a goalkeeper of promise.

Scott enjoyed a remarkable introduction to League football when coming off the substitute's bench after Mark Ovendale had received a red card at Brentford in May 2001. His first job was to face a penalty from the Bees' Lloyd Owusu which he turned round the post before acquitting himself well in an eventual 2-2 draw.

Sadly, Hatters manager Joe Kinnear preferred to use the more experienced Ovendale and Carl Emberson between the sticks the following season leaving no chance for the frustrated Scott who departed from Luton in 2002.

Scott was last playing for London Colney.

■ John WARNER

Another player who made only a single appearance for the Hatters, Ashington born but Hemel Hempstead raised John made a meteoric rise from the club's fourth team to making his League debut in a Division One clash at home to Burnley in October 1959.

A part-time professional, John had been pushed into a friendly match against Banik Ostrava at Kenilworth Road earlier that season and had starred on the left wing. This gave rise to his elevation to the League eleven but the occasion was a little too much for him and he was not given another opportunity.

After leaving Luton, John had spells at Yiewsley and Amersham before returning to Hemel Hempstead where he lived until recently.

■ Charles (Charlie) WATKINS

Charlie made his name at Glasgow Rangers in war-time football but after the end of hostilities found that he was often marginalised at Ibrox due the huge professional playing staff there at the time.

Following the advice of old playing colleague Billy Arnison, Charlie accepted a move to Luton in 1948 and there began a love affair with the town which never waned apart from a five year spell in South Africa in the late 1950's where he went as a coach.

A clever and skilful wing-half or inside-forward, Charlie made over 200 League appearances for the Hatters and signed off with two goals against Bristol Rovers in 1955 which virtually assured promotion to the top flight.

Charlie held a physiotherapist and chiropodist practice in the town for many years, came back to Kenilworth Road as a coach under George Martin and was still playing football for the local Round Table well into his 60's.

Charlie sadly passed away in 1998.

■ Julian WATTS

Tall and mobile central defender Julian had played only a handful of games for Rotherham when he was snapped up by Sheffield Wednesday in 1992 for £130,000.

Julian found it tough to break through at Hillsborough, but it was still a surprise when he moved to Leicester in 1996 and the Owls fans were proved right when he helped his new club to promotion to the top flight.

After moving on to Bristol City in 1998, Julian came to Luton a year later and was virtually ever present for 18 months until falling out with new manager Joe Kinnear and deciding on a fresh start with Northern Spirit in Sydney. After returning to these shores in 2004 Julian has set up a business in Worksop.

■ Mark Robert WATTS

After several brilliant displays on the wing for Luton reserves, Welham Green born Mark was suddenly thrust into the Hatters first team in a home FA Cup Third Round clash with Peterborough in January 1983, replacing the injured David Moss.

With Moss still injured the teenager, who had come up through the ranks at Kenilworth Road, did enough to keep his place the following week for the visit of Tottenham in a top flight League fixture.

The return of Argentine maestro Ossie Ardiles to the Spurs line-up for the first time since the end of the Falklands war swelled the gate to 21,231, a figure never subsequently bettered at Kenilworth Road, and in this tense atmosphere Mark set up the Luton goal in a 1-1 draw.

Surprisingly, Mark was never given another first team chance and he is now living in Cheshunt and works in London as a market trader in fruit and vegetables.

■ William (Billy) Lindsay WAUGH

Stationed at Bicester during the war, Billy was alerted to Luton officials by his father leading to him signing for the Town in 1944.

A super-fast winger, Billy was nicknamed 'Rabbit' by the Hatter's fans and although not a prolific goalscorer, laid on many chances for the likes of Hugh Billington. After becoming the first Luton player to top 100 League appearances after the war, Billy fell out with manager Dally Duncan and transferred to QPR in 1950.

Following a three year spell at Loftus Road, Billy enjoyed a season at Bournemouth before several stints at non-League clubs which he combined with a job as an insurance agent.

Billy then spent thirty years as general secretary for Electrolux Sports before retiring in 1986. A sprightly 86, Billy has recently moved from Luton to Felixstowe.

■ Roy Connon WEGERLE

Born in South Africa, Roy was only young when he moved to the USA and was turning out for Tampa Bay when he was poached by Chelsea.

Used only sparingly at Stamford Bridge, Luton took a gamble on him in 1988 and he soon became a favourite with his superb close control, balance and scoring ability, with his performances helping the Hatters to a second successive date at Wembley for the Littlewoods Cup final.

Sadly, finances dictated that a £1 million bid from QPR, a record for both clubs at the time, was accepted in December 1989 followed by further big money moves to Blackburn and Coventry.

Roy re-invented himself when returning to the States, becoming a star in the MSL and earning call-ups for the national side.

Now involved in media work in the USA, Roy is also a golfer of note.

■ James (Jimmy) WEIR

Glasgow born Jimmy was playing for Clydebank Juniors when Fulham scouts enticed him to Craven Cottage but after three years and only three League appearances he moved on to York in 1960.

Winger Jimmy proved a revelation at Bootham Crescent, netting 38 goals in 82 starts for the Minstermen, and the supporters were mightily disappointed when he left to join Mansfield who he helped to promotion to the old Division Three.

Joining Luton at the end of August 1963 for £5,000, Jimmy failed to show his previous form as a goalscoring winger in a poor Luton side and after losing his place to teenager Ray Whittaker moved on to Tranmere. Jimmy finished his football career at Midland League side Scarborough, and then settled in the town working as a coachbuilder until retirement.

■ Michael (Micky) Graham WEIR

Micky joined his local club, Hibernian, from school and after working his way up at Easter Road embarked on a long time infatuation with the club and its supporters.

Already a terrace favourite at Hibs, the 21 year old was not happy when contract terms broke down leading to a tribunal set £230,000 move to Luton in 1987.

A classic Scottish winger, Luton fans never saw the best of him although he did score the goal at Wigan that set the Town up on their road to Wembley in the 1987/88 Littlewoods Cup. Four months after signing for Luton the homesick Scot returned to Hibs to resume what was to become a long career, which only ended when he took on a coaching role at Motherwell.

■ Alan WEST

After being spotted by Burnley scouts while playing for his school team in Hyde, Alan joined one of the best youth set-ups in the country and became part of the Clarets side that lifted the FA Youth cup in 1968.

A midfielder of skill and vision, Alan made over 50 appearances for Burnley and picked up an England Under-23 cap before a big bid from Sunderland was accepted in 1973. Amazingly, Alan failed a medical because of a back problem but Luton manager Harry Haslam immediately stepped in, leading to an eight year stay at Kenilworth Road and 285 League appearances!

Since leaving the professional game, Alan has been a church minister in Luton for many years and has recently recovered from serious illness. He is now also the club chaplain at Kenilworth Road.

■ John (Jackie) Richard WHENT

Although born in Darlington, Jackie was brought up in Canada but played his early football in California.

After joining the Canadian Army in 1942, Jackie came over to England and was posted near Brighton where he was asked to assist the Albion junior team. He eventually signed on with the Seagulls and became a regular in their Division Three (South) side as a strong and capable centre-half and was awarded the captain's armband in his last two seasons at the Goldstone.

At the age of 30, Jackie was transferred to Luton in exchange for Jim Mulvaney and Peter Walsh and was asked to play in the forward line where he met with only limited success although he did score on his Hatters debut.

Jackie's stay at Luton lasted only a year before he moved to Kettering and then back to Canada where he has since settled.

■ Adrian Richard WHITBREAD

Tough and influential central defender Adrian started off his football career as a Youth Trainee at Leyton Orient, before making his League debut in December 1989 and then becoming club captain at the young age of 20.

His battling performances earned him a £500,000 move to new Premiership side Swindon in 1993 and an even bigger fee changed hands when he switched to West Ham a year later. He failed to settle at Upton Park and moved on to Portsmouth where he was soon made skipper.

After falling out with manager Steve Claridge, Adrian joined Luton on loan in November 2000 and his commitment shone through as he tried to save the Hatters from relegation. Sadly, a transfer could not be arranged and Adrian joined Reading before finishing his League career at Exeter.

In recent years Adrian has acted as number two to Martin Allen in his various managerial posts.

■ Brian Kenneth WHITBY

Luton born Brian played for the Bedfordshire Youth team and Vauxhall Motors before joining the Hatters as an amateur and then signing part-time professional forms in May 1957 whilst continuing to work at the car factory.

A fast and two-footed winger, Brian made his League debut for the Town at Newcastle in March 1958, scoring in a 2-3 defeat, and kept his place for the remainder of the season. The signing of Billy Bingham by Luton that summer effectively ended his career at Kenilworth Road as he made only one more first-team appearance before throwing in his lot with Bedford in 1960.

After spells with St Neots and Milton Keynes, Brian hung up his boots to concentrate fully on his job with Vauxhall before using his skills in a sales environment. He still lives in the town in retirement.

■ Alan WHITE

After joining Middlesbrough as a Youth trainee, the tall and aggressive centre-half struggled to earn a first team chance at the Riverside so when his old manager, Lennie Lawrence, came calling in September 1997 to ask him to come to Luton he jumped at the chance.

The Hatters were suffering from a major injury crisis at the time which gave the £40,000 signing an opportunity to earn himself a regular spot in the side with his no-nonsense style and he was virtually ever present until losing his place to Julian Watts.

Alan has since enjoyed successful spells at Colchester, Leyton Orient, Boston and Notts County and is currently with Darlington, his home town club.

■ Stephen (Steve) James WHITE

Honest and dependable goalscorer Steve, played almost 650 League games for seven clubs in a twenty year, virtually injury free, career.

Starting with Bristol Rovers, Steve caught the eye of Luton manager David Pleat after scoring a brace against the Hatters and moved to Kenilworth Road for £175,000 in December 1979. Unable to displace Bob Hatton initially, Steve had to wait until the 1981/82 season before he earned a regular start when his goals helped the Town to promotion to the top flight.

Sadly, Steve was forced to move to Charlton that summer as part of the deal that brought Paul Walsh to Luton but he put his disappointment behind him and went on to prove a credit to the game.

After finally hanging up his boots, Steve assisted Bath City and managed Chippenham Town.

■ Raymond (Ray) Henry WHITTAKER

A great career was mapped out for tiny winger Ray after he gained a winners medal for England in the Little World Cup of 1963 and was then awarded a contract at Arsenal.

Unfortunately, he failed to make the breakthrough at Highbury and joined Luton in March 1964 just in time to help the Hatters avoid the drop to the football basement. Quick and accurate with an eye for goal, Ray could not prevent the Town from being relegated in 1965 on his own but was a mainstay in the side that romped to the Division Four title three years later.

After losing his place to Mike Harrison, Ray moved to Colchester and had spells at various non-League clubs before a broken leg ended his career.

Ray then worked for a merchant bank for 22 years and lives in Upminster in retirement.

■ Paul WILKINSON

Another well travelled striker who turned out for ten League clubs in a long career, which included four caps at England Under-21 level, although he could have been lost to the game as he had trials for Nottinghamshire CCC as a youngster.

Starting with Grimsby, Paul's goalscoring form soon had the scouts flocking to Blundell Park leading to a £250,000 move to Everton in 1985. From there he moved on to Nottingham Forest, Watford and Lennie Lawrence's Middlesbrough for increasingly larger fees.

Out of favour at the Riverside, Paul was remembered by new Luton boss Lawrence leading to a loan transfer to the Hatters in March 1995. The Town were desperately fighting relegation and needed Paul's goals but typical of the club's luck at the time the tall forward broke a toe in only his third game!

Paul is now on the coaching staff at Cardiff City.

■ Martin Keith WILLIAMS

Although born in Luton and the nephew of ex-Hatter Ray Daniel, Martin started his football career as a Youth Trainee at Leicester before being enticed to Kenilworth Road and signing professional forms in 1991.

Over the next four years, the popular winger made 40 League appearances for the Town, although most of the time he came on as a 'supersub' when the team was chasing a game and his pace could be used to full advantage.

After a loan spell at Colchester, Martin moved to Reading where after a slow start he was converted into a striker and was top scorer for the Royals in 1998/99 even though he was out injured from the February.

The injury ended his Reading career and after short spells at Swindon and Peterborough, Martin moved down into non-League and is now at Windsor.

■ Steven (Steve) Charles WILLIAMS

One of the finest midfield players of his generation, Steve started his League career at Southampton and in ten years at the Dell played over 300 first team games as well as earning six England caps.

Brilliant control and distribution were sometimes let down by an impetuous streak but he still attracted a £550,000 bid from Arsenal in 1984 and on the bigger stage his talents shone through.

A fall-out with manager George Graham just before the Gunners were due to play Luton in the 1988 Littlewoods Cup final meant a parting of the ways and he perversely joined the Hatters that summer for a record fee of £300,000.

Sadly, he failed to show his England form at Kenilworth Road and was eventually packed off on a free transfer to Exeter in 1991.

Steve still lives in the Exeter area where he is involved in property.

■ Christopher (Chris) Alan WILLMOTT

Bedford born Chris joined Luton from school and after working his way up through the ranks at Kenilworth Road suddenly found himself thrust into the first team following the Hatter's double sale of Graham Alexander and Steve Davis in 1999.

A tall and powerful defender, Chris filled in reliably at either full-back or centre-half for the remainder of the 1998/99 campaign before an amazing £350,000 bid came in from Premiership Wimbledon that summer which was too good to turn down.

Chris could never carve out a regular place in the Dons team and came back to Luton for two loan spells in 2003 before making a permanent move to Northampton where he enjoyed greater success.

Chris is now at Conference side Oxford United.

■ Daniel (Danny) Joseph WILSON

Wigan born Danny started his football career with Bury before moving to Chesterfield where his strong, forceful midfield performances caught the eye of Nottingham Forest manager Brian Clough, leading to a transfer in January 1983.

Surprisingly, Danny did not settle at the City Ground and switched to Brighton but returned to the top flight when he became Luton manager Ray Harford's first major signing in the summer of 1987.

Slotting straight into the side, Northern Ireland international Danny was virtually ever present over the next three seasons with his all action displays as the Hatters made four trips to Wembley, appeared in an F.A.Cup semi-final and diced with the threat of relegation.

After spells with Sheffield Wednesday and Barnsley, Danny settled into management and is currently in the hot seat at Hartlepool.

■ James (Jim) Allan WILSON

Hailing from Musselburgh, Jim turned out as an amateur for Peterborough whilst serving in the RAF during the war. After demobilisation he signed professional forms with Posh, then in the Midland League, before he was spotted by Luton scouts leading to him moving to Kenilworth Road for a sizeable fee and the promise of a friendly match.

Making his League debut for the Hatters in 1947/48, the quick and tenacious full-back, who could play on either flank, enjoyed a long run in the side in the following campaign before losing out to the consistent pairing of Billy Cooke and Bud Aherne.

Jim moved on to Northampton in 1951 and then had a short spell at Chesterfield before settling back in Scotland where he died in 1997.

■ Marc David WILSON

Belfast born Marc joined Portsmouth from school and soon earned a reputation as a talented midfielder, comfortable on the ball with an eye for goal.

After a spell on loan at Yeovil in March 2006 which lasted only two games, Marc enjoyed a much longer run at Bournemouth, starting in January 2007 which ran to the end of the season by which time he had notched up 19 appearances and scored three goals.

Although Bournemouth would have loved to have kept him, Pompey would not sell but after a further spell in the reserves at Fratton Park he was sent out on loan once more, this time to Luton.

After making his debut for the Hatters in a 0-0 draw at Walsall in November 2007, Marc went on to make four starts, and was only on the losing side once, before returning to Fratton Park where he has just signed a new three year deal.

■ Robert James WILSON

After joining his local club Fulham from school in 1977 and then signing professional forms two years later, Robert was converted into an attacking midfielder from full-back and enjoyed five successful seasons at Craven Cottage during which time he helped his side to the brink of Division One.

Surprisingly transferred to Millwall in 1985, Robert only lasted a year there before he rejoined his old manager Ray Harford at Luton in a £40,000 deal. Despite scoring on his home debut, Robert soon lost his place to Mark Stein and for the rest of his stay at Kenilworth Road was used as a utility man in a variety of positions none of which he made his own.

Robert moved back to Fulham in 1987 and then enjoyed stays at Huddersfield and Rotherham before taking up a position at Huddersfield in their youth development office.

■ Robert (Robbie) WINTERS

Robbie had been plying his trade in Scotland for ten years before trying his luck south of the border at Luton, but he then saw only 45 minutes of action at Kenilworth Road!

Starting with Dundee United in 1992, Robbie soon earned a reputation as a brave striker which won him a big money move to Aberdeen where he became a prolific scorer, although his most memorable performance came in the Scottish FA Cup final of 2000 when he replaced injured goalkeeper Jim Leighton and conceded four goals as Rangers romped home!

By now a Scottish international, Robbie came to Luton in August 2002 but played only the first half of the opening day defeat at the hands of Peterborough without making an impact. He then decided on a complete change of scene and joined Brann in Norway who he still turns out for.

■ Maurice (Matt) WOODS

Matt started off at Everton in 1947 but after nine years and only eight League appearances he moved to Blackburn for £6,000.

Immediately becoming a mainstay in the heart of the Rovers defence, Matt helped his new side to promotion to the top flight and was reckoned to be the best un-capped centre-half of his era, showing superb timing and power in the air.

Matt eventually left Blackburn in 1963 for a spell in Australia, before coming back to England two years later and joining Luton. By now 33, Matt was a tremendous influence in a Hatters side that narrowly failed to win promotion from Division Four in 1965/66 but stayed only one season before leaving, following a row over bonuses, to help Stockport to promotion.

Matt later managed Stockport before becoming an HGV driver. He now lives in Cheadle in retirement.

■ Jamie Marcus WOODSFORD

Ipswich born Jamie joined Luton from school and after learning his trade at Kenilworth Road signed professional forms in March 1995.

A quick and clever striker, Jamie made his League debut coming on as substitute in a 1-0 win at Port Vale in September 1994 and with an England Youth international call-up following swiftly afterwards his career seemed set.

Sadly, Jamie could not then manage to push his way into the League eleven on a regular basis and despite being loaned out to Portadown for first team experience he was eventually forced to accept the inevitable.

Jamie now works for Royal Mail.

■ Robert (Bobby) Jack WYLDES

Strong and fast left winger Bobby was turning out for United Counties League side Desborough Town when he was noticed by Luton who signed him on professional forms in October 1949.

The following month Bobby was making his League debut in a 5-2 home win over Blackburn and although in and out of the side for the remainder of that campaign he seemed to have sealed a permanent slot on the wing in 1950/51 until breaking an ankle at Birmingham in November 1950.

Sadly, Bobby was never able to regain his form and joined Kettering in 1952 before taking on a coaching and then a managerial role at Desborough. An electrician by trade Bobby lives in Kettering in retirement.

■ George McArthur YARDLEY

Kirkcaldy born George played in goal for East Fife reserves and Scotland amateurs before moving to Forfar and Montrose. Unable to establish himself in his favoured strikers position he emigrated to Australia where he played for Sydney side St George Budapest while working as a draughtsman.

He came back to these shores in October 1966 to try his luck once more and was taken on by the Hatters who handed him his League debut in the number nine shirt in a 2-2 home draw with Bradford Park Avenue. He failed to impress but was given another chance by Tranmere the following month.

At Prenton Park, George finally fulfilled his potential and netted an amazing 68 goals in only 123 starts in two spells at the club and becoming a terrace hero at the same time!

After hanging up his boots, George returned to Australia where he lives in retirement.

■ Landry ZAHANA-ONI

Much travelled forward Landry was born on the Ivory Coast but moved to France as a youngster, being capped for his new country at under-15 level.

After playing for Le Havre and Ancenis in France, Landry made a baffling move to Stirling Albion and then on to Bromley where he was watched by Luton manager Lennie Lawrence who eventually took the plunge, signing him in January 1999.

Landry made eight League appearances for the Hatters over the remainder of that season, without making much impression, before being sidelined for most of the following campaign with a bad knee injury.

Released in 2000, Landry had spells with three Scottish clubs, and four non-League outfits in England before making another curious move to Limassol in Cyprus in 2004 and then diverting to Molde in Norway.